The

SCIENCE

of

LEADERSHIP

The

SCIENCE

of

LEADERSHIP

Nine Ways to Expand Your Impact

JEFFREY HULL AND MARGARET MOORE

Berrett–Koehler Publishers, Inc.

Berrett-Koehler Publishers, Inc.
1333 Broadway, Suite P100
Oakland, CA 94612-1921
Tel: (510) 817-2277
Fax: (510) 817-2278
bkconnection.com

ORDERING INFORMATION

Quantity sales. Special discounts are available on quantity purchases by corporations, associations, and others. For details, please go to bkconnection.com to see our bulk discounts or contact bookorders@ bkpub.com for more information.

Individual sales. Berrett-Koehler publications are available through most bookstores. They can also be ordered directly from Berrett-Koehler: Tel: (800) 929-2929; Fax: (802) 864-7626; bkconnection.com.

Orders for college textbook / course adoption use. Please contact Berrett-Koehler:
Tel: (800) 929-2929; Fax: (802) 864-7626.

Distributed to the US trade and internationally by Penguin Random House Publisher Services.

The authorized representative in the EU for product safety and compliance is EU Compliance Partner, Pärnu mnt. 139b-14, 11317 Tallinn, Estonia, www.eucompliancepartner.com, +372 5368 65 02.

Berrett-Koehler and the BK logo are registered trademarks of Berrett-Koehler Publishers, Inc.

Printed in the United States of America

Berrett-Koehler books are printed on long-lasting acid-free paper. When it is available, we choose paper that has been manufactured by environmentally responsible processes. These may include using trees grown in sustainable forests, incorporating recycled paper, minimizing chlorine in bleaching, or recycling the energy produced at the paper mill.

Library of Congress Cataloging-in-Publication Data

Names: Hull, Jeffrey W. author | Moore, Margaret, MBA author
Title: The science of leadership : nine ways to expand your impact / Jeffrey Hull & Margaret Moore.
Description: First edition. | Oakland, CA : Berrett-Koehler Publishers, Inc, [2025] | Includes bibliographical references and index.
Identifiers: LCCN 2024059075 (print) | LCCN 2024059076 (ebook) | ISBN 9798890570765 paperback | ISBN 9798890570772 pdf | ISBN 9798890570789 epub
Subjects: LCSH: Leadership | Executive coaching
Classification: LCC HD57.7 .H846 2025 (print) | LCC HD57.7 (ebook) | DDC 658.4/092— dc23/eng/20250416
LC record available at https://lccn.loc.gov/2024059075
LC ebook record available at https://lccn.loc.gov/2024059076

First Edition

33 32 31 30 29 28 27 26 25   10 9 8 7 6 5 4 3 2 1

Book production: 1000 Books / Susan Geraghty
Cover design: Ashley Ingram
Interior design: THE COSMIC LION
Author photos: Jeffrey Hull, by Dave Pelham Photography; Margaret Moore, by Matthew Guillory

To Jason and Paul

Contents

Preface   ix

Introduction: From Science to Impact   1

1   **Conscious:** See Clearly, Including Myself   19

2   **Authentic:** Care   37

3   **Agile:** Flex   53

4   **Relational:** Help   71

5   **Positive:** Strengthen   90

6   **Compassionate:** Resonate   104

7   **Shared:** Share   120

8   **Servant:** Serve   139

9   **Transformational:** Transform, Including Myself   156

10 Putting All Nine Together   176

Conclusion: Moving into Action   194

Discussion and Study Guide   203

Notes   231

Acknowledgments   249

Index   255

About the Authors   267

Preface

We met in 2012 at the Institute of Coaching, which supports a global community of coaches committed to coaching research and to applying scientific findings in coaching practice for leadership, health, and well-being. The institute is based at McLean Hospital, the prestigious psychiatric hospital and research institution that is part of the vast Mass General Brigham health care enterprise in Massachusetts. Most of the institute leaders have teaching appointments at Harvard Medical School.

Margaret's career is a unique blend of leadership, coaching, and science, including thirty years in C-suite roles, coleading four successful start-ups in biotechnology and coaching (including the Institute of Coaching), and two decades of professional coaching and coach training. Since 2000, she has been a prolific translator of science into coaching, training, and leadership practice. Jeffrey has had a thirty-year career focused on leadership, as an HR director with multiple corporations, cofounder of a leadership development consultancy, and psychotherapist. His focus over the last two decades has been coaching leaders across the globe, along with coleading the Institute of Coaching, which has grown to over four thousand members. He brings years of translating science into leadership as a consultant, psychologist, and teacher at New York University and Harvard Medical School.

Over the past two decades, we have played instrumental roles in bringing scientific integrity to coaching worldwide. We have helped coaches apply the latest research on high-quality motivation, behavior change, creativity, and insight generation. Our commitment to constructing a solid scientific foundation for coaching led us to this book, bringing the scientific foundation of leadership to you.

This book shines a light on the science of leadership for everyday leaders accountable for the performance of small and large teams and organizations, along with coaches and anyone else who wants to help leaders, including their bosses. The fifty years of research underpinning leadership practice is, for the most part, out of sight and out of mind for most leaders. Most research-based insights on what improves results are buried in scientific journals that few read.

Getting a study of an effective leadership practice, such as forgiveness or humility, published in a scientific journal requires hundreds of hours and thousands of watts of brain power, only to reach a small island of readers and miss an ocean of leaders.

It's hard to digest the science of leadership because it isn't organized into a unified whole. Groups of researchers come together to create, define, measure, and study a multicomponent model, such as authentic leadership or servant leadership, which generally overlaps significantly with other models.

To simplify the complexity, we distilled the main leadership research topics into nine distinct leadership capacities, each made up of a set of well-studied elements. For example, the authentic capacity includes authenticity, character, virtues, values, and purpose. Each leadership capacity and its elements are based on scientific findings that are worth knowing, remembering, and putting into your everyday practice. Bringing the science to life, we have illustrated the nine capacities with true, real-life stories (well disguised to preserve confidentiality) and actionable advice.

Most leaders are naturals at some of these capacities; they lean on them most of the time, finding other approaches unnatural. For example, you may be good at serving others, but find it difficult to be agile. You may be agile, yet not so good at cultivating high-quality work relationships. From your own base of strength, you can learn and practice capacities that are less comfortable for you.

In the pages that follow, you will hear the chorus of leadership scientists singing in harmony for the sake of better leadership. Their work to uncover what improves performance and well-being of followers and organizations will open your eyes, surprise or shake up your understanding, and galvanize your interest in becoming a better leader.

By applying more of the capacities now and over your next months and years, you will not only grow your impact but also accomplish more with less strain. Inspiration, expansion, impact, and ease. That's where the science of leadership will take you in this book.

FROM SCIENCE TO IMPACT

Be a self-scientist; there is no end of discoveries to be made.

Leaders know how to ask good questions. Let's start with four. You answer the first one, and we'll answer the next three.

WHAT BRINGS YOU HERE?

Perhaps you're already a leader who is accountable for others' performance, looking to get better by expanding your mindset and skill set. You could be a leader of leaders looking for insights from the science of leadership. You might be a coach or consultant who wants to integrate more leadership research into your professional practice. Or maybe you aspire to become a leader yourself, and you're looking to better understand what it takes. Whatever your answer to this question, you'll find good value between these covers.

HOW CAN THIS BOOK HELP YOU?

No doubt there is an art to leadership, captured in thousands of books and stories of famous leaders. But there is more to guide us—there is a *science* of leadership that we bring to you in this book. We've reviewed hundreds of scientific articles on leadership, particularly those published recently in the most respected journals. The articles we cite in the book were produced by at least seven hundred researchers. All together, their articles cited and analyzed more than fifteen thousand scientific studies or related articles.

Leadership research is a global endeavor; we summarized studies conducted by researchers collaborating across twenty-two countries in Africa, Asia, Eastern Europe, the Middle East, North America, and Western Europe:

AFRICA

- South Africa

ASIA

- Australia
- Cambodia
- China
- India
- Pakistan
- Singapore

EASTERN EUROPE

- Czech Republic
- Latvia

MIDDLE EAST

- Israel
- Turkey

NORTH AMERICA

- Canada
- US

WESTERN EUROPE

- Denmark
- Finland
- France
- Germany
- Netherlands
- Norway
- Sweden
- Switzerland
- UK

We've organized, synthesized, and translated this scientific literature into nine leadership capacities. Our ability to simplify leadership science for everyday leaders is based on decades of hands-on roles as leaders, leadership coaches and trainers, and translators of science into practice.

By turning science into leadership practice and delivering actionable advice in this book, we want to inspire you to expand your repertoire and your impact. The self-coaching exercises will set you on the right track.

WHAT DO WE MEAN BY LEADERSHIP?

Over the past fifty years, definitions of leadership have multiplied in the scientific literature. The following multipart definition, published in 2024, was pulled together from diverse sources by psychology professor Alexander Haslam in Australia and collaborators in Sweden and the UK:

> Leadership can be defined as the process whereby one or more people motivate one or more other people to contribute to the achievement of collective goals (of any form) by shaping beliefs, values, and understanding. . . .
>
> Leadership is more about getting people to want to do things than about making them do them.[1]

Notice that although leadership starts with motivation, it's not ideal for leaders to focus on "motivating others," as the definition here shifts to clarify. More precisely, according to the most respected theory of human motivation, self-determination theory (SDT), the highest-quality, most stable motivation is internal—that is, based on what is important to a person, not what is imposed by others, even bosses or senior leaders. SDT teaches that good leaders help followers motivate themselves, to find their own whys—their own reasons to contribute to collective goals.

"Leadership is not a solo process but one that is grounded in relationships and connections between leaders and those they influence."[2] A good deal of leadership science concerns relationships of leaders with followers, and how those relationships support followers' performance. Your success as a leader depends in large part on the high-quality relationships that you have cultivated.

"The ultimate proof of leadership is not what leaders are like or do but what their followers do." Leadership researchers study followers—measuring the signs of effective leadership, including their attitudes, perceptions, beliefs, behaviors, well-being, and their performance. Along with performance of individuals, researchers measure team and organizational performance.[3]

More than ever before, our world needs leaders who inspire and empower everyone to do great work. The quality of leadership matters, and the science shows us what qualities to improve. We can use science to separate the signals of good leadership from the noise.

NINE LEADERSHIP CAPACITIES

The nine capacities we selected draw upon well-known models of leadership, translating them into practice. These models are often used by leadership coaches in support of the frontline needs of leaders. They generally fall into three categories: widely studied, popular but not widely studied, and emerging.

Five leadership models have been widely studied. Transformational leadership is the most studied leadership topic. (The second most studied topic is human capital, which we discuss in the positive leadership chapter.) Relational leadership, renaming what scientists call the leader–member exchange, is the third most studied topic. Authentic, servant, and positive leadership are also supported by many studies and scholars.

Two popular leadership models lack significant study: conscious and agile. We bolster them by pulling out their unique capacities and supporting them with relevant science, including research on emotional intelligence, mindfulness, cognitive agility, and well-being.

Getting the attention of scientists are two new models. One is shared (or distributed) leadership, and the other is compassionate leadership.

In each chapter, we begin with a brief description of a core capacity that makes, for example, a leader agile or conscious or positive.

Then a leadership story, sometimes two, bring the capacity to life. The stories (real-life stories combined and altered to protect confidentiality) draw upon our coaching experiences with hundreds of leaders over the past two decades.

The section titled "Understanding the Science" assembles the main lessons from the scientific literature having to do with each capacity and its elements, and their impact on others' performance and well-being. Outlined in the "Practice" section are reflection questions, practices, and action steps that can help you upgrade your capacity. The "Integration" section explores the interdependence of the capacities. It also helps you see and regulate the ego states that drive underuse or overuse of that capacity, and ultimately integrate these states into a quieter ego with more ease and grace.

We use the term *capacity* because it's broad and inclusive. Adapting a definition of capacity development,[4] we intend for a leadership capacity to integrate related elements studied by researchers. That said, bear in mind that many elements can contribute to a capacity's impact beyond what has been studied. Elemental examples are awareness, values, motivations, intentions, identity, attitudes, knowledge, skills, abilities, processes, behaviors, resources, experience, and competence.

What makes being a leader challenging is that leadership capacities operate simultaneously at three levels: leading yourself, leading others, and leading a system, such as a team or organization. You will see that all nine capacities are vital to leading at all three levels. It's easier to help others and ultimately an entire system to improve once you have upgraded your own capacities.

That said, these capacities have a natural order of increasing complexity, moving from self, to others, to a system. Let's have a quick look at the nine capacities, organized into these three levels.

SELF-ORIENTED CAPACITIES

Conscious leadership (See clearly, including myself). As a conscious leader, you are aware of your ego. You manage your ego well to stay calm, stable, and objective. Then you can see things more clearly, including yourself. You are able to transcend your agitated emotional states, ultimately turning your noisy ego into a quieter ego with more strength and calm. You work to accept and see yourself and others objectively.

Authentic leadership (Care). As an authentic leader, you care about excellence in character, quality, and outcomes for yourself and your team and organization. You model integrity, genuinely walking your talk in communication, action, and decisions. You help an organization align around a shared purpose that fulfills shared values. Being open and sincere, you create high-quality work relationships and inspire the workforce to fulfill the team's or organization's purpose.

Agile leadership (Flex). As an agile leader, you move flexibly and gracefully across many tasks, perspectives, polarities (opposing views), and conflicts. You zoom in and out, zip up and down from detail to big picture, from adversity to opportunity, from knowing to not knowing, from deep focus to mind-wandering, from rest to driving forward, from stability to disruptive change, from conflict to resolution, and on and on. Agile leaders adapt and bounce forward, going beyond resilience to turn adversity into growth.

OTHER-ORIENTED CAPACITIES

Relational leadership (Help). As the name suggests, you cultivate high-quality relationships. You are able to shift from prefrontal task focus to heart-centered connection. Relational leaders build rapport, trust, and psychological safety by empathizing with others through high-quality listening. You seek to understand others' perspectives and emotions, and what is meaningful and important to them. You accept and forgive others' (and your own) limitations and mistakes. You work to help others, without trying to impress, dominate, or control them.

Positive leadership (Strengthen). As a positive leader, you mobilize followers by helping them cultivate psychological capital and well-being. Five key sources of psychological capital and well-being are autonomy (feeling a sense of agency), confidence (feeling competent), positive emotions (feeling good), optimism (feeling optimistic), and meaning or fulfillment of values (feeling fulfilled). These resources energize everyone's work engagement, productivity, perseverance, resilience, and growth.

Compassionate leadership (Resonate). This capacity brings together all the previous five into compassion. As a compassionate leader, you understand the everyday stresses and strains of organizational life. You combine the warmth of concern—the desire and ability to make work life better, for example, less distressing and more rewarding—with a focus on accountability, being tough on performance.

SYSTEM-ORIENTED CAPACITIES

Shared leadership (Share). Also known as collective or distributed leadership, this capacity involves a shift from "I" to "We." Leadership roles are shared and distributed throughout an organization or even a system of organizations, as in a global corporation. You empower everyone to learn how to lead in their own contexts. Your open, inclusive approach to figuring out the direction to take your organization includes team or organizational visioning, defining purpose, designing strategy, setting goals, and making decisions.

Servant leadership (Serve). As a servant leader you are a humble steward of your team and organization. You foster the autonomy, agency, development, and service orientation of followers, which in turn increases their motivation and engagement in meaningful work. While there is an evolutionary basis for other-focused service (e.g., the parenting role), the servant capacity develops with psychological maturity.

Transformational leadership (Transform, including myself). As a transformational leader, you are an inspirational visionary as well as an influential role model. You enable creativity and facilitate innovation by fostering the motivation and confidence of followers. You stimulate others intellectually to challenge, expand, and diversify their perspectives. And as a transformational leader, you model courage, a virtue in short supply.

HOW TO USE THIS BOOK

Now let's prepare for the journey from science to practice. You can quickly engage with the nine capacities by writing down a top-of-mind self-rating using table I.1 as a guide. Use a paper or digital journal to track these ratings; you'll be coming back to them later. You can also walk through the self-rating exercise with a partner, mentor, or friend, or both of you could even do it together. We will then ask you to reflect on your readiness to change (see figure I.1)—choosing a capacity or two to work on and getting ready for action.

The purpose of this exercise is to reflect on and then expand your self-awareness. Self-reflection and self-awareness are key attributes of effective leaders. In their review of critical reflection in leadership development, Yingting Wu and Oliver Crocco explain that the ongoing practice of updating your assumptions about yourself and followers is essential to leading better over time.[5]

Now on to an initial dose of critical reflection on your leadership as you consider the following self-ratings:

1. **Strengths.** In the first column, rank each capacity from 1 to 9, from your strongest to your weakest. Number 1 is your top strength.

2. **Importance.** In the second column, rank each capacity from 1 to 9 based on its importance to your current leadership dynamic. Number 1 is the most important.

3. **Strategic priorities for growth.** For the third column, look at the first two columns together. Identify one or two capacities that are high in importance (scores of 1–3) and low in strength (scores of 4–9). These may become

your priority capacities that you want to improve or even transform into new strengths.

TABLE I.1   SELF-RATING OF NINE LEADERSHIP CAPACITIES

LEADERSHIP CAPACITY	KEY ELEMENTS OF CAPACITY	RANK MY STRENGTHS (1–9)	RANK WHAT'S IMPORTANT NOW (1–9)	RANK PRIORITIES FOR GETTING BETTER (1–9)
SELF-ORIENTED CAPACITIES				
CONSCIOUS See clearly, including myself.	I am calm (quiet ego). I am stable. I am objective.			
AUTHENTIC Care.	I express my highest values (walk my talk). I am genuine and sincere. I balance my concern for my values and others' values.			
AGILE Flex.	I am open and curious. I navigate easily between opposites. I embrace and drive change.			
OTHER-ORIENTED CAPACITIES				
RELATIONAL Help.	I cultivate high-quality relationships. I empathize. I foster trust and psychological safety. I forgive. I support others to learn and grow.			
POSITIVE Strengthen.	I support agency. I support competence. I support positivity. I support optimism. I support fulfillment.			

(continued)

TABLE I.1   SELF-RATING OF NINE LEADERSHIP CAPACITIES
(*CONTINUED*)

LEADERSHIP CAPACITY	KEY ELEMENTS OF CAPACITY	RANK MY STRENGTHS (1–9)	RANK WHAT'S IMPORTANT NOW (1–9)	RANK PRIORITIES FOR GETTING BETTER (1–9)
COMPAS-SIONATE Resonate.	I have compassion for humanity. I practice showing compassion. I foster accountability with compassion. I cultivate resonance.			
SYSTEM-ORIENTED CAPACITIES				
SHARED Share.	I share visioning, pur-pose, values, strategy and goal-setting, decision-making. I empower others to lead. I elevate leadership in others.			
SERVANT Serve.	I cultivate humility. I am a good steward. I serve the higher good and help others do the same.			
TRANSFOR-MATIONAL Transform.	I cocreate a vision. I model courage. I am committed to personal growth. I inspire others to be visionaries. I foster creativity and innovation.			
SUMMARIZE YOUR RATINGS		What are your top strengths?	Which strengths do you most need now?	What are your priorities to improve that are higher in importance and lower in strength?

You've made good progress with self-reflection. You have now ranked your first take on what you are good at, what's important now, and your priorities for improvement (the ones with higher importance and lower strength scores). Again, it's ideal to keep track of these rankings in a paper or digital journal to reflect on your progress and how the rankings change over time as you read this book. We will nudge you to revisit your journal notes at the end of each chapter and to repeat table I.1 self-ratings in the conclusion.

Even with some reflection, you still might not be sure what to improve first. You could have several equal priorities for improvement. You may even want to work on all of them. The next step will help you figure out which capacities you are truly ready to improve now.

Your readiness to improve a capacity depends on two resources: your motivation and your confidence. (This is based on well-studied theories of motivation and change—self-determination theory and the transtheoretical theory of change.[6]) You can think of motivation and confidence as twin engines that need to be fueled and refueled to fly you to your destination of sustained improvement. When setbacks arrive, you may need to restart your motivation and confidence engines to get you back up in the air.

For a capacity to earn a place on your priority list, your motivation to improve it (what makes it important to *you*, not determined by outside influences) needs to have a score of at least 6 out of 10. Your confidence (belief in your ability to be successful) when it comes to improving this capacity needs to have a score of at least 6 out of 10. The 6/10 target is a coaching rule of thumb used to help people change something difficult, such as eating or exercise habits. When change is hard, there is a high chance of failing if the scores are lower, which depresses future engagement.[7]

In figure I.1, you can see that your scores on both motivation and confidence need to be around 6/10 to be ready to improve. This is the *getting ready* stage, when you are preparing—putting things in place to make the change by, for example, inviting a peer, mentor, coach, or friend to support you.

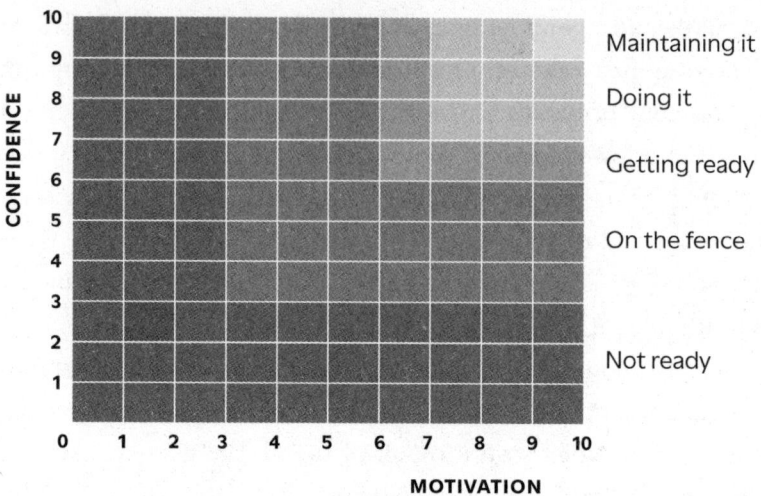

FIGURE I.1.
READINESS-TO-IMPROVE CHART

Notice a few other things about figure I.1:

- When either your confidence or motivation is below 3/10, you are *not* ready to improve.

- Scores between 4 and 6 indicate you are thinking about it, but not decided or committed.

- At around 6–7 you are ready to commit, and you can get ready to improve.

- Between 7 and 9 you are in action, practicing new skills and habits, observing the impact of your actions, getting better, and learning a lot from your experiences.

- Between 9 and 10 you have created new mindsets and habits that feel automatic and that you can maintain. Your motivation is reinforced by enjoying the increased impact of your actions. Your confidence is improved with practice.

You may now be ready to name your top two or three (tentative) priorities for getting better. While you read the book's ten chapters as your coaching tool, keep a lookout for things that increase your motivation, your confidence, or both. As a reminder, we will keep these six questions in the front of your mind, revisiting them at the close of each chapter:

- What makes this capacity valuable to you?

- What is inspiring you?

- What did you learn?

- What did you know that was confirmed?

- What questions come up?

- How has this chapter

  - Confirmed your strengths?

  - Increased your motivation and confidence?

  - Impacted your interest in getting better at this capacity?

In the conclusion, you will find a brief guide for self-coaching on whatever capacities land as your top priorities. Then you can turn science into action and impact.

TWO THINGS TO BE AWARE OF

Before you start the book's tour, there are two things we want you to be aware of. First, significant criticisms of leadership science have been published by leadership scholars, which we will consider in this section. Second, we have organized the scientific literature in a novel way so that it's easier to apply.

CRITICISMS OF LEADERSHIP RESEARCH

Studying leadership phenomena is a difficult, complex, and imprecise endeavor. Critiques abound. One paper starts with "Our field has lost its way."[8] Another paper warns of "excessive positivity."[9] A third asks, "Are the effects of servant leadership only spurious?"[10] A fourth is titled "Does Leadership Still Not Need Emotional Intelligence? Continuing 'the Great EI Debate.'"[11]

Key concerns are that survey questionnaires rather than the study of observed behaviors are the main sources of data and that unintended methodological flaws and biases (called endogeneity) are widespread.[12] In particular, the majority of research outcomes show only associations and correlations, not evidence of causation (i.e., a leader does something that changes follower behavior, which then produces a desirable, measurable outcome that is sustained—for individuals, teams, or the organization).

Even if causation between a leader's action and others' performance could be shown, it would be context specific. Leadership dynamics vary widely in small organizations compared to large ones, and across regions and countries. Leadership research is conducted in widely diverse sectors—for example, education, health care, technology, manufacturing, nonprofits, governments, e-commerce, and retail—and in a wide array of regional and local cultures and economies.

What can we do about these limitations? Should we just end the book here?

No.

Here's why.

These same scientific limitations—self-reported data, correlations not causation, and wide variability in contexts—plague the entire fields of psychology and social sciences. In response, a methodology called action research was created by social psychologist Kurt Lewin in the 1930s to show ordinary people how to do their own research attuned to their own contexts.[13]

Action research allows everyday leaders to use scientific approaches—reflecting on challenges, designing hypotheses and experiments, observing and learning from impacts, then adjusting, adapting, and moving forward in new ways. In fact, coaches use the action research approach to help people see themselves more objectively and find their own ways to reach their own aspirations.

Consider the science of leadership as a gift. It offers signs of what might work for you in your context, signs that are worthy of your consideration and experimentation.

ORGANIZATION OF LEADERSHIP RESEARCH

The second thing to be aware of is that our development and organization of the nine capacities differ from the way leadership science is organized in the literature and textbooks. For example, fifty-six topics were identified and clustered into five domains in a computerized analysis of leadership research led by management professors Hao Zhao (US) and Chaoping Li (China).[14]

We are covering many of these topics, but not all of them. For example, we didn't include characteristics that leaders can't easily change, such as age, intelligence, personality, and identity. We left out research on toxic, destructive, and narcissistic leadership; it won't surprise you that these approaches are harmful to leadership results, including workforce well-being.[15] We didn't cover research on gender, race, and cross-cultural leadership, which merit another book.

In the academic textbook *Leadership: Theory and Practice*, first published in 1997 and now in its tenth edition, Peter Northouse and his collaborators describe fifteen models and topics of leadership theory in four categories—traits (including personality and cognitive and emotional intelligence), skills, behaviors, and processes (leadership models).[16] We are using the term *capacity* to combine these four categories into one.

Here's more background on our thinking behind organizing leadership science into the nine capacities.

The goodness part—values, virtues, character, ethics, collective good—common to conscious leadership, servant leadership, positive leadership, ethical leadership, and others, is assigned to authentic leadership. The self-oriented half of emotional intelligence (self-awareness and self-regulation) helps give conscious leadership a scientific foundation. We moved what some scholars refer to as relational leadership to shared leadership, which also includes distributed leadership and collective leadership. We expanded shared leadership from the team to the organizational level and added strategic leadership because sharing the strategy-making process is important to followers' engagement and performance.

We integrated other leadership models into the selected nine where they fit. Meaning-based and values-based leadership are included in authentic leadership. Inclusive and complexity leadership are in shared leadership. Resonant leadership is in compassionate leadership. Strategic leadership and strategic management are in shared leadership. Visionary leadership and inspirational leadership are in transformational leadership.

We also integrated studies of other phenomena that are valuable to leaders: virtues and purpose (authentic); empathy, listening, trust, and forgiveness (relational); intrinsic motivation (positive); humility (servant); and creativity, inspiration, and innovation (transformational).

The nine capacities build on coauthor Hull's book *Flex: The Art and Science of Leadership in a Changing World*, which unpacks flexibility in applying diverse leadership approaches.[17] The nine capacities align with the science of well-being presented by coauthor Moore as nine capacities in her coauthored Harvard Health book *Organize Your Emotions, Optimize Your Life*.[18] They overlap with core coaching capacities in her coauthored *Coaching Psychology Manual*, used by fifty thousand coach trainers and coaches.[19]

All this to say, this book organizes and ties together the scientific foundation of well-being, coaching, and leadership into a common whole.

CLOSE

Given the hard-to-avoid limitations of leadership research, you can safely assume that improving any one element or capacity by itself will have a small to moderate effect on others' performance and well-being. From our leadership stories, you will see that leaders upgrade a few capacities together to produce substantial improvements and that these projects take months to a year or more. After you read the book, you could start improving one or two capacities for the next few months, trusting that there's more growth potential coming in your future.

Over months and years, expanding your playbook by improving the nine capacities will yield more and more impact on others' performance. You will feel more fulfilled as a leader as your impact grows. Leading will feel more like flying than trudging uphill, with more ease, less strain, and more pleasure. That's what we have learned through our experience in applying science as leaders and coaches.

Let's find out about the science of leadership! We'll start with an in-depth look at being a conscious leader.

CHAPTER 1

CONSCIOUS

See Clearly, Including Myself

Quieting a noisy ego is your path to leading better.

As a conscious leader, you are calm, stable, and objective. As a result, you see things clearly, including yourself. You are fully present in each moment. You have a high level of self-awareness. You reflect on your emotional states and are able to set them aside to be fully present in each moment. You see yourself and others objectively and without judgment—strengths, limitations, and growth opportunities. You recognize your leadership shadows, which are agitated, fear-based states in which you overuse strengths or avoid taking action, particularly under stress. By taking time to feel self-compassion and then process and transcend your shadow states, you transform them into new strength and calm.

LEADERSHIP STORY

Our first story is about Sidney, who reached a heady career peak as the human resource (HR) director at a major investment bank when he was promoted to senior vice president of global HR and asked to move from New York to Asia. Sidney began his HR career in Brazil, later joining the Latin American division of the investment bank that brought him to New York.

Excited about his move to Singapore, Sidney successfully took charge as the head of HR for the Asian division. Yet despite his strengths in intelligence, communication, and efficiency, Sidney received feedback that he was snappy, impatient, and critical; he also wasn't attuned to the Asian business culture's aversion to self-promotion, which was considered normal in New York.

While his hard work and attention to detail made him a star, for him to excel in broader leadership roles, he needed to improve his emotional intelligence, listening, coaching, and collaboration skills. The new role in Asia would provide him the chance to stretch (or fail). When first offered coaching, Sidney initially felt reluctant, ironic given that his HR role involved hiring coaches. Even though he recognized the benefits of coaching, his pride was hurt by the negative feedback from peers and subordinates. However, he committed to becoming more of a team player and signed up for coaching in spite of his resistance.

Sidney's enthusiasm for coaching grew as he realized that his sense of self was adaptable, not hard-wired, and that he could foster more effective team behaviors with a shift in work habits. He read Carol Dweck's book *Mindset: The New Psychology of Success*, which helped him view his challenges as growth opportunities (a sign of a quiet ego, which we will discuss in the science section).[1] He could then appreciate coaching as part of a lifelong journey of personal growth.

When asked what success looked like for him, Sidney expressed his desire to be an impactful global HR executive who was attuned to cultural differences. He had come a long way since his days as a clerk in a manufacturing organization in São Paulo, where he learned time management and efficiency. While he had many work relationships, they had not always gone smoothly. Despite his strengths, his long work hours and ambition sometimes caused resentment among colleagues.

LEARNING TO SELF-REGULATE

Sidney's father, a small shopkeeper in Brazil with limited education, was a role model but also critical and demanding. Sidney recognized that his impatience and critical nature mirrored his father's style. Through coaching, Sidney came to understand the importance of self-awareness and self-regulation and of balancing efficiency with relationship building, central to emotional intelligence. If he had completed the readiness-to-improve exercise in figure I.1 (in the introduction), his motivation and confidence scores likely would have risen above 6 out of 10. He learned that being liked and respected would advance his career more than perfect spreadsheets.

As we discuss in the science section, researchers have identified self-awareness and self-regulation as two of four core elements of emotional intelligence. They are self-oriented signs of conscious leadership. Fortunately for Sidney, he was highly motivated to become more conscious. He was open to slowing down, being less reactive, and becoming more reflective. He became conscious of his desire to grow as a person and have a positive impact on others. These were core values that would support his journey; they were also signs of values-driven leadership, which we will explore in chapter 2 on authentic leadership.

Sidney attended a leadership development workshop that included mindfulness exercises, which revealed his difficulty in sitting still and paying attention to his breath. Struggling with meditating for even two minutes (a challenge for many investment bankers; Sidney was hardly an outlier), he came to see the importance of being present and observing himself with calm acceptance. By taking short breaks between meetings to breathe and reflect, Sidney found he could reset and calm down his emotional landscape to show up better for his colleagues.

He chose to use a touchstone as a physical reminder to pause and become mindful. Sidney selected a piece of weathered glass from a

Caribbean beach, placing it on his desk to remind him of moments of joy and relaxation. This simple practice—holding the glass object and breathing deeply, even for a few seconds—helped him become more conscious of his emotional states. As we discuss in the science section, setting aside your mind's emotional activity and becoming present, moment by moment, enables you to be conscious and (more) objective about yourself, others, and the situation you're in.

ATTUNING TO OTHERS

By scheduling breaks and quieting the noise in his head, Sidney calmed down and his interactions improved. He became more consistent, positive, and, in the perceptions of his colleagues, trustworthy. He made time to encourage dialogue and demonstrate his interest in others' perspectives. He practiced asking open-ended questions and active listening. He turned off his phone so that he could give others his undivided attention, also expressed in his body language. By attuning with others emotionally and mentally, he could show empathy and understanding.

This approach not only improved his relationships but also fostered a collaborative work environment. Sidney developed his coaching skills, beginning to see the value in guiding his team members with positive reinforcement, curiosity in how they learned, and supportive suggestions, rather than just directing them. He learned to provide constructive feedback that balanced both strengths and areas for improvement. This shift in his approach improved trust and respect within his team, leading to better morale and increased productivity.

One significant breakthrough came when Sidney realized the value of authentic sharing of his vulnerability as a leader. Sharing his own challenges—for example, the struggles he had experienced as a young clerk in a factory—and admitting that he was a work in progress made him more relatable and approachable. His team appreciated his honesty and began to open up more, creating a culture of transparency and mutual support.

SEEING LEADERSHIP SHADOWS

Reflecting on his childhood, Sidney recognized that his father's demanding nature had triggered defensive responses that were now obstacles. Earlier in his life, his young, developing ego had responded to his father's harsh behavior with overdrive, hypercontrol, and even arrogance, all to protect him from feeling hurt and anxious. He could now see where his tendency to be critical of others, and himself, had come from. Sidney is not alone—we are all, in many ways, the product of patterns set in place early in life—emerging to support us and strengthen our egos.

While his "shadows," his darker ways of being, were well intended to be protective, now that he was an adult, they became derailers. Reacting negatively toward others took Sidney away from leading consciously. He began to understand that he was not controlled by these patterns or thoughts but could be free of them. He could develop his own leadership style. He learned to manage his reactivity by becoming aware of his triggers and implementing practices to stay grounded.

Sidney also realized that his work ethic and organizational skills, though they were strengths, got in the way of conscious leadership. Instead of being reactively critical and impatient, he needed to be proactively present, emotionally self-aware, and emotionally available to others by sharing and being receptive to others' emotions.

INTEGRATING LEADERSHIP SHADOWS

Sidney's breakthrough moments and changes in behavior are examples of what psychologists call integration, which is a growth process we explore in the science section.[2] His integration process started with a deeper, more objective awareness of his reactive patterns that were fueled by fear and insecurity. Once he realized that old patterns didn't serve him as a leader, he saw new options and could make better, more conscious choices.

His journey from a highly skilled but impatient executive to a conscious leader models the importance of mindfulness, self-awareness, self-regulation, and continuous personal growth. Sidney not only achieved his career goals but also inspired those around him to strive for leadership excellence. His transformation shows that you can achieve more when you lead with a calm, conscious presence—the starting point for all the other capacities to come.

UNDERSTANDING THE SCIENCE

With Sidney's story in mind, what do we mean by a conscious leader? A conscious leader is calm, stable, present, and objective, not activated and reactive. You see things clearly, including yourself.

This is a different take on conscious leadership than what is described in most of the leadership literature and the popular movement called conscious capitalism, exemplified by Whole Foods founder John Mackey's book on conscious leadership and how business can elevate humanity.[3] Here's why.

Along with John Mackey and others, Czech leadership scientists Kubátová and Kročil, in defining conscious leadership competencies, start with the idea of becoming conscious of virtues and virtues-driven purpose rather than embodying consciousness per se.[4] In Mackey's words: "I think [that purpose is] beginning to penetrate into more mainstream thinking about business, meaning it's not just about making a profit; it's about a higher purpose and creating value for others."[5]

Virtues are a special form of excellence—combining quality with benefits to humanity. Virtues are responsible, ethical, altruistic values that motivate us to improve the thriving of humans and our earthly home. Attuning to our virtues influences how we lead—how we arrive at good strategy and decisions and then implement them.

For now, we are going to set aside virtues in describing conscious leadership. Being virtuous is not the same as being conscious and objective. We will talk about virtues when we discuss authentic leadership, where it fits well. Here let's ground conscious leadership in well-studied concepts of emotional intelligence, self-awareness, and mindfulness—seeing things clearly, including oneself—because this is where many of us—not just Sidney—trip up.

SELF-AWARENESS AND SELF-REGULATION

In his book *Leadership: The Power of Emotional Intelligence*, Daniel Goleman makes the case for two self-oriented dimensions of emotional intelligence in leadership: self-awareness and self-management. Notes Goleman: "People with high self-awareness are able to speak accurately and openly about their emotions [and values] and the impact they have on their work . . . including a self-deprecating sense of humor. . . . Self-aware people know and are comfortable talking about their limitations and strengths, and they often demonstrate a thirst for constructive criticism."[6] Goleman's exploration of self-awareness sounds like Sidney's, and aligns with the sincerity of authentic leaders, which we discuss in chapter 2.

On self-regulation (or self-management), Goleman summarizes: "The signs of emotional self-regulation are easy to see: a propensity for reflection and thoughtfulness; comfort with ambiguity and change, and integrity—an ability to say no to impulsive urges."

We saw self-regulation in action with Sidney. He took the time and made the effort needed to reflect on his own behavior. He learned to pause, become present, and self-regulate—to behave in new ways.

Goleman goes on to say, "If there is one trait that virtually all effective leaders have, it is motivation—a variety of self-management where we mobilize our positive emotions to drive us toward our goals. . . . Interestingly, people with high motivation remain optimistic even when the score is against them. In such cases, self-regulation combines with achievement motivation to overcome the frustration and depression that come after a setback or failure."

South African researchers Gina Görgens-Ekermans and Chene Roux studied the association of components of emotional intelligence with effective leadership. Their study confirmed Sidney's experience—that high emotional self-awareness starts a cascade that enables self-management and empathy for others. Both are vital to the high-quality work relationships that allow leaders to enhance followers' moods and motivations.[7] We will unpack further how leaders can cultivate high-quality relationships in chapter 4 on relational leadership.

Psychologist Eva Bracht in Germany led a team from Singapore, the US, and China studying the impact of leaders' self-awareness and self-efficacy (self-confidence) on the evolution of followers into leaders. Their study concluded that a leader's self-awareness and self-efficacy were associated with followers' engagement in self-leadership, emergence as leaders, and nomination for promotion to a leadership positions.[8]

SEEING CLEARLY—BEING CONSCIOUS

Being conscious is being awake to what is going on—seeing things objectively. For leaders, becoming more conscious is a big undertaking, an energetic and agile exercise in focusing one's attention on one thing at a time. Leaders need to quickly shift their attention from themselves to people and situations close at hand. Next, that attention travels outward in ever-expanding concentric circles to teams, organization, stakeholders, industries or sectors, and on and on.

The starting point of conscious leadership is challenging—objective awareness of one's inner self. It's hard because awareness must override the brain's automatic processes. Canadian American neuroscientist Lisa Feldman Barrett's groundbreaking work on how emotions are made reveals that the brain's automatic mode of processing information isn't designed to directly perceive and experience internal and external reality—to be, in a nutshell, conscious or objective.[9]

The brain is designed to continually monitor, evaluate, and predict. To do that, it's focused on tracking your internal resources, abilities, needs, and desires along with ever-changing external demands across all of your life's domains. Your brain's calculations are entirely based on your past experiences, coded in your memories and learning.

Without conscious intervention, your brain is *not* focused on detecting reality in the present moment or observing yourself objectively.

Your brain sends messages to your conscious self in the form of emotions. Your emotions are not created by your brain as direct responses to the current reality. They are constructed by your brain to advise you on how you are doing and what to do next, based on a prediction of what may happen. Your continuous stream of emotions creates an internal reality—a continuous flow of emotional activity.

What happens next? You've likely noticed how your thinking brain tries to make some sense of the emotional swirl. In order to more objectively experience reality, you need to set aside your emotions-based internal "reality" just as if you were taking off a pair of virtual reality glasses.[10] You shift your mind from thinking to experiencing, in order to more accurately perceive, detect, and discern what is actually happening right here, right now.

Sidney's foray into mindfulness practices of grounding, breathing, and putting a stop to distractions (e.g., setting down his smartphone) enabled him to become present and more self-aware. He began to observe and set aside, rather than act on, his physical, mental, and emotional states, including his snappiness.

MINDSIGHT

Now you are beginning to see a way to become more intelligent about your emotions. You can step into your mindful self, a state of meta-awareness that UCLA psychiatrist Dan Siegel calls mindsight.[11] You can become conscious of your emotions; you can observe them and not react to them, just as Sidney did in his mindfulness practices.[12]

With mindsight you can notice and act on emotions that serve you well. Emotions that express your values—your desire to feel empathy and to help others—are important to act on. Sidney did this well. Emotions that motivate you to create or strive or persevere without excess also serve you well, including achievement motivation. Emotions that tell you to take care of your body are important to attend to. You can also notice the noisy emotions that are not helpful to act on, such as anxiety. Acting on noisy emotions is risky and may bring turmoil or regret. Instead, they need a good sit-down to settle down (see our practice later in this section).

THE LEADER'S SHADOW

As leaders take on bigger roles and more responsibilities, they do their best to project the confidence and optimism and potential that these roles call for. But, of course, the higher you rise the further you can fall. That realization leads the brain to produce what European coaching psychologist Erik de Haan calls the leader's shadow.[13] The shadow is a personal mixed bag of behaviors driven by agitated emotional states, such as fear and anxiety.

Shadow-driven behaviors include overdrive, hubris, hypercontrol, arrogance, self-promotion, and avoidance. The brain intends these emotional states to be protective, but instead they block or distort access to objective awareness and understanding. Leadership shadows are sometimes called leadership derailers because they take you away from leading consciously.

We saw Sidney's leadership shadows in action. His childhood experiences with a tough, harsh parent led to shadow-driven behaviors when he was under stress as a leader, including being hypercritical and impatient. Sidney was able to tap into his growth mindset and transform his shadow states into self-awareness, self-regulation, and growth—what psychologists call integration, and what mindfulness experts call self-transcendence, as you will see in the practice section.

INTEGRATING THE SHADOWS

The next frontier of emotional intelligence is what Dan Siegel (who defined mindsight) and Richard Ryan (cofounder of self-determination theory), call integration—the place where noisy, uncomfortable emotions go to settle.[14] Integration is a natural process that transforms one's internal noise into new clarity, calm, and strength.

Siegel describes integration as a process of linking differentiated brain networks—that is, connecting a neural pathway "groove" to other neural networks so that your mental activity is released from the groove. These neural grooves can feel chaotic (out of control—anxious, afraid, or hopeless) or rigid (too controlled—impatient or angry). By contrast, an integrated state after connecting to other brain networks feels relaxed and balanced, at least for a while until the next agitated emotions arise.[15]

In the best moments of coaching, coaches work with leaders in the zone of potential integration. Emotional arousal is the call to integrate agitated emotions into more clarity and objectivity. Moments of integration can emerge out of playing with different vantage points, ideas, and perspectives. They arrive with a sense of insight, of resolution: *So that's what is going on here. Now I see. That's an interesting perspective. I think I can do that. Never thought of that before.*

Over time, with plenty of integration, a leader's noisy ego gets quieter, even in a crisis. A quieter ego enables cleaner, more conscious leadership—where your focus is unimpaired and your goodness can shine through.

You can now understand how mindsight and integration brought about a more relatable Sidney with a quieter ego. A more conscious Sidney was better at listening and collaboration. His team trusted him more than when he was snappy, impatient, and critical.

INTRODUCING THE QUIET EGO

American psychologists Jack Bauer and Heidi Wayment have defined the quiet ego as being mindful, emotionally intelligent, compassionate, and growth oriented, in a balanced state of concern for self and others.[16] The quiet ego is just beginning to be studied by leadership researchers. Even without research, we can see that conscious leaders like Sidney develop a quieter ego over time. Given that shadow states generate a noisy, self-focused ego, aspiring for a quieter ego certainly sounds like a good compass setting for leaders—"perhaps for all of us."

Interestingly, Heidi Wayment and her team published a study of business-to-business salespeople in which they concluded that a quiet ego improves selling behaviors, especially in conflicts. They note that a quiet ego means "having the quiet strength to ask for what you need in a way that is good for you and good for others."[17]

PRACTICE

In this section, we introduce you to a mindfulness framework developed by neuroscientist David Vago and Harvard psychiatrist David Silbersweig: the S-ART framework, which stands for three steps: self-awareness, self-regulation, and self-transcendence.[18]

We are applying the S-ART framework (adapted by coauthor Moore for coaching and leadership) to help you transcend your agitated emotions—your leadership shadows, which distort and bias your mind's perceptions of yourself, other people, and the world.

The S-ART framework was derived from extensive study of the brain networks engaged in varied states of mindfulness. Neuroscientists use the term *brain network* to describe a particular brain activity or process. A brain network is a network of interconnected neurons (also called a neural network) that brain imaging studies have shown to be associated with a particular brain activity. We use the metaphor of dialing up and down, or switching on and off, brain networks as a way to imagine controlling your brain's activities. For example, you could say to your brain, "Hello, brain. Please dial down thinking. Please dial up listening."

The following four steps operationalize the S-ART model in service of transcending your leadership shadows and quieting your ego noise.

STEP ONE: PREPARATION

In Step One you stabilize and prepare your mind for integration.

1. Mental dial. Imagine you have a mental dial in your brain that you can use to dial various brain networks up or down.

2. Pause thinking. Dial DOWN your frontal networks (in your forehead) for thinking and judging. Then you are not analyzing and judging yourself.

3. Detach from emotions. Dial UP your mindsight brain network that detaches from aroused emotions. Rather than feeling strong emotions, you observe them. For example, rather than feeling ANGRY, you notice a feeling of anger.

4. Focus your attention. Dial UP your attention network and focus your attention as if it's a spotlight that you can move around your brain, expanding or narrowing at will.

5. Focus on experiencing. Focus your attention spotlight on networks in the back of your brain that are open and receptive, and take in sensory information. Focus on experiencing (not thinking or feeling) your mental and emotional activity.

STEP TWO: AWARENESS

Now that your mind is stable and receptive, experience your shadow state. Bring to mind an uncomfortable state of emotional arousal triggered by a leadership challenge.

1. Experience fully. Experience the agitated emotional state in your brain and body. Dial UP the emotional volume— let it rise and expand, to move up and out as if it were a cloud or wave of emotional energy that can move up and out. Stay neutral and observant. (As much as possible, keep the thinking and judging networks dialed DOWN.)

2. Give the emotional state a name. Describe the aroused emotional state in a granular way. Perhaps it's impatient frustration or irritated impatience or disappointed irritation. The more granular you are, the more your brain can detach and loosen the Velcro grip of your ego noise.

STEP THREE: REGULATION

Now it's time to regulate your shadow.

1. Self-compassion. Dial UP kindness toward your aroused state. Feel compassion for our shared humanity—you are not the first or last leader to feel this way.

2. Acceptance. Dial UP acceptance. Accept that this agitated state is a necessary, though unpleasant, experience on your leadership path.

3. Understand the purpose. Appreciate that the purpose of the aroused emotional state is not to derail you but to offer a healthy path to integration into something good—new calm, strength, and even wisdom.

STEP FOUR: TRANSCENDENCE

Now it's time to transcend your shadow.

1. Expand your perspectives. Try out the intellectual stimulation process we describe in chapter 9, one of four components of transformational leadership you can apply to self-transformation. Dial UP the brainstorming brain network. Seek, generate, and welcome a wide variety of views and perspectives on the situation that is arousing or agitating you.

2. Set aside. Change the channel by shifting your focus to other activities, such as relaxing, sleeping well, exercising, or going for a walk. You are giving your brain the space it needs to automatically perform its natural function of integration when you are not focused on the agitated state.

3. Notice when you feel a shift. The uncomfortable state has relaxed or faded. Maybe after a good night's sleep. Maybe during or after a generative conversation or coaching session. Maybe after a walk or workout. Integration is a gentle

receiving process; it is not an effortful push like getting through a to-do list.

As you can see, the integration process is a natural growth process. You can trust that integration will lift you out of your ego noise and increase your consciousness and objectivity. You will welcome new and bigger challenges that generate new ego noise, switching ON your growth mindset. When you make time for self-awareness, regulation, and transcendence or integration, your leadership will become calmer and clearer and stronger. You will lead with more pleasure and less strain.

INTEGRATION—UNDERUSE

The main focus of conscious leadership is seeing yourself and your influence objectively, with minimal interference from your noisy ego. The vast majority of leaders are navigating a good deal of ego noise, so we are focusing this section on underuse rather than overuse of the conscious capacity.

The self-oriented elements of emotional intelligence show up in conscious leaders: They regulate their behavior—that is, how they present themselves to others, which in turn determines how they are perceived by others. Leaders who have a strong ego, or self-identity, sometimes lack awareness of how they're perceived by others. They may have an inflated and unrealistic sense of themselves. They may believe that their ego is quiet and confident, but their behavior, at least some of the time, may reveal anxiety and insecurity. The body expresses the true state of its owner, putting the inner world of a leader on full display.

Good leaders are open to feedback; they listen closely to somebody who tells them how they are coming across. Preferably that person is a trusted mentor, colleague, or coach who provides psychological safety (an element of relational leadership). Followers can provide valuable feedback if they trust their leaders. This feedback can help leaders become aware that they may not be as conscious as they think they are.

LEADERSHIP EXAMPLE

Mike, the CEO of a fast-growing travel services organization, had a positive and perhaps overly inflated sense of himself, believing he was self-aware and self-controlled in feelings and actions. He tended to be introverted and quiet, yet decisive and fast moving, with a strong sense of authority and belief in himself. Although still young for a CEO, he spent a few years working successfully in investment banking, where the competitive culture taught him to communicate with confidence, vision, and a strong presence. He was transformational in his focus on innovation, risk-taking, and work ethic.

A 360-feedback assessment, along with discussions with his colleagues, revealed dissonance between how Mike shows up in one-on-one situations versus group presentations (to the board of directors, investors, senior team, and even the larger organization of about a hundred staff during town hall meetings). In the latter, he comes across as competent, focused, intentional, even inspirational. By contrast, in more intimate situations, colleagues noted that his physical presence contrasts with his public persona: He tends to be distracted, terse, and directive. He sometimes asks questions, but doesn't take time to listen to the answers. He becomes impatient if a colleague is not quick to respond.

Physically, he comes across as anxious and uncomfortable, with shaking knees, bouncing legs, and an inability to sit still. He continuously taps his pen on the desk and continually glances at his watch or smartphone. He appears overworked, tired, and unaware of how he's coming across, causing many to feel uncomfortable and doubt his confidence. He sometimes barks orders and cuts meetings short, leaving colleagues confused and nonplussed. There is a major disconnect between his public and private personas.

Feedback on this behavior was tough for Mike to accept. But ultimately, with self-reflection and coaching, he developed the ability to first self-regulate and then self-transcend—to turn the agitation into calm. It wasn't immediately obvious to Mike that his physical presence in smaller intimate settings contradicted his sense of self as grounded and centered, and that his anxiety, although hidden behind strong speaking skills, left his team wondering whether he was insecure or uncomfortable in his role.

While this chapter emphasizes that the ability to become present to one's emotional, mental, and physical states improves with consistent practice, showing up with heightened awareness in one context doesn't guarantee it will spread to every domain. Mike was highly self-aware and self-regulated in group settings—where the stakes were high. But his awareness of himself and others was offline in intimate settings, where he reverted to his "lower self."

Recognizing and regulating his agitated states with his colleagues were important steps forward for Mike. Once he became aware of the disconnect, he could see the benefit of incorporating mindfulness practices into his routine. In fact, taking a few moments to calm himself, breathe deeply, center, and focus were practices that he dusted off. He had learned them in programs to develop presentation skills—to get ready to speak eloquently and with executive presence in group settings.

Taking just a small amount of time to calm his anxiety, get clear on who he wanted to be with his colleagues—steady, curious, connected, grounded—helped him show up as more relaxed, open, and ready to listen.

Chapter Summary

- As a conscious leader, you are calm, stable, and objective, and see clearly, including yourself.

- As a self-aware leader, you observe your emotional states and select the good ones to act on (create, strive, persist, take a break) and the ones to set aside (agitation, reactivity).

- In common with most leaders you may exhibit leadership shadows, states of ego overdrive, or avoidance based on stress, worries, and fears, which can be derailers.

- To become a more conscious leader, you integrate your shadows by implementing the S-ART framework—self-awareness, self-regulation, and self-transcendence.

- Your leadership ego gets quieter with experience, integration, and maturity; your objectivity increases, and leadership gets easier.

FROM SCIENCE TO IMPACT ON YOU

- What makes conscious leadership valuable to you?
- What inspires you to become a more conscious leader?
- What did you learn about being a conscious leader?
- What did you know that was confirmed?
- What questions come up?
- Revisit your self-ratings in table I.1 in the introduction: How has this chapter
  - Confirmed your strengths?
  - Increased your motivation and confidence?
  - Impacted your interest in getting better at being a conscious leader?

CHAPTER 2

AUTHENTIC

Care

When well-being comes from engaging our strengths and virtues, our lives are imbued with authenticity.

—MARTIN SELIGMAN[1]

As an authentic leader, you model character with integrity, walking the talk in communication, action, and decisions. Self-awareness includes reflecting on your personal values—what you care about; what's important about your leadership role; and what positive contribution you want to make to new leaders, the workforce, the organization, other stakeholders, and beyond. You think about what excellence means, both personally and collectively. You help a team or organization align around a shared purpose that fulfills shared values. By being open and sincere, you create high-quality work relationships and inspire the workforce to fulfill the organization's purpose.

LEADERSHIP STORY

"I know who I am, and I know what I want." These were Jennifer's words in her first coaching session. Jennifer was head of sales for a large global legal software organization. It was immediately clear that she was headstrong, talented, ambitious, and wholly committed to her career success. Considering Jennifer's strong sense of self and belief in her capabilities, one might ask: Why would she need coaching?

Jennifer confided that she had been successful for many years at a top software company, moving from a sales assistant role to one of sales manager, always excelling by "making her numbers." When she was recruited to her current role, she was excited to be at the pinnacle of sales, and eager to make a significant leap in financial remuneration.

Having worked for years with highly educated software engineers, Jennifer was comfortable transitioning to a software firm led by lawyers. She was smart; they were smart. Early in her tenure, she was enthusiastic about her role, believing in her team's and colleagues' abilities to achieve great things together. Her team included several professionals who reported to her; she was their leader.

She had faced setbacks, however. Her performance reviews had not gone as well as she had hoped. She sought coaching on her own initiative, and prepared by putting together a PowerPoint presentation outlining her strengths and growth opportunities. Notably, Jennifer's definition of success was tied to her title, compensation, and achievements—not to her effectiveness as a leader.

Jennifer was not new to the benefits of coaching. She had worked with a coach multiple times earlier in her life as an athlete. Coaching had helped her elevate her basketball game.

This time, coaching was different. With her coach, she delved deeper into what it would take for her to upgrade her leadership skills. Coaching was a huge wake-up call, in terms of becoming not just a more conscious or self-aware leader but a truly authentic one.

Despite Jennifer's transparent and direct approach to leading, her focus on success was self-centered. While she claimed to care about her team's success, it became clear that this was true only if it made her look good to senior management and prepared her for the next rung on the leadership ladder.

Jennifer's stated desire for greater collaboration was undermined by her competitive nature, especially with peers and sometimes with her own team. When her coach asked her about effective collaboration, she sighed in frustration, believing she was already good at it and disagreeing with feedback suggesting otherwise.

Jennifer described herself as a gifted storyteller. Yet she was told in feedback sessions that she wasn't particularly collaborative or inspirational. It became clear that although she excelled in front of clients, her communication gifts did not translate to her team. She was poised, present, articulate—impressive—in client presentations but failed to inspire her own people.

When asked why she didn't hit it out of the park with her team, she reacted defensively. She believed her team needed to up their game and was committed to coaching them, but felt they lacked her intrinsic drive. On one level, her response made sense, but something felt off. It wasn't clear whether she genuinely believed she needed a coach or whether she was using coaching to reinforce her belief in her capabilities, hoping to prove her bosses wrong.

VALUES DRIVEN

Digging down into her motivations, Jennifer probed more deeply into her ambition: When would she consider her professional life a success? This question was challenging for Jennifer. She had always equated success with having the big corner office, respect from senior colleagues, and increasing financial rewards.

In a broader conversation about success, she discussed the purpose of the organization and how her values aligned with their mission. She grew quiet, realizing she hadn't thought much about the connection between her values and the company's purpose. She respected the legal technology services offered to clients, but, in a moment of candor, she admitted she didn't love legal software; she was a driver of sales, regardless of the service line.

At the same time, it wasn't difficult for her to understand that for her team to feel committed and passionate about their jobs, they needed to hear from their leader that she believed in the value of their contributions. They needed to hear how their leader's values aligned with their own values along with the company's goals.

Initially, Jennifer dismissed this as obvious, but on further discussion, she realized that her focus on sales targets overshadowed her interest in inspiring her team. Jennifer's sales team meetings were data driven. She talked about past successes and future goals. She saw her own hard work as role modeling, but it failed to inspire her team.

When asked about her virtues as a leader (excellence in both quality and benefits to humanity, as we discussed in chapter 1), Jennifer listed ethics, integrity, work ethic, transparency, and fairness. When pressed to think about what virtuous behaviors she could express to inspire her team beyond just making numbers, she was stumped.

This chapter's science section confirms that authentic leaders operate with keen awareness of their values. They seek to align their personal purpose with what is meaningful and valuable to others and the collective. Jennifer modeled some virtues explored by scholars, including drive, integrity, and judgment. Yet the expression of virtuous leadership that was missing from Jennifer's self-portrayal was a strong sense of caring about what is good for others—for her team and the whole.

Jennifer's coach asked her whether she felt compassion for her teammates, her boss, even for herself. Catalyzing a deeper level of reflection and, ultimately, purpose, this question hit home: If it weren't for the lofty paycheck, what would get her out of bed in the morning?

Through reflection, Jennifer recognized that in her work life she had paid scant attention to humanistic elements such as empathy, compassion, and caring. These skills were outside her comfort zone. But when she discussed the importance of a leader demonstrating benevolence, a passion for the success of her team and the entire organization—not just herself—a spark inside her was ignited.

FROM CONSCIOUS TO AUTHENTIC

It was in these revelatory moments that Jennifer softened her stance and opened herself to a new level of self-reflection, to becoming *conscious*, not unlike Sidney's breakthrough in chapter 1. Becoming a conscious leader was an important first step toward seeing herself objectively—strengths, warts, and all.

Jennifer discovered her commitment to being authentically good. It surprised her that she didn't have to lose her competitive edge to be virtuous. But she did need to raise her periscope and be less myopically focused on her own success. She needed to scan the organizational horizon and attune to what was important and valuable to others. She became conscious of the potential for all to be virtuous—together.

This realization was a turning point. Leadership was not just about building a competitive team to win but about becoming an authentic leader, inspiring others by linking personal and shared values to a greater purpose. Using her storytelling abilities in new ways, she showed her team members how to make a positive impact on clients' lives. This coaching journey would take Jennifer on an expansive journey toward becoming not just a better leader but a more fulfilled person.

UNDERSTANDING THE SCIENCE

In their article "We Don't Need More Leaders—We Need More *Good* Leaders," a Tasmanian team of scientists led by Toby Newstead put it simply: "To be a good leader one needs first to be of good character, and good character is built of virtues."[2] They define virtue as "the human inclination to feel, think, and act in ways that express moral excellence and contribute to the common good."[3] Being a good leader involves acting on what's good for others.

Models of virtue-based leadership, including authentic leadership, came alive in the early 2000s following multiple ethical leadership failures, including those at Enron and WorldCom.[4] We witnessed in these organizational failures the important role leaders play in modeling integrity or, in these cases, unethical values and behaviors.[5]

Another Tasmanian team led by Joseph Crawford updated prior definitions of authentic leadership to better reflect the role of character in good leadership: "An authentic leader influences and motivates followers to achieve goals through their sincerity and positive moral perspective." The authors explain that "positive moral perspective is the commitment to one's intrinsic ethical framework, and a willingness to subdue personal interests and ego to facilitate collective interests."[6]

We will come back to character later and talk about the leader character framework developed by professors at Canada's Ivey Business School.[7]

OUTCOMES OF AUTHENTIC LEADERSHIP

To compare outcomes of authentic leadership and transformational leadership, George Banks in North Carolina and his Texan collaborators evaluated one hundred studies.[8] They recounted the four components of the research-based definition of authentic leadership: self-awareness, relational transparency, balanced processing, and an internalized moral perspective.

In this chapter, we focus on relational transparency: showing one's true self to others, the self that is anchored in one's values, purpose, and desire to make a difference. Recall in chapter 1 on conscious leaders that we introduced the importance of a leader's self-awareness or self-objectivity. Balanced processing refers to an open, objective approach to decision-making that considers multiple perspectives.

The comparison by Banks et al. concluded that while the two models, authentic and transformational, produce similar outcomes, authentic leadership had a greater impact on organizational performance and organizational citizenship (serving the collective good) than transformational leadership.

By contrast, transformational leadership (chapter 9) had a higher impact than authentic leadership on individual performance—including task performance, leadership effectiveness, and follower satisfaction with the leader.

Aspiring to be both authentic and transformational makes sense. The virtuous caring of authentic leaders seems to spread and improve organizational performance, while the intellectual stimulation of transformational leaders improves individual performance.

A report on a study led by Niklas Steffens and collaborators in Australia, titled "Knowing Me, Knowing Us," concludes that a leader's genuine support of collective interests, even more than a leader's sincerity, is associated with elevated levels of organizational performance. The researchers concluded, "Leader personal self-awareness tended to have stronger effects on perceptions of authentic leadership than it did on people's support for leaders; leader collective [awareness] had stronger effects on people's support than on perceptions of leader authenticity.[9]

Simplifying the study's takeaways, the authentically good character of leaders, in terms of collective awareness and serving the collective interest, delivers better follower support and organizational results than simply being authentic. Notice how well this ties into the quiet ego in our discussion of conscious leadership. A quiet ego effectively balances self-interest, vital to a leader's own thriving, with the thriving of the collective.

Bottom line? Being authentic is good for the leader. Being authentically good is good for followers and the organization.

VIRTUES

Which virtues are most important in a leader's character? While the application of any particular virtue is context specific, a well-cited values model developed by American Israeli psychologist Shalom Schwartz is a good place to start. In his model, two lower-level self-oriented values are *self-enhancement*, through achievement and power, and *conservation*, through tradition and conformity. Higher-level values are *self-transcendence*, through heightened humility and benevolence for the workforce, family, and society, and *openness to change*, through a high level of new stimulation and challenge.[10] We will come back to the openness-to-change virtue in our chapter on agility.

A comprehensive model of virtues was published in 2004, a most ambitious contribution by positive psychology leaders Christopher Peterson and Martin Seligman. Peterson and Seligman note that the idea of virtue as an orientation toward excellence and flourishing is remarkably consistent across time and cultures.[11]

Peterson and Seligman identified six universal virtues, encompassing twenty-four character strengths, essential to the survival of human communities.[12] Their work was based on deep study of ancient Chinese, Greek, and Middle Eastern traditions. The six virtues are courage, justice, humanity, temperance, transcendence, and wisdom.[13] Individual assessment of virtues and character strengths is mainstream, readily available in forty-five languages, and widely used in coaching to help people connect to their better selves.[14]

Recall that Sidney had traversed the globe in his leadership evolution, from São Paolo to New York City and then Singapore. In his experience on three continents, he was exposed to a wide variety of cultural differences. He came to see the virtues of the best leaders as remarkably similar, even when considering cultural differences, which included the varied ways that hierarchy and power structures were handled. His growth into a conscious and authentic leader was grounded in these shared, universal virtues.

LEADING WITH VIRTUE

Positive organizational psychologist Kim Cameron and colleagues, many at the University of Michigan's Center for Positive Organizations, integrated the Peterson-Seligman work on virtues into leadership in the early 2000s. More broadly, they defined positive organizational behavior as the study of individual and collective flourishing in organizations.[15] (We discuss their work outside virtues in our chapter on positive leadership.)

Management professor and Institute of Coaching research leader David Bright and colleagues offer three virtue-related principles relevant to leaders. First is that the human inclination to be virtuous has an evolutionary basis. It is a basic moral instinct to draw upon. Second, being virtuous is a capacity that can be developed. Third, "People feel empowered and energized when they experience virtuousness. . . . Witnessing virtuous actions tends to inspire more of the same."[16]

Bright and colleagues caution that virtues are more than behaviors. Virtues need to have an underlying association with a kind of excellence that also generates well-being, making it authentically good. Otherwise, so-called virtues can have dark sides. For example, forgiveness can perpetuate abuse, and optimism can promote risky behaviors. They also note that a virtue is an ideal point on a continuum in a particular context, ranging from too little (e.g., curiosity) to too much (e.g., humility). This means leaders need to be wise in calibrating the dose of virtuous behavior for a specific context.[17]

How does a leader demonstrate virtue? Once you consciously tap into your virtuous motivation, your desire to improve some form of human (or even planetary) thriving generates small habits of virtue. And much of what a leader does, including acting in virtuous ways, is a form of modeling. The bottom line on being authentically good? The more frequently you communicate and model virtuous intent in words and actions, the more you can improve others' support and performance.

It's worth noting the synergies of conscious and authentic leadership, which were robust for both Sidney and Jennifer. You saw the improvements in team engagement as both Sidney and Jennifer became more grounded, then present and awake. They aligned their values with what was good for their teams. They both rose to the occasion, answering the call to be more conscious AND authentic.

LEADER CHARACTER FRAMEWORK

An Ivey Business School team of professors, Mary Crossan, Gerard Seijts, and Jeffrey Gandz, developed a framework of eleven character dimensions, emerging from their research on leadership character.[18] Ivey research has demonstrated that moving from weak to strong character has shown positive impact on many outcomes, including leadership effectiveness, employee voice, and job satisfaction.[19]

In the list that follows, we connect the eleven character dimensions (capitalized) in the leader character framework to our nine capacities (not capitalized), not as a definitive map but simply to show that values and virtues underpin each of the nine capacities. Note that the first seven leader character dimensions (italicized) are the Peterson-Seligman character strengths and virtues with the same name:

1. *Judgment*—conscious, agile
2. *Humanity*—compassionate
3. *Humility*—servant
4. *Temperance*—conscious
5. *Courage*—transformational
6. *Transcendence*—transformational
7. *Justice*—shared
8. Accountability—shared
9. Collaboration—relational
10. Drive—positive
11. Integrity—authentic

The point we want to make is that each of the nine capacities works best as a motivated expression of your values or virtues. This makes each capacity personally meaningful. For example, you are authentic because you care about integrity. You are a servant leader because you value humility. You share leadership because fairness is important to you. This is why we ask the question at the end of each chapter—what makes this capacity valuable to you?

The Ivey team's findings on trends in character suggest that many leaders would benefit from improving their conscious, relational, and compassionate capacities: "Our research reveals a consistent overweighting of the character dimensions of drive, accountability, and integrity and an associated under-weighting of temperance, transcendence, humility, and humanity. When the traits associated with integrity—being authentic, candid, transparent, principled, and consistent—are overweighted without being counterbalanced by the under-weighted dimensions—self-awareness, vulnerability, empathy, compassion, patience, and calm—a person can end up being a bully, abrasive, dogmatic, and toxic."[20]

MEANING AND PURPOSE

Scholars debate the roles and interrelationships of values, meaning, and purpose for leaders and workforces. Norwegian business school professor Rune Todnem By proposed simplifying all of the complexity by defining leadership as an activity simply *in pursuit of purpose.*[21] A purpose can be thought of as one's values and virtues expressed as a central aim and direction, which makes a purpose meaningful, and meaning purposeful.

Dutch professor of organizational behavior Daan van Knippenberg lays out a concept of meaning-based leadership grounded in a shared organizational purpose. He explains that all organizations have a purpose, even in the absence of a vision, and that a shared purpose can deliver high-quality meaning-based motivation.[22] Said another way, putting our personal or shared values into action toward an organizational purpose makes our work meaningful.

In his third True North book, former Medtronics CEO Bill George encourages leaders to set an organizational compass in the direction of a true north—a purpose, making a difference, and having an impact.[23] McKinsey partners Dewar, Keller, and Malhotra studied the practices of CEOs of high-performing organizations, concluding that what matters to excellent CEOs is not a fine graining of vision, values, mission, meaning, and purpose but "to have a clear and simply articulated North Star for the company that redefines success, influences decisions, and inspires people to act in desired ways."[24]

Bill George's True North and the McKinsey partners' North Star point everyone toward leading in virtuous ways in the direction of a virtuous purpose or vision. A virtuous compass direction provides the inspiration and deep meaning needed for all to perform together at their best.

PRACTICE

You have likely encountered values statements prominently displayed in the entryways of corporate offices. These statements often convey such ideals as teamwork, customer service, excellence, and a commitment to being the best. Of course, one has to wonder whether these values are genuinely embraced and practiced or merely displayed for show.

For leaders dedicated to fulfilling authentic and meaningful corporate values, a crucial first step is to align your personal values with the values you wish to be actualized in the organization's work. This process begins with introspection to clarify your own core values. By understanding what is truly important to you, you can arrive at coherence between your own values and the corporate values you advocate for.

Following are two approaches to self-reflection on your personal values. You can do these exercises alone, although working with a coach, spouse, or mentor can amp up the results.

First, consider doing an evidence-based character assessment. One example is the VIA (values-in-action) Character Strengths assessment, developed and tested by psychologist Christopher Peterson. A free assessment is available online; it will give you a quick rundown of your top character strengths, which will help you uncover your core values.[25] Another option is the leader character assessment included in a character development app called Virtuosity developed by the Ivey team.[26]

Alternatively, you can reflect on the aspects of your life that feel indispensable and journal about your fundamental drives and motivations. One powerful way to tap into your values is to ask a confidant who knows you well to quickly list what they consider to be your top five virtues or strengths. You may be surprised by what you hear!

With this feedback, you can reflect on how your virtues are perceived by others. When we use this exercise with coaching clients, they often discover deeper values that are not accessible through self-reflection alone.

Once you have identified your personal values, the next step is to consider what action steps you can take to manifest these values in your daily leadership practice. It is important to actively role-model your values through your communication and behavior; this reinforces two key attributes of an authentic leader:

- Aligning your personal values with your actions

- Expressing virtues that serve the collective, which can inspire others to reflect on their own values

The final step is to align your values and followers' values into a purpose that resonates powerfully with everyone. Ultimately, the integration of personal values into corporate values can lead to a more cohesive, values-driven culture that inspires and empowers all its members to accomplish more.

INTEGRATION—OVERUSE

It may seem strange to think of authenticity as something that could be overused or show up as an ego state that becomes a problem. How could one's values, if expressed with honesty and integrity, become an obstacle to effective leading? Core virtues including ethical behavior and honesty may stand the test of time with an inherent sense of justice, but one's personal values may evolve throughout a lifetime, and often may not align with the values of others.

VALUING DIFFERENCE

Leaders can become so attached to their values that they lose the ability to listen, be open, and be respectful of those with different values. The overly driven ego state of authentic leaders can show up as righteousness or rigidity. If a leader demonstrates a great deal of commitment to their values but doesn't have the space to listen openly to the values of others, the rigidity may become an obstacle to welcoming diverse viewpoints and perspectives.

Many organizations have teams of people from all walks of life—different countries, races, and cultures. Authentic leaders are culturally humble, respectful, and open to learning about the values of cultures different from their own. They are able to see and forge common ground: alignment around values shared by all.

BELIEFS: NOT VALUES

It is helpful for authentic leaders to explore the distinction between core beliefs (ideas and opinions they hold as true) and core values (what is important and meaningful). The historical basis of their beliefs and how they evolved—from childhood experiences, from spiritual or religious communities to which they belong, and so on—may cause a leader to have a strong attachment to beliefs and see them as values. But values are deeper, more stable phenomena than beliefs. The distinction between beliefs and values is illustrated in our example here.

LEADERSHIP EXAMPLE

Mary, the chief operating officer of a nonprofit organization of mechanical engineers, is highly ethical, honest, and well intentioned. Working in a nonprofit environment, she's passionate about serving her constituency. She leads a team that delivers educational programs, conferences, and other services for the engineers in a way that shows up as highly ethical, transparent, and having integrity. At the same time, however, Mary demonstrates a tendency to espouse what she considers values and express their religious foundation in such a manner that those who don't hold similar beliefs feel at times unwelcome and diminished.

Mary's background in a religious, conservative family supported her in building a foundation of integrity. However, she assumed that her beliefs and her values were the same. Hence, her personal narrative became a public expression not only of her conservatism but of her sense of moral superiority. Mary was unaware at first that her personal definition of values-driven leadership was driving a wedge between her and some members of her diverse team, who had come from different backgrounds and different religions. They didn't feel heard.

The good news is that Mary was committed to leveraging the full diversity of her team. She had made a commitment to hire people with different backgrounds from her own, different races, different genders, and different cultures. When the feedback from colleagues, a mentor, and a coach indicated that Mary needed to be more sensitive to the varied backgrounds of others and draw upon universal values they could all share, not just those based on her personal experience, it wasn't a huge leap for her to look for common ground.

This shift in perspective led Mary to a deeper level of authenticity. It required her to become a student of differences at a level she hadn't yet pursued. She found herself excited and motivated to learn about the cultures of her diverse team and to bring their unique stories, beliefs, and rituals into the team dynamic. This process enlivened everyone. She did not need to relinquish her own beliefs to welcome diverse perspectives—in fact the opposite was true.

Once she came to see that the core values of her team members, even those from extremely different backgrounds, were fundamentally similar, she was able to be less strident and rigid. She was more open to looking for the common themes that underpinned the organization's success. Those themes were service, humanity, quality, and teamwork. This was important for Mary to take to heart: Core values cross the divides of religion, culture, and nationality.

Chapter Summary

- As an authentic leader, you combine sincerity and being true to your values, with authentic caring about the interests and values of the collective.

- Virtues combine excellence in quality with excellence in outcomes in serving collective interests.

- Being authentic benefits the leader. Being authentically good benefits followers and the organization.

- Virtues need to be adjusted to the context—for example, forgiveness may not be appropriate in an abusive situation.

- Virtues and values are expressed as purpose—a central aim or compass direction for a leader and an organization.

FROM SCIENCE TO IMPACT ON YOU

- What makes authentic leadership valuable to you?
- What inspires you to become a more authentic leader?
- What did you learn about being an authentic leader?
- What did you know that was confirmed?
- What questions come up?
- Revisit your self-ratings in table I.1 in the introduction: How has this chapter
    - Confirmed your sense of being authentic?
    - Increased your motivation and confidence to act authentically?
    - Impacted your interest in getting better at expressing your core values in action?

CHAPTER 3

AGILE

Flex

Setting oneself on a predetermined course in unknown waters is the perfect way to sail straight into an iceberg.

—HENRY MINTZBERG[1]

As an agile leader, you move flexibly and fluidly across many tasks, perspectives, emotional states, polarities, and conflicts. You zoom in and out, zipping up and down from detail to big picture, from adversity to opportunity, from knowing to not knowing, from deep focus to mind-wandering, from rest to driving forward, from the stable status quo to disruptive change, and on and on.

LEADERSHIP STORY

Peter is the executive director of a nonprofit with a purpose of developing innovative ways to combat climate change. He has the impressive ability to pull together a diverse team of researchers, engineers, and project managers, all working closely together. In order to take his team's performance to the next level, Peter hired a coach.

Peter was adamant, right at the outset of his coaching, that he was not a typical entrepreneur: "I'm no Steve Jobs," he said. "I'm actually an introvert. Even though I have a strong vision and a sense of mission for my organization, I'm a big believer in collaborative work and consensus decision-making. I often lead, as they say, from behind."

Peter operated from a deeply authentic place of integrity. He was emotionally intelligent, sensitive to the needs of others, a good listener (maybe too good), and even willing to be vulnerable at times.

What he wasn't, as it turned out, was flexible. He had a particularly structured, organized, and habituated approach to managing his team that, when things were stable, brought out the best in everyone. Under his leadership, Peter's team was highly engaged and full of creative solutions. Then, in early 2020, COVID-19 arrived, disrupting the organization's normal operations and forcing a sudden transition to remote work.

In March 2020, Peter and his team were required to switch from being together in their big city offices to working virtually. Peter floundered. When he could no longer check in on his team in person on a regular basis, it became even more important to ensure that the team was still fully engaged. When it was suggested to Peter that the circumstances might require him to exhibit a more extraverted and directive style, he was initially reluctant. "I've never been comfortable being a bossy boss," he said, "and I'm not sure the team will respond well to that kind of shift."

FROM CONSISTENCY TO FLEXIBILITY

He talked about the anxiety and uncertainty everyone was feeling, fearing that their funding would dry up, key people might get sick, or their climate change agenda might just completely drop off everyone's radar screen, leaving them with not only no office to go to but no work at all.

Agile leaders change things up, sometimes dramatically, when the need arises.

The shift to virtual work created significant challenges. Peter initially attempted to re-create the office environment virtually, maintaining the same meeting schedules and workflows. However, he soon realized that the new circumstances required a different approach. Team members, each grappling with their unique challenges, found it difficult to adhere to the old routines. The previously successful consensus-driven approach now felt forced and ineffective.

Recognizing the need for change, Peter began to reassess his leadership style. Without the ability to check in regularly in person, he needed to rely on his team members to manage their tasks independently. This required a significant shift, moving from a hands-off approach to one that emphasized clear direction and accountability.

As we discuss in the science section, he needed to be agile and shift his approach. Peter adopted a more extraverted and directive leadership style rather than relying on nudging in check-ins. When confronting his reluctance to drive the team, as he would put it, he reflected on the many times in his life when he had been directive, extraverted, and forceful. "Of course I can be forceful," he noted, "when I present at conferences. I walk out on stage, and even though I'm nervous, I'm quite capable of giving a presentation for over an hour to hundreds of people." The question for him to consider: Where does that sense of presence, the comfort as front person in the spotlight, come from?

Peter began to engage his inner extravert. Initially, he was concerned that showing up as strident or authoritarian, especially in a virtual setting, might be a real turnoff to some who were used to a more collegial, partner-like style. Yet he also immediately saw the deeper truth: He wouldn't lose his ability to lead from behind. It was more a matter of being flexible and curious, experimenting in the moment.

Recognizing that the situation called for being not only empathic and comforting but also directive, Peter didn't have to be stuck in an either/or dynamic. He could integrate his introverted tendencies and find ways to be authoritative without being authoritarian.

Peter experimented with this new style, being transparent and self-deprecating about the shift. He engaged his team in discussions about leadership during a crisis, which sparked camaraderie and renewed energy. He shared with his team the reason behind his more directive stance and made it clear that his goal was to maintain momentum on their projects, while still listening and providing emotional support during this difficult time. His newfound three-part balance among authority, vulnerability, and empathy helped the team adapt and maintain their productivity.

ENGAGING POLARITIES WITH HUMILITY

A crucial lesson for Peter was about the importance of empowerment and trust. He was forthright and direct about the need for his team to continue to focus on work output despite lockdowns (empowerment), and this clarity enabled him to rely on his team members to manage their tasks independently (trust).

Communication also played a vital role in Peter's transition. By being transparent about the changes, maintaining open lines of communication, and being a supportive listener when needed, he was able to address concerns and keep the team aligned with the organization's goals. Regular check-ins, even if virtual, helped maintain a sense of connection and support among the team members.

We discussed in chapter 2 on authentic leadership that being humble and candid about one's struggle through change, so long as it connects with core values that are consistent, strengthens the trust and camaraderie needed to get through difficult times—like a pandemic.

Peter's story serves as a powerful reminder that agile leadership is not defined by a single style or approach. Instead, it is characterized by the ability to adapt and respond to the ever-changing landscape in work and in life.

UNDERSTANDING THE SCIENCE

The concept of agile leadership was born with the 2001 Agile Manifesto signed by seventeen software developers after a meeting at a Utah ski resort.[2] Its tenets aimed to humanize the development process and reduce bureaucratic drag. They valued human talents and interactions over business processes and collaboration with customers over contractual matters.

Although these tenets are popular in software and beyond, and spawned the field of agile coaching,[3] agile leadership has not been supported by a tribe of researchers or a large scientific literature.

Alignment on a science-based definition is yet to come, and there is a lack of outcomes studies showing whether and how agile leadership is effective.

With these scientific gaps in mind, we are grounding agile leadership in the research on a variety of agile and flexible phenomena relevant to leadership. We start our tour by looking at the nature of an agile mind and other agile phenomena. Then we take a look at polarities (opposites) and some relevant leadership constructs.

THE AGILE MIND

An agile mind is able to shift attention swiftly and fully from one state or one activity to another, a process that neuroscientists call attentional set-shifting.[4] Set-shifting involves single-tasking (shifting from one single task to another), which is distinct from multitasking whereby you scatter your attention across multiple activities simultaneously and shallowly, with none getting a proper focus.[5]

Thanks go to psychologist Wilma Koutstaal for her 763-page scholarly book *The Agile Mind*. Dr. Koutstaal breaks down cognitive agility into two dimensions and four domains; figure 3.1 illustrates our adaptation of her model.[6] Here are the two dimensions:

- One dimension ranges from **high control** (e.g., evaluating a detailed financial spreadsheet) to **low control** (e.g., being in a state of creative flow, such as brainstorming).

- One dimension travels from **high specificity** (e.g., today's to-do list) to **low specificity** or high abstraction (e.g., organizational vision).

An agile mind travels quickly along the wide range from high to low control, and high to low specificity.

Koutstaal proposes four domains of cognitive agility, each operating across the two dimensions of high and low control and high and low specificity. We list the domains here in their own descending order of degree of control:

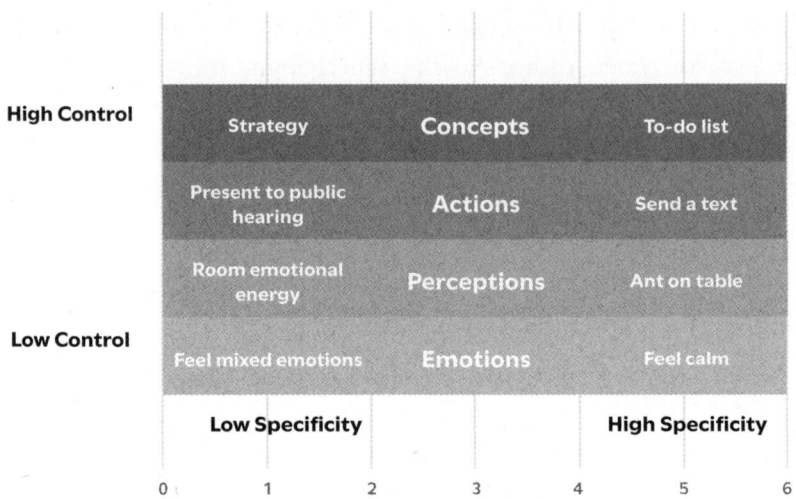

FIGURE 3.1. THE AGILE MIND—

TWO DIMENSIONS AND FOUR DOMAINS

1. **Thinking**—concepts (from strategy and vision to granular tasks and to-dos)

2. **Doing**—actions (from presenting in a public hearing to sending a quick text to a colleague)

3. **Perceiving**—perceptions (from sensing the collective emotional energy in an all-company session to seeing an ant on the meeting table)

4. **Feeling**—emotions (from arousal of multiple emotions to stable calm)

PSYCHOLOGICAL FLEXIBILITY

Psychological flexibility is the capacity to flex in two ways: be open and accepting of your emotional reactivity to the present circumstances and then to move forward into action based on your values. A robust evidence base has shown that psychological flexibility improves well-being.[7] Psychological flexibility is valuable to leaders as an agile combination of conscious leadership (open and aware) and authentically good leadership (values based).

In her book *Emotional Agility*, Harvard psychologist and Institute of Coaching cofounder Susan David lays out the practice of psychological flexibility in leadership, work, and life. First, you welcome and fully experience your emotions in productive ways. You then shift to align with your authentic values and move into action. David calls the action stage "walking your why," an example of authentic self-leadership.[8]

We added integration (or self-transcendence) to psychological flexibility in the chapter on conscious leadership. Beyond navigating your emotions, moving through self-oriented awareness, acceptance, compassion, and regulation, you then transform your emotional reactivity into calmness and strength. In fact, the hidden invitation of opposites is for you to head toward integration—solutions that integrate the opposites into something new and better.

CURIOSITY AS AGILITY

Turkish professor Büsra Müceldili and her team studied the importance of open-minded curiosity to being agile. People at work who are curious to explore and learn are comfortable with change and innovation.[9] Curious people are agile. They are interested in what's new, traveling far from the opposite—what's already known.

CREATIVITY AS AGILITY

Creative activities are by nature agile processes. Flow researcher Mihaly Csikszentmihalyi ("Me-high-lee Cheek-sent-me-high") describes the natural agility of creative people along many dimensions (what's called a dialectic personality).[10] These individuals

- Have a great deal of physical energy, but also are often quiet and at rest
- Combine playfulness and discipline, or responsibility and irresponsibility
- Alternate between imagination and fantasy, and a rooted sense of reality

- Tend to be both extraverted and introverted

- Are humble and proud at the same time

- Transcend rigid gender-role stereotyping

- Are both rebellious and conservative

- Are passionate about their work, yet can be extremely objective about it as well

INNOVATION AS AGILITY

In the innovation process, the tension between opposites as the new comes into contact with established ways is inevitable, calling for agility. Management professor Mary Uhl-Bien and Michael Arena while at GM describe this situation as an adaptive space, where there is by necessity a creative tension that recombines the status quo with the novel into a new, integrated whole.[11]

AGILITY, RESILIENCE, AND WELL-BEING

Setbacks, failures, and obstacles present opportunities for agility. Mengye Yu in Australia and collaborators in China and the UK explain, in their analysis of research on leaders and resilience, that leaders are more resilient when they are agile—when they welcome adversity as an opportunity to learn and adapt.[12]

When you are navigating more serious losses and disappointment, including grief, finding rays of hope and opportunity is an exercise in agility. You go back and forth between the emotional pain and the emerging growth and well-being, which, as we've learned from studies of posttraumatic growth, includes more meaning, better relationships, new strength and possibilities.[13] Agility isn't the whole story though— resilience and posttraumatic growth are also supported by high-quality relationships (chapter 4) and psychological resources (chapter 5).

Now that we are talking about agility and well-being, remember that an agile mind is working hard to flex and expand, even more so in the face of adversity, stress, and loss. Everyone, not just a leader, is prone to fatigue and burnout. Your physical body is a key resource for mental agility—the usual suspects (rest, good nutrition, and exercise) are vital to agile recovery, learning, and expansion.[14]

AGILE MINDSET

Let's head to a research definition of an agile mindset by Mordi and Schoop in Germany, which includes being open and willing to continually learn, adapt, improve, and grow.[15] Continuous learning and change, which may feel unsettling to followers, is then balanced with stabilizing forces—being responsible, accountable, and trustworthy. The agile mindset itself is good at balancing opposites, enabling you to go back and forth between change and stability as needed.

NAVIGATING POLARITIES AS AGILITY

Koutstaal notes that "agile thinking thrives in stimulating environments."[16] The word *stimulating* pretty well sums up today's world, although it may not be the first word that comes to mind. It's stimulating because organizational life is full of internal and external polarities—opposing and conflicting perspectives, values, and activities. The more we stretch (or our environment stretches) our minds to experience both ends of a polarity, the more agile our minds become.

Examples of polarities abound, beyond the lists of opposites we've already shared:

- Structured versus flexible

- Individual versus team

- Risk-taking versus stability

- Relationships versus results

- Thinking versus feeling

- Action versus reflection

- Hierarchy versus network

- Looking good versus getting better

In his book *Flex: The Art and Science of Leadership in a Changing World*, this book's coauthor Jeffrey Hull summarized qualitative surveys from a series of focus groups with executive coaches, who described the leadership behaviors on which they were most often called on to coach. The results pointed to polarities in behaviors, domains where leaders work with a coach to expand their agility.[17] The six most common leadership polarities were as follows:

- Decision-making (directive versus consensus driven)

- Communication (data/fact oriented versus narrative/storytelling)

- Emotional agility (stoic/restrained versus emotionally skilled)

- Authenticity (strong/competent versus humble/vulnerable)

- Collaboration (delegating/advising versus coaching/empowering)

- Engagement (productivity/results oriented versus innovation/creativity oriented)

We can see Peter's situation in the decision-making and emotional agility polarities. In the midst of lockdowns, he shifted his leadership style to support an anxious and disrupted team by becoming more directive (despite his natural home as a consensus builder) and emotionally skilled.

None of these attributes or behaviors are right or wrong. Agile responses to the context call for leaders to recognize and build on what they do naturally and to practice new ways of operating.

The book *Both/And Thinking* by American management professors Wendy Smith and Marianne Lewis describe the upside of working deeply with polarities, or paradoxes, as they call them. They organize paradoxes into four types:

- **Who** (identity)—e.g., conflicting roles as leader versus colleague

- **Why** (outcomes)—e.g., profit versus well-being

- **When** (time frame)—e.g., short term versus long term

- **How** (style)—e.g., control versus autonomy

Smith and Lewis describe people who are agile at using paradoxes: "These people leveraged paradoxes to solve their most challenging problems. They went beyond the presenting dilemmas to identify the underlying paradoxes. Doing so allowed them to find new, alternative approaches to their toughest problems. . . . Both/and thinking brought underlying paradoxes to light and opened new, more creative, and longer-lasting possibilities."[18]

CONFLICT RESOLUTION AS AGILITY

The agile flexing in navigating polarities is particularly helpful when you are seeking resolution of a conflict. An agile leader fully values, respects, and hears both sides of the polarity. The way forward integrates the polarities into learning, growth, and solutions that have common ground, with differences respected.[19]

THE AGILE LEADER

Moving along from an agile mind navigating many dimensions and domains, to polarities, we arrive at the basic capabilities of an agile leader, derived by German researcher Marco Brand and colleagues.[20] An agile leader

- Responds quickly and flexibly to changes and uncertainties

- Drives change proactively

- Integrates a fast-changing environment

What does agile leadership look like? There are two general scenarios: in one, you are an entrepreneurial leader driving internal change;

in the other, you are a leader responding to external shifts, such as a market shock or competitor innovation (or the pandemic, in Peter's leadership story). In both scenarios, as an agile leader you traverse multiple polarities. You honor formal structures while unleashing more responsive, fluid structures. You are directive at the right moments, while at the same time empowering followers to take charge and pursue innovation, balanced with an eye on stability and efficiency.[21]

In the Institute of Coaching qualitative study of leadership trends during the pandemic, we noted that the best leaders understood how to foster workforce agility in a global crisis. They recognized that if they went the extra mile in deepening relationships and supporting well-being, people would go the extra mile to adapt to new strategies and directions.[22]

Peter's team responded this way when they were forced to go virtual. His willingness to be vulnerable, open, and supportive—and directive when needed—created a psychologically safe space (even on Zoom) where the team could rally together and maintain high levels of productivity and creativity, even during the worst phase of disruption.

An important thing to note about polarities as opposing forces is that the leader's goal isn't to reduce the differences but to make space for both to come alive and function, and to be agile in moving back and forth between the opposite states. A good example of agility comes out of our discussion of being conscious. In one moment, you befriend your brain's well-intended but distracting emotions. In the next moment, you shift your mind to fully experience (perceive) the present moment. Another example of agility is being an authentic leader. On the one hand, you are true to your own values. On the other hand, you shift fast to hold equally sincere concern for what is good for a diverse set of others, who may well have interests and values that conflict with your own.

MODELS OF AGILE LEADERSHIP

While the scientific literature on leadership introduces multiple overlapping models with themes of agility—agile leadership, adaptive leadership, complexity leadership, versatile leadership, and ambidextrous leadership, to name the main ones[23]—at the core, leaders share a common experience. You are first managing your own personal polarity—balancing calm and stability with the impatient urge to save the day—then you are navigating the external polarities that arise from disruptive change.

The science of adaptive leadership, codeveloped by psychiatrist and leadership expert Ronald Heifetz, has not moved forward into outcomes research.[24] However, the concept of adaptive challenge is widely taught. Technical challenges can be resolved by the directive authority of leaders, whereas adaptive challenges require agile collaboration on solutions that integrate the old with the new.

CONCLUSION—AGILITY FOR LEADERS

Where might you begin improving your agility, given so many possibilities? Consider first how you can be more agile throughout your day—dialing up an agile mind that moves fully from task to task, self-regulating your activated states, engaging your values, being open and curious, being creative, resolving conflicts, leading innovation and change, and bouncing forward from setbacks. You can also be agile in the moment by dialing up or down one or more of the nine capacities in this book as needed—more on that in the conclusion.

When you are navigating polarities, becoming more agile is a two-step dance. First, recognize the opposing forces at play in disruption and help everyone avoid a reactive black-and-white mindset where one force seems positive and the other seems negative. Second, reflect with your team on the variety of options available to meet the moment. Following your agile reflection on many possibilities and opposites, it will be time to be strategic, choose wise action, and be ready to shift again as needed.

PRACTICE

We bring you two practices on navigating polarities in an agile way. The first entails adopting the opposite perspective. The second is called polarity mapping. Both are excellent tools for generating either individual or team insights amid disruption.

ADOPTING THE OPPOSITE PERSPECTIVE

The first practice is described by finance professor Alex Edmans (UK) in his book on managing psychological bias, *May Contain Lies: How Stories, Statistics and Studies Exploit Our Biases—and What We Can Do about It*.[25] Edmans suggests that whenever a strong sense of "right" or "wrong" appears in a strategy or decision-making forum, take the extra time to step back, reflect, and make a strong case for the opposite position.

Edmans points out that when emotions run high around an organizational initiative or innovation, it is very likely that confirmation bias—seeing what we want to see in the data—is aroused. The way to move with agility through these human dynamics is to ask yourself—and others, especially those whose position feels heightened with emotion—to advocate for and experience, literally, the possibility that the opposite is true.

This exercise can help you develop a more nuanced and balanced approach to managing paradoxes and integrate your own emotional and cognitive biases into new understanding.

POLARITY MAPPING

Developed and popularized by Barry Johnson, an organizational consultant and author of the book *Polarity Management: Identifying and Managing Unsolvable Problems*, polarity mapping exercises leverage the interdependent nature of polarities in complex situations to arrive at balanced solutions.[26]

This practice can be done alone, with a coach, or as a facilitated team process, following these steps:

1. **Identify the polarities.** Begin by identifying a polarity that is relevant to your leadership context. A polarity is a pair of interdependent and complementary elements

that are both necessary but often in tension. One common example: the need to achieve productivity and innovation at the same time.

2. **Create a polarity map.** Draw a simple diagram with two opposite poles of the polarity at the ends of the map. In the case of productivity and innovation, the two would be at opposite ends of a horizontal pole.

3. **Identify positive aspects.** On the line connecting the two poles, identify the positive aspects of each pole. For productivity, this might include results, profit, and efficiency. For innovation, it could include new initiatives, growth, and enthusiasm for creativity.

4. **Identify negative aspects.** Identify the potential negative aspects associated with each pole. For productivity, this could include burnout, repetition, and stagnation. For innovation, it could include high risk, failure, and unpredictability.

5. **Explore interdependencies.** Reflect on how the two poles are dependent on each other. For example, efficiency and strong results can free up resources for creative activities that require investments of time and energy.

6. **Develop action steps.** Develop action steps that leverage both ends of the pole in tandem. In this example, it might look like setting up a rotating "skunk works" program that enables highly productive teams to have a creativity sabbatical to explore new opportunities; in other words, one side of the polarity rewards the other.

INTEGRATION—OVERUSE

If agile leadership is a strength for today's leader, how could it become an obstacle? Is it possible to be too agile or overly flexible? Unfortunately, it is not only possible but relatively common. Often situations require multiple perspectives and have many options. There may not be an immediate or obvious right or wrong direction or strategy.

An agile leader works with a team to identify the target outcome (vision), then the areas of focus (strategies) that provide the greatest likelihood of success. The team moves forward through an iterative process that tests possible approaches (implementation). Agile initiatives, once committed to by the leader and team, may be updated and shift as needed. However, it's important to avoid destabilizing agile projects by moving the goal posts—changing the desired outcome and focus areas. The goal posts are retained for stability, barring any major disruptions that demand a reboot of vision and strategy.

A leader who tends to overuse agility may not be able to find clarity in decision-making: on the one hand, seeing many options; and on the other hand, struggling to choose. An overly flexible leader may create a team dynamic where team members lose respect for the leader because what might appear to be a strength—a willingness to embrace the multiplicity of options and frequently shift priorities—can present as a lack of clarity and consistency.

LEADERSHIP EXAMPLE

Head of IT security at a major insurance firm, Bob was highly respected as a top-notch software engineer, someone who had worked his way up the career ladder over many years in several international technology firms. He had an almost encyclopedic knowledge of security software—the technology that prevents breakdowns, hacking, or cybercrime that could knock the firm's systems offline. So, as the CIO of information security, he was extremely agile due to the constantly changing nature of software and systems.

The challenge for Bob and his team was that he was such an expert in his field, which was constantly changing, that he struggled at times to know the right direction to go in. New products and new technological innovations were coming online rapidly, and with his insatiable curiosity and a substantial budget, he was eager and able to invest in the latest and greatest security capabilities.

NOT EVERYTHING IS EQUAL, OR POSSIBLE

His boss, the CEO, would often remind him that they must have the most innovative, up-to-date, forward-thinking security software solutions. This made sense, except that it put Bob in a situation where his ability to change his mind, regularly invest in new software, and initiate new projects became frustrating for his team: He seemed to want to do everything (i.e., he kept adding new goal posts).

When given an opportunity to provide feedback, team members shared that although they respected Bob's capabilities and ability to navigate complexity, he tended to shift like the wind (their words) and often spent money without thinking through the implications. They were never quite sure whether the projects they were working on would be kept alive through to completion because he was constantly updating his thinking and striving for the latest and greatest innovation (changing the goal posts).

A senior leader's excessive flexibility and responsiveness to situations that change regularly can become problematic. Bob needed to see that although his willingness to sail the choppy seas of technological innovation was a strength, for his team it was not. To have a sense of clarity and purpose, and to enable follow-through, they also needed to have his unwavering commitment to completing projects before shifting to new goal posts.

DIALING BACK AGILITY

Once Bob became aware that, to everyone's detriment, he tended to focus on the "latest shiny object," he was able to commit to a course and control his budget. More important, he came to recognize that too much flexibility undermined his desire to be decisive. Instead, his willingness to change his mind made him appear indecisive.

Bob's story shows that an optimal dose of agility, not too much and not too little, improves your team's confidence in your leadership and their confidence that they can follow through with the right level of your support at the right time.

Chapter Summary

- As an agile leader, you navigate easily across many tasks, perspectives, mindsets, emotional states, conflicts, and polarities.

- You lead change or respond flexibly to imposed change by balancing disruption and stability.

- Navigating polarities using a mindset of both/and thinking, particularly during conflicts, enables your deep engagement with opposites to arrive at creative solutions (another kind of integration).

- Innovation generates polarities between the old and new which you can handle with an adaptive mindset, recombining the status quo with the novel into new solutions.

- Agility is mental exercise for your brain, which may cause fatigue that can be averted with a healthy lifestyle.

FROM SCIENCE TO IMPACT ON YOU

- What makes agile leadership valuable to you?
- What inspires you to become a more agile leader?
- What did you learn about being an agile leader?
- What confirmed what you know?
- What questions come up?
- Revisit your self-ratings in table I.1 in the introduction: How has this chapter
    - Confirmed your strengths as a flexible leader?
    - Increased your motivation and confidence to be more agile?
    - Impacted your interest in getting better at being an agile leader?

CHAPTER 4

RELATIONAL
Help

Relationships are the agar agar in the Petri dish of life. They are the context for sustained, desired change.

—RICHARD BOYATZIS[1]

As a relational leader, you focus on cultivating strong, high-quality relationships. With high self-awareness and sincere respect, you build rapport and trust by empathizing with others' experience through high-quality listening. You seek to understand others' thoughts and emotions, and what is meaningful and important. You accept and forgive others' limitations and mistakes. Then you find out the best way to help others, without self-interest in impressing, dominating, or controlling relationships.

LEADERSHIP STORY

"Move fast and break things," Anita declared emphatically during a coaching chemistry session in the atrium of the corporate offices in the northeastern US. It was clear that she embodied this motto attributed to Mark Zuckerberg during Facebook's early days. As the sales director of the health and wellness division of a global pharma conglomerate, Anita was fast-talking, high-energy, and passionate about her self-care including vitamins and skin regimens. A dedicated athlete and runner, she took great care with her exercise routine and diet. She seemed to be always on the move, working at all hours and traveling with her team worldwide.

As she prepared to step into a new leadership role as a division vice president, Anita sought coaching. Despite her polished sense of self and impressive accomplishments, it was apparent she needed help in aligning her relentless work style and authoritative management approach with her leadership goals.

Feedback collected from her peers, superiors, and subordinates highlighted a misalignment: Such phrases as "unnecessarily competitive," "self-aggrandizing," and "hyperbolic about her own role" emerged. Anita's tendency to operate at the center and take credit for team successes raised eyebrows in the C-suite.

BECOMING EMPATHETIC

Anita was proud of her team's accomplishments in terms of revenues and their adaptability during the pandemic. Despite her belief that she was working well with her team, feedback suggested otherwise: Her team felt that she could be overbearing, a micromanager, and a poor listener. Her approach was described as robotic and emotionless. They appreciated her strategic sense, but wished she could slow down, listen more, and show empathy toward their challenges.

She was prompted during a coaching session to reflect on the value of her relationships with colleagues. She took note of the request for more empathy; it became a central theme for Anita. She was quick to use the adage "putting yourself in someone else's shoes." But when first pressed, she admitted she rarely had time for empathy.

As she reflected more on her need to build a supportive, collaborative reputation, she began to see the importance of emotional and cognitive empathy. Her realization aligns with research findings we describe in the science section: Empathy is the foundation of high-quality relationships at work and elsewhere.

While cognitive empathy involves understanding others' thoughts and perspectives, emotional empathy requires a willingness to acknowledge and resonate with ambiguous emotional states such as anxiety and fear—a challenging path for Anita, who preferred action over dwelling on negative emotions.

Anita's newfound understanding of empathy led her to realize that addressing emotions was not about resolving them immediately but about acknowledging them. By doing so, she created a space where her team felt heard and valued. This shift in perspective was instrumental in transforming her leadership style from directive to supportive.

Reflecting on her almost constant state of exhaustion, she had to admit that between the workload, the clamor for results, and the relentless pace, she did at times feel emotionally drained. It wasn't such a big leap to consider that these feelings of overwhelm might extend to her team. She began to recognize that she had typically placed little emphasis on relationships in her personal life—and her friendships and family connections had suffered as a result.

It then didn't take a major shift for her to see that focusing on relationships at work had received the same lack of attention; she tended to focus on clients, which made sense on one level, but she paid a price for not extending the same attentiveness to her own team.

LISTENING WELL

In the science section, you will learn that better listeners are perceived to be leaders, and more likely to be seen as influential. Where could Anita begin to make a change? Feedback indicated that she often dominated conversations, repeating herself and taking up unnecessary space. Hence an important focus area for Anita would be learning to listen in all areas of her life. Anita was a good listener when it came to tuning in to potential clients. Her listening strength inherent in her sales role could be applied in all aspects of her work and private spheres.

Practicing good listening would require her to pause, ask open-ended questions, and focus her attention on the other person (and not looking at her computer or phone). A simple sticky note with the word *listen* on her screens became a helpful reminder. Spending more time listening to her team members, not just her clients, propelled Anita toward a deeper level of connection with her team.

BUILDING TRUST AND PSYCHOLOGICAL SAFETY

Building trust was another crucial element for Anita. She recognized the importance of nonverbal cues such as body language and facial expressions in establishing trust with her clients. She explored how she could apply this same level of attention to her relations with colleagues. Paying close attention to eye contact, body language, and facial expressions would become essential in her team interactions.

Professor Amy Edmondson studies psychological safety in team dynamics.[2] Her research, covered in the science section, shows that teams with a sense of psychological safety take risks, admit and bring mistakes to the surface, and focus on growth and learning instead of blame. Creativity requires transparency about missteps and mistakes, and Anita needed to foster an environment where her team felt safe to take risks and learn from them.

Creating psychological safety involves encouraging open communication, supporting team members through their failures, and promoting a culture of learning. Once Anita realized the value of psychological safety for her team, she shifted from being primarily self-congratulatory to recognizing her team's efforts. She made sure they spent time and energy on lessons learned from setbacks. This approach not only boosted the team's morale but also led to more creative and effective solutions.

This evolution required Anita to shift her priorities from her own achievements to the well-being and development of her team and colleagues. It was a journey of self-discovery and learning, one in which she embraced her vulnerabilities and strengths. In doing so, she became a more effective and inspiring leader, ready to take on the challenges of the C-suite.

Anita redefined her leadership style. Her new empathy and listening built trust and psychological safety. She learned that being a leader was not only about moving fast and breaking things but about building strong, trusting relationships that could withstand challenges and drive collective success.

This shift toward a relational style had broader implications: her cross-company relationships improved. There was a powerful ripple effect—leaders senior to Anita, not just her team and peers, learned from her good role modeling.

The HR leader she worked with commented that "everyone in Anita's division is on better behavior these days, which is a testament to her as a role model." An organization's culture can improve below, across, and above when a leader steps up and embodies relational skills.

UNDERSTANDING THE SCIENCE

We are parting ways here from the leadership researchers who use the term *relational leadership* to describe what fits better with our chapter on shared leadership, also known as distributed or collective leadership. The big idea there, well summarized by leaders of the Center for Creative Leadership, is that there is a distinction between "building a person's capacity to be effective in leadership roles and processes (i.e., leader development) and building a collective's capacity to produce leadership (i.e., leadership development)."[3] Leadership lives in a collective web of relationships, not where the individual leader herself lives.

We are contributing here to a rethink of the leadership model called the leader–member exchange, or LMX, the third-most studied leadership topic (after transformational leadership and almost tied with human capital, discussed in chapter 5 on positive leadership).

LMX theory focuses on leader-follower relationships and interactions as central to leadership, a widely endorsed premise. That said, the term *exchange* is thought to be an inadequate formulation of human relationships, even at work. Here's a critique (citing the same issues we brought up in the introduction) led by management professor and coach Ryan Gottfredson:

> We believe leader-follower relationships are an essential part
> of leadership effectiveness. . . . We, likely similar to most

leadership researchers, believe that these leader-follower relationships are a critical aspect of the leadership process and
appreciate the monumental amount of research that has gone
into the study of these relationships, which has almost solely
been through the lens of LMX. . . .

Despite LMX being a focus of much leadership research,
we have identified and summarized issues with LMX that
are so problematic that it is impossible to have confidence in
findings that rely upon the construct and its measures. . . .

Collectively, these issues lead us to conclude that LMX is
not a valid construct and therefore incapable of serving the
needs of the theories it has traditionally served, and as cur-
rently constituted, unlikely to advance leadership theory and
practice in significant or meaningful ways. We are left to conclude that there is little value for its continued use.[4]

RELATIONSHIPS FIRST

The good intentions behind LMX make sense, as noted by Gottfredson et al. It's important to focus on relationships in leadership at multiple levels—dyadic, team, and workforce, as we saw in Anita's story.
Here we are talking about what produces good relationships through
empathy, listening, trust, psychological safety, and connection—all vital
to a leader's impact on others' performance and well-being at work.

Putting people, putting relationships, first is hard for many leaders like Anita because of the intense demands—the need to zoom in
on getting things done, stay on track with goals, track the environment, and zoom out to strategy making and goal setting. How easy it
is to look past others to the tasks and goals, especially under pressure
and stress, rather than first connecting as fellow humans sharing the
present moment.

Relating to others as a leader is an exercise in mental agility (chapter 3) that involves moving from frontal cortex–centered task focus to
heart-focused connection and empathy.

RELATIONSHIP MANAGEMENT

Emotional intelligence in leadership, which we introduced in the chapter on conscious leadership, has a component called relationship management, which fits well here. Daniel Goleman, in his book on emotional intelligence in leadership, talks about how good leaders use relational skills to influence and inspire others: "People tend to be very effective at managing relationships when they can understand and control their own emotions and can empathize with the feelings of others. . . . They are expert persuaders—a manifestation of self-awareness, self-regulation and empathy combined. . . . Motivation, when publicly visible, makes such people excellent collaborators; their passion for the work spreads to others, and they are driven to find solutions."[5]

In the chapter on conscious leadership, we introduced a study by South African researchers Gina Görgens-Ekermans and Chene Roux. They studied the association of components of emotional intelligence with effective leadership and also found that leaders skilled in relational management were influential role models; role modeling is one of the four components of transformational leadership we discuss in chapter 9. Their study also concluded that being an influential role model improves followers' "perceptions of supervisor support," separately shown to improve employee retention and effectiveness.[6] We saw that Anita's empathetic listening made her team members feel more supported.

EMPATHY AT WORK

Empathy researcher and Harvard psychiatrist Helen Riess notes that the history of empathy started with the German word *einfühlung*, which is a feeling of emotional resonance with a work of art. Later, psychologist Theodore Lipps expanded empathy to mean resonance with another person; philosopher Martin Buber took empathy a step further, beyond human resonance to the expression of humane respect and concern.[7] It turns out that resonance with another shows up as a mirroring of neural activity, as though you are yourself experiencing a little of what the other is experiencing.[8]

In his paper "From Empathic Leader to Empathic Leadership Practice," Guowei Jian expands the role of empathy beyond moments of understanding another's perspectives (cognitive empathy) and how they feel (emotional empathy) to empathy being the continuous process by which relationships are developed and sustained.[9] Basically, the quality of relationships equals the quality of two-way attuning and understanding. Empathizing is relating, and relating is empathizing.

This two-way process of relating and empathizing is virtuous—it has the authentically good intentions of generosity (giving of undivided attention), of care (watchful concern), and of responsibility (feeling accountable for the other's welfare at work).[10]

LISTENING AT WORK

Listening in coaching is central to relationship building. Coaches aim for Olympic-level listening. They are trained to give their undivided attention and to listen on multiple dimensions—to the other's words, thoughts, voice intonation, energy and pacing, emotions, meaning (expressed values), facial expressions and body language, and what's not said.[11]

Jeffrey Yip (Canada) and Colin Fisher (UK) synthesized studies of listening in organizations. High-quality listening reduces the other's anxiety and defensiveness, improves their storytelling, and increases their self-awareness. It clarifies their attitudes and generates more disclosure and new insights. Better listeners are perceived to be leaders and are more likely to be seen as influential. "Good listeners acquire more information than poor listeners do, allowing them to customize their influence attempts to the situation."[12]

There is a cost—good listeners expend a good deal of motivational and cognitive effort in listening, which take its toll, especially in emotionally charged situations. Listening to people vent is particularly costly to listeners.[13] Coaches set a boundary on venting—allowing a few "BMW" moments, just a little time for bitching, moaning, and whining—and then move on to strengths-spotting and insight generation.

A false belief that is hard to shed for leaders, and maybe one you can relate to, is that time spent listening to frustrated or stressed followers is time wasted. Big mistake. Taking just a few moments to show you care—to be available, supportive, and genuinely attentive to the struggles of your team—makes you a more influential leader, what Daniel Goleman called an expert persuader. "Listening empathically" is an effective coaching skill for leaders, as modeled by Satya Nadella, Microsoft's fourth CEO.[14]

Israeli researchers Kluger and Itzchakov study listening in the workplace. They note that listening is a common way we empathize.[15] Good listeners focus on the other's message (paying attention), adopt the other's cognitive and emotional frame of reference (comprehending), with the benevolent intention (being true to one's values) of helping the other gain insight and solve problems on their own.

Good listening behaviors include good responding to convey understanding and support paraphrasing (reflective listening), reflecting emotions (e.g., "You sound concerned"), asking relevant and open-ended questions, asking for clarification or repetition where needed, conveying a nonjudgmental attitude, using silence effectively, asking sensitive questions, and showing verbal and nonverbal signs of your interest (e.g., saying "uh-huh" or using body posture to convey you are paying attention).

Bad listening behaviors include changing the topic, using a tone that conveys impatience, interrupting, offering unsolicited advice, dual-tasking (e.g., looking at one's smartphone), physically disengaging from the conversation, or raising an eyebrow. These signs of poor listening signal that the listener doesn't respect the other and is already preparing a response, rather than focusing on the other's message.

Good listening or empathic listening is an important precursor to trust. If you sense that a leader is generous and caring, and feels a sense of responsibility because they are trying to understand your perspectives and emotional states, you will more likely trust that they have your best interests in mind. Going further, empathic listening creates psychological safety, and others are more likely to speak up, self-disclose, and speak authentically.

An authentic conversation creates a sense of togetherness—the sign of a good relationship. In the words of Kluger and Itzchakov: "Participation in the togetherness experience leaves both conversation partners with clarity, novel plans, new knowledge, heightened well-being, and strengthened attachment to each other."[16]

TRUST AT WORK

Neuroscientist Paul Zak studies trust at work, noting that when you trust others, your brain releases the hormone oxytocin—the "I want to help" hormone—in proportion to the amount of trust you are experiencing. Oxytocin in turn increases your ability to correctly assess others' emotions, your empathic concern for others, your understanding of others' perspectives, and your motivation to cooperate and reciprocate—for example, to serve others and collaborate as teammates.[17]

This phenomenon came alive in Anita as she focused more on how her team was feeling rather than just focusing on her clients. She became motivated and energized to elevate her relationships across her organization. Trust-building was inspiring to Anita and to everyone else as well.

Oxytocin release is stimulated by positive (trust-building) social encounters and stays active for about thirty minutes. Oxytocin release is impaired by chronic high stress, including negative social interactions, and by too few positive social interactions.[18] Over time, regular social connections are vital to your health and well-being, and reduce the risks of premature mortality.[19]

An evaluation of the impact of trust in leadership, based on 185 studies, found that the relationship between "affective [emotions and values] trust in the leader and organizational performance outcomes was significantly stronger than that of cognitive [facts and logic] trust. . . . Employee affective trust is driven by a perception that the leader has good intentions towards them and cares for their wellbeing." In team performance, affective trust and cognitive trust were equally effective.[20]

It's also worth noting that trust-building at work is about much more than what we have explored in the context of relationships. While leaders build trust in their leadership through relationship building—showing respect for others and openness to others as demonstrated in empathy and good listening—just as important is their demonstration of competence and reliability, fostering the perception that they have the expertise and skills to fulfill their roles.[21] We call that the "what" of leadership in chapter 7 on shared leadership.

FORGIVENESS AT WORK

Outside of work, forgiveness "is an essential aspect of well-functioning and lasting relationships."[22] Organizational psychologist Wenrui Cao and colleagues in the Netherlands conducted three studies of the impact of forgiveness on work outcomes. They concluded that forgiveness in close work relationships improves job satisfaction and work engagement and reduces burnout (outcomes related to well-being), which can indirectly improve performance outcomes. They also assembled a simple definition from others' research that goes like this: Forgiveness is a transformation in one's motivation in response to hurtful actions by an offending party: moving from negative motivations—a desire for revenge and to retaliate, and/or maintain estrangement—toward positive motivations, a desire for benevolence, conciliation, and goodwill.[23]

Forgiveness is framed in a respected survey of servant leadership as interpersonal acceptance, defined as the ability to forgive when confronted with offenses, defensive arguments, and mistakes. This kind of acceptance is thought to bring out the best in people.[24]

PSYCHOLOGICAL SAFETY

We are including psychological safety, which we introduced in Anita's story, as an implicit element of relational leadership, both a contributor to and indicator of high-quality relationships. In their latest review of 185 studies of psychological safety in organizations, Amy

Edmondson and Derrick Bransby confirm that psychological safety is a sense of safety in taking interpersonal risks by being oneself and openly sharing ideas, concerns, and mistakes with respect and without concerns of retribution. Leaders' empathy, listening, acceptance, trust, and forgiveness, as we've just discussed, contribute to a climate where personal risks are low.

Edmondson and Bransby found four topic clusters of research showing positive outcomes of psychological safety: getting things done (performance), learning behaviors (including creativity and innovation), experience of work (including trust, authenticity, inclusion, and well-being), and leadership (including transparency, listening, humility, and two-way feedback).[25]

You might find it interesting that a key influencer of psychological safety is a leader's character, reported by the Ivey Business School professors we cited in chapter 2 on authentic leadership.[26] Leaders with good character are more trusted and feel safer to work with.

How might high-quality relationships improve results? Our synthesis goes something like this:

- **Conscious.** First, quiet your ego so you can be present with others.

- **Authentic.** Show you care by bringing your empathy online.

- **Agile.** Be open and accepting, not judging or resisting what you hear when you don't agree.

Voilà—now relational trust emerges, which enables psychological safety. Feeling safe, without fear and anxiety, improves others' performance, creativity, and innovation.

HOW TO HELP

So far we have shown that high-quality relationships with leaders help followers reach their goals. Helping goes further, as an active, direct intervention. There is not yet a substantial body of research on how best to help others do their work, such as through giving advice, mentoring, coaching, or teaching. However, three studies on helping at work are worth mentioning.

One study, led by Blaine Landis in the UK, shows that employees prefer to receive advice from leaders when they ask for it (not unsolicited) and when their leaders show a genuine motivation to help without a desire for personal gain in their advice giving (not self-focused on controlling or impressing).[27]

The second study, by Colin Fisher (UK), Julianna Pillemer and Teresa Amabile (US), analyzed the helping phenomenon in a design agency with a well-rooted culture of helping, contrasting with highly competitive cultures. The researchers called this phenomenon "deep helping on a timely basis," an intense process of helping a team through a difficult juncture or overcoming a difficult deficit.[28]

The third study used a set of strategic games conducted by management researcher Ghufran Ahmad (Pakistan) and Christoph Loch (UK). The study concluded that followers primarily want leaders to step in when they are stalled—when team coordination is failing and/or conflicts need resolving. Followers also prefer facilitative leadership, whereby leaders make recommendations, rather than enforcing leadership, whereby leaders make and enforce decisions.[29]

PRACTICE

Our practices for elevating your relational skills as a leader leverage our experience as coaches. In coaching, listening skills enable strong relationships with coachees. Coaches also model listening behaviors. Having a "leader as coach" is what today's knowledge workers want, especially millennials and members of Gen Z. The next generation of emerging leaders expects to be coached, mentored, and advised, making relational skills crucial to a leader's impact.

THREE Ps OF LISTENING

Developed by this book's coauthor Jeffrey Hull and European leadership coach Andreas Bernhardt, the following practice is designed to help you take your listening skills to an Olympic level. You may want to make note of the following three Ps as a prompt to be a good listener all day long.

Many leaders are rightly concerned that coaching takes time, but listening is about quality not quantity. Even a short, focused session, as little as ten to fifteen minutes, can be a potent experience that leaves a team member walking away feeling not just seen but heard and supported.

- **Presence (conscious).** Prepare to listen well: pause to be calm, present, and more available—mentally, emotionally, and physically. Set aside all distractions (smartphones, etc.). Use a warm, calming voice tone. On video or in person, pay attention to your body language, posture, eye contact, and facial expressions. Spend more time listening (80 percent) than speaking. Ask open-ended questions and hold space for silence.

- **Perspective (agile).** Prepare to be open and curious; reflect on where you are coming from before entering a helping conversation. Ask yourself: Do I have a strong position or opinion about this topic? If so, can I mindfully set those feelings aside to accept and explore, with curiosity, the position of the other?

- **Purpose (authentically good).** Reflect on your "why" (the purpose) and the best role to play to serve the purpose. What would be most helpful—playing mentor? teacher? advisor? friend? accountability enforcer? We have multiple selves that we could use to help. Deciding on the best role to play beyond leader, and why, is a purposeful approach. Then you can be transparent and open about your purpose and role, which reinforces trust and perceived support.

CLEAR THE PATH

A second practice that combines your relational skills with effective helping is known as guiding and path clearing. The guidelines outlined here draw from an article on helping by Fisher, Amabile, and Pilleme.[30] They enable you to help effectively while avoiding the trap of micromanagement.

- **Choose the right time.** Practice paying close attention to the timing of your involvement in advising and coaching. Too soon may feel overbearing; too late may feel suffocating (and unnecessary) to subordinates. If you have strong relationships with your team, it is perfectly OK to make it explicit that you are available to support them and to ask them to let you know when they might need you.

- **Explain your role clearly—your role is to help.** Because you are in the power position as the leader, it may not always be obvious to subordinates that your intention is to help. Being explicit about your intention can reinforce a sense of autonomy and psychological safety: You are not taking over, trying to rescue, or pushing your authority; rather you are stepping in to offer support, as needed.

- **Understand people's needs.** Pay particular attention to understanding what is needed by the individuals you are seeking to help. Each person is unique. Some may welcome more support, coaching, and involvement. Others may wish to know you are supportive, but prefer to take initiative and seek you out only when they need your help.

INTEGRATION—OVERUSE

Key to relational leadership, as we have learned, is valuing human relationships for their own sake along with valuing their impact on performance. But there are situations in which a leader's commitment to strong relationships and team alignment can become an obstacle. Overemphasis on relationships can lead to what is known in psychological circles as groupthink, where the collective's desire to be liked, to please others, for everyone to get along, and for social cohesion become overly important.

We might call this the "Kumbaya effect"—an overemphasis on unity and harmony, so much that the team loses sight of productivity and avoids taking risks. Overuse of relational leadership can slow innovation in order to meet needs to be liked and to feel good about everything and everyone.

LEADERSHIP EXAMPLE

Barbara, the head of clinical trials at a pharmaceutical research organization, was extremely well liked—actually loved—by her team. It wasn't unusual to hear that her team would go to the ends of the earth to support her. Barbara and her team spent a great deal of time together outside of work; there was a strong sense of trust, openness, and willingness to learn. Barbara had created an environment where there was a strong commitment to personal growth. What could go wrong?

THRIVING RELATIONSHIPS NEED CONFLICT

As a highly relational leader, Barbara was allergic to disagreements and uncomfortable with conflict. Her commitment to building consensus, listening, dialogue, and brainstorming created an environment where people would relax and be fully engaged during team meetings. However, anyone observing from the outside would notice that there was rarely any display of a counternarrative to the one her staff signed up for; naysayers, if there were any, always "went along" with the majority.

As much as Barbara created an environment filled with curiosity and empathy for diverse perspectives, there was very little tolerance for outright disagreement. When there was a clash of opinions, Barbara acted as a consummate diplomat, often taking participants aside, coaching them to work through their differences, come to consensus, and get back into alignment. They were missing opportunities to "juice" their polarities, turning them into innovation.

CREATIVITY THRIVES IN VARIETY

Creativity requires experimentation, varied perspectives, and even taking risks on new ideas or unproven initiatives. Barbara's team members, however, were unwilling to take risks or stand out from the crowd. When confronted with the observation that her team wasn't innovative, Barbara was initially dismissive, arguing that she was fully committed to brainstorming, curiosity, listening, and having empathy for different perspectives.

Yet, as she came to see, very little disagreement surfaced in her highly relational environment. There was also a fine, permeable line between social and professional activities. Barbara firmly believed in having a strong social connection with her team, investing a lot of time, energy, and money in what she considered team building. They often blended social events with work events, switching from one to the other at a barbecue or in other settings outside work.

Her initial belief was that having people relaxed, friendly, connected, and supportive of one another would bring out the best ideas, and she wasn't completely wrong. But Barbara got a wake-up call when she learned about research showing that conflict improves innovation, and that taking risks and working through disagreements improves psychological safety.

DISAGREE WITH RESPECT

Barbara came to see that productivity and innovation did not have to be sacrificed for a focus on relationships. She needed to encourage a good amount of dissonance and disagreement to ensure that her team members were speaking the truth to her and one another. A new practice for Barbara in brainstorming sessions consisted of asking specifically for a varied or unpopular viewpoint, pointedly asking, "Who will disagree? I'd love to hear it."

Fostering enough safety, she encouraged her team to speak up and engage with creative tension and conflict, without loss of respect and care. Being genuine, honest, and candid were values she now supported.

With coaching, Barbara was able to help her team step up and take a risk to disagree with one another and even with her, knowing that she wouldn't like and respect them any less. When everyone prioritizes getting along, they risk missing wake-up signals—e.g., new customer pain points or a competitor's strategic move or new product. Failure may result from too much getting along.

Success for Barbara's team was relational agility, balancing high-quality relating with respectful and creative conflict and disagreement.

Chapter Summary

- As a relational leader, you develop high-quality relationships as a basis for your influence and impact.

- Your high-quality relationships are built on respect, empathy, listening to understand, acceptance, and forgiveness.

- High-quality relationships help you generate trust and psychological safety, which improves your followers' engagement, well-being, resilience, and performance.

- You support followers in a timely way by helping them navigate conflicts and challenges and offering advice and support when they ask for it.

FROM SCIENCE TO IMPACT ON YOU

- What makes relational leadership valuable to you?
- What inspires you to become a more relational leader?
- What did you learn about being a relational leader?
- What did you know that was confirmed?

- What questions come up?
- Revisit your self-ratings in table I.1 in the introduction: How has this chapter
    - Confirmed your relational strengths?
    - Increased your motivation and confidence to relate with others effectively?
    - Impacted your interest in getting better at being a relational leader?

CHAPTER 5

POSITIVE
Strengthen

What you appreciate, appreciates.
—SOURCE UNKNOWN

As a positive leader, you leverage the key drivers of human well-being and performance at work that have been identified by researchers. You help followers cultivate sources of psychological capital and well-being as foundational resources that motivate and energize work engagement, productivity, perseverance, resilience, and growth. Five key sources of psychological capital are autonomy (feeling a sense of agency), confidence (feeling competent), positive emotions (feeling good), optimism (feeling optimistic), and meaning, or fulfillment of values (feeling fulfilled by doing good).

LEADERSHIP STORY

Hospitals are challenging environments in which to foster and sustain positivity. Most people associate hospitals with dangerous and negative experiences. It's remarkable when a world-class cardiac surgical center applies positive leadership to transform the morale and motivation of surgeons, staff, and the entire care support team from demoralized and burned out to inspired and reenergized. This transformation suggests that positive leadership can be effective anywhere.

Ahmed, the leader of the "heart center" at a major European hospital, led a team conducting high-risk, life-or-death cardiac surgeries. Ahmed and his team were responsible for very ill patients in grave danger. They saved many lives, but patients often didn't survive. He recognized that positive leadership was crucial for sustaining peak performance in such a tough setting.

The team's challenge was to create an environment that fostered high-quality motivation, care, and positive energy despite frequent setbacks and painful losses. Sharing the death of a loved one with a distraught family happened often.

Positive leadership had initially seemed counterintuitive to Ahmed and his team. Ahmed's primary concern was efficiency and speed, with zero tolerance for mistakes. At first, he dismissed the idea of "staying positive," believing it unrealistic in their environment. "We face death *every day*," he said, "and failing at surgery is inevitable and never pleasant."

STAYING POSITIVE AND REALISTIC

Positive leadership is not about happiness or joy. In a hospital setting, especially where patients are extremely ill, it's about tuning in to core values that make work fulfilling (a source of positive psychological capital we discuss in the science section). Those values include relational empathy and care, surgical excellence, a growth mindset, and team well-being. Then you look for opportunities to communicate and reinforce what makes work fulfilling. Leaders need to ensure that their team stays present to the grave dangers they face, while performing at their best, taking care of themselves, and being good to one another.

The first step in introducing positive leadership was to appreciate positive outcomes and not take them for granted. The surgical team often brushed aside affirmations. "All in a day's work," Ahmed would say. Acknowledging and expressing gratitude and celebrating positive outcomes, much as sports teams do when they win, were new experiences. Ahmed started to see the value in sharing and harvesting success with his team, realizing it could foster a more supportive and motivated environment.

Physicians like Ahmed are trained to seek out and diagnose problems, focusing on fixing them with precision. Ahmed's upbringing, continuing a lineage of doctors in his family, reinforced a black-and-white approach to evaluating oneself and one's team as a doctor: Success meant life; failure meant death.

This mindset extended to the M&M (morbidity and mortality) meetings. While the intention was to foster learning and improvement, the meetings often devolved into sessions full of blame and denial, creating a psychologically unsafe environment for learning and growing. Just like Anita's lessons showed in the previous chapter, psychological safety is vital for collaboration and helps people to stay motivated, despite setbacks. Ahmed had some work to do.

The hospital's climate survey highlighted the cardiac surgery team's low morale and high burnout rate. Ahmed's initial response— to drive the team harder—only worsened the situation, making the team feel even more demoralized. M&M meetings sometimes ended in shouting matches, exacerbating the negative energy.

Ahmed realized that a shift in mindset was necessary. Positive leadership wasn't about ignoring problems or failures but about balancing them with sincere, positive energy. He began to appreciate the importance of taking moments to express gratitude and acknowledge his team's hard work. This small change in his behavior had a significant impact, boosting team morale and even improving Ahmed's own well-being as a leader.

The positive change also resonated with other leaders. Department-level physician managers under Ahmed, who had seen him model a tough stance, now began to note the shift toward appreciation. They saw him honoring competence and celebrating moments of brilliance and agency in risk-taking by surgeons. All of this reinforced an appreciation of "what is working" throughout the department.

Researchers have shown that positive feedback and gratitude at work are associated with improved collaboration and psychological capital.[1] Ahmed's own struggles with being optimistic helped him see that positive leadership was needed for his own well-being, as well as for his team. By focusing on what worked, even when surgeries didn't go as planned, Ahmed could cultivate a more positive and resilient mindset. He also began to remind his team of their purpose and celebrate their purpose-aligned wins, helping them reconnect with their sense of fulfillment.

Ahmed also realized the importance of creating a sense of efficacy for his team. Positive leaders create better outcomes by improving confidence, a robust belief in their team's competency. What coaches call strengths-spotting,[2] acknowledging the valued contribution of every team member, including nurses and technicians, empowered the entire team by flattening the hierarchy. Highlighting everyone's positive contributions increased confidence. It also improved psychological safety, helping them better work through mistakes and challenges with a desire to learn and get better and without toxic blame and denial.

Ahmed began to talk about how uplifted he felt when he remembered how meaningful their teamwork was to him. He consistently reminded his team of their fundamental "why"—that despite exhaustion, setbacks, and occasional missteps, their shared purpose was big: to save lives.

APPLYING THE SCIENCE

Once Ahmed, a researcher himself, learned about research findings on positive psychology interventions in health care settings, he discovered that even in difficult situations, acknowledging what worked well could boost morale. He began to see that celebrating small wins and appreciating efforts increased agency and efficacy, sources of psychological capital we'll talk about shortly.

Ahmed's positive leadership was not just about transforming his team's outlook but also about changing his own mindset. The journey wasn't easy, but the results were profound.

The cardiac surgical team, once marked by low morale and high burnout, began to thrive in a more supportive and gratitude-filled environment. Ahmed understood that appreciating what's good in a surgical setting energized the team to speak up, share ideas, and support one another.

This balanced approach created a more resilient, motivated, high-performing team. By implementing positive leadership, Ahmed didn't just improve the morale of his team; he also set a new standard for how leadership could be practiced in high-stress, high-stakes environments.

UNDERSTANDING THE SCIENCE

The research case for positive leadership in improving organizational performance sits at the intersection of psychological well-being or thriving and performance. In fact, thriving (aka well-being) and performance are interdependent. Good work increases human thriving, and people who thrive are more engaged and perform better at work.[3] Researchers have made profound, easy-to-understand contributions in psychology over the past forty years, pertaining first to human thriving, and then extending to thriving at work.

WELL-BEING AT WORK

Operationalizing well-being at work has a long way to go. Employee engagement is a proxy for work well-being, and global levels are low. Gallup reports annually on the global employee engagement gap, which is holding steady at only 23 percent of employees who are enthusiastic about their work; 62 percent are uninspired and unengaged. Gallup also notes that the low levels of engagement are mainly associated with the low quality of managers.[4] The engagement gap is for the most part a leadership gap.

The memo to leaders from well-being researchers calls for investing first in your own thriving so that you are strong enough to consistently energize your work climate and help others do the same.[5] Recall that Ahmed's journey toward becoming a positive leader included upgrading his own positive energy, resources, and well-being.

Three German psychologists led by Antonia Kaluza completed a review of leadership styles and leaders' self-reported well-being. They concluded that change-oriented (transformational) and relational-oriented leadership styles were associated with greater well-being, compared to transactional, destructive, and laissez-faire styles. (We are not presenting these last three styles in this book.) Recall how Ahmed's toxic meetings were harmful to collaboration and well-being.

As a leader, improving your own well-being through relationships and positive change, and the nine capacities in this book, is not just good for performance. It's good for you too.

High-performing work cultures can generate rather than consume well-being—for you and everyone you influence.

PSYCHOLOGICAL CAPITAL

We are unpacking positive leadership by reconstituting the scientific term *psychological capital*, or PsyCap. Psychological capital is an excellent frame because it conveys that leaders and followers need to have capital, here meaning psychological resources, to energize their challenging work lives and lift them back upright when they're knocked down by hard situations.

We will summarize positive leadership as comprising five sources of psychological capital that improve well-being, along with resilience and work performance. All together they make up a strong foundation and strengthen leaders and followers for what lies ahead. All of them will be familiar topics, so this chapter will feel like a light read, although big in impact.

The scholarly definition of PsyCap includes hope, efficacy, resilience, and optimism, also known as HERO.[6] We are adding agency, positive emotions, and fulfillment. Resilience, introduced in chapter 3 as a kind of agility, has been set aside. Resilience is an outcome of high-quality relationships (chapter 4) and the positive resources discussed in this chapter.

While we are talking about capital, we diverge for a moment to comment on the topic of human capital, the second-most studied leadership topic after transformational leadership.[7] Human capital isn't addressed elsewhere in this book. While research on human capital is well intentioned and aspires to upgrade training, education, expertise, and social resources, the use of the term *human capital* doesn't resonate with the values we discuss in chapter 2 on authentically good leadership.

A good leader doesn't view humans as capital or resources to be spent or used. Humans are not capital; they *have* capital, including psychological capital as well as social, financial, and physical health capital. Human betterment is every leader's purpose, one connected to authentic values and virtues.

Let's talk about how leaders can increase the psychological capital of humans at work. We are introducing five kinds of capital—autonomy/agency (which support hope), competence (self-efficacy), positive emotions (feeling good), optimism, and fulfillment.

FEELING A SENSE OF AGENCY

You have a sense of agency when you feel that you have the autonomy or the psychological freedom to choose how you work, to live by your own values, to make a difference, and to do work that matters. Autonomy is not the same as independence, which is to a great extent an illusion in our interdependent world. Autonomy is about having a sufficient sense of control in one's life and in one's work life, of being able to actively influence both. Agency is simply the ability to act. They go together in that having a sense of control enables you to act.

According to psychologists Richard Ryan and Edward Deci, who cofounded self-determination theory, the need for autonomy is the most potent of human psychological needs.[8] An absence of autonomy causes languishing; our work, our lives wither without it.

The burnout tragedy of physicians today around the world is in good part due to physicians' loss of autonomy in the bureaucracy-heavy state of health care that weighs down—financially, technologically, and emotionally—the real work, the real value in health care of caring for patients.[9] A research review of seventy-two studies by a team of Australian scientists led by Gavin Slemp concluded that when leaders support follower autonomy, followers have more internalized motivation (based on their own values) and greater well-being, and they engage more in positive work behaviors that improve performance, engagement, and proactivity.[10]

A core insight of self-determination theory is worth sitting with: The human organism has "evolved tendencies toward growing, mastering ambient challenges, and integrating new experiences into a coherent sense of self. These natural developmental tendencies do not, however, operate automatically, but instead require ongoing social nutriments and supports. That is, the social context can either support or thwart the natural tendencies toward active engagement and psychological growth."[11]

We can now understand how Sidney, Jennifer, Anita, and Ahmed became agents of others' self-determination. They stepped up to provide social nutriments (improving agency, confidence, and optimism) that supported their followers' engagement and growth.

Whether you are a parent, teacher, mentor, friend, or leader, you are supporting the natural agentic tendency of people to be proactively engaged, to lean into mastering work challenges, and to learn and grow. You are unleashing these natural forces, more like a gardener or a coach than a bossy boss.

FEELING COMPETENT

The third core psychological need of humans as uncovered by self-determination research (along with autonomy mentioned previously and relatedness in chapter 4 on relational leadership) is competence. Competence is aligned with the psychological term *efficacy* or *self-efficacy*. We need to feel competent, confident, and effective in mastering our work and our lives. Applying our strengths to important tasks and goals, learning new skills, becoming more competent—all of this is central to our work satisfaction and performance. Followers particularly need work relationships that support their competence and its positive trajectory.

FEELING GOOD

Feeling good is a catchall for the things that give us pleasure or make us feel good at work, all of those experiences that generate positive emotions and states. They include getting our top three core psychological needs met: for autonomy, a sense of competence, and a feeling of being supported and giving support in work relationships. Feel-good moments can also be small moments of savoring—a fresh, aromatic cup of morning coffee, or a shared laugh with a colleague. It might be enjoying work, mobilizing our intrinsic motivation for activities that are interesting and enjoyable for their own sake.[12]

An enjoyable activity could be the social interactions that generate camaraderie in a team meeting, a productive conversation, a deep flow state, engaging in an interesting project, accomplishing something hard, or feeling gratitude for learning something new. It could be feeling inspired by seeing someone doing a good job or solving a tough challenge or helping out a colleague in a crisis.

Social psychologist Barbara Fredrickson's seminal research on positive emotions helps us appreciate their positive impact on our brains in the moment: opening minds, reducing bias, and enabling more strategic and creative thinking. Cumulatively over time, positive emotions support well-being by promoting positive relationships, physiological health, and resilience. From an evolutionary perspective, Fredrickson's work situates the function of positive emotions as building intellectual, social, and physical capacities that support adaptation and long-term survival.[13]

Feeling good is good for you and for your performance.[14] It's not a luxury at work; it's a necessity. When leaders prioritize enjoyment of meaningful work for all, followers cultivate the psychological and physical resources needed to keep going in a tough world.

FEELING OPTIMISTIC

A leader's key role is to generate optimism, the belief that there is a promising future ahead. Optimism is a vital resource because our relationship with the future is a major regulator of our mood, motivation, and engagement. When we feel even slightly depressed, our relationship with the future is depressed. Optimism, even if a little irrational, is what fuels our perseverance.

Psychologist Martin Seligman, who led the founding of positive psychology in 1998, which launched the field of positive leadership, made a scientific mark earlier in his career studying the nature of optimism. Seligman explains that optimists view setbacks as temporary, as challenges to overcome that are not of your personal making. However, pessimists "tend to believe bad events will last a long time, will undermine everything they do, and are their own fault."

The good news for pessimists is that they can train themselves to adopt a positive explanatory style—that bad events are temporary, situation-specific, and not their fault.[15]

More recently, in Seligman's autobiographical book *The Hope Circuit*, we learn that the role of agency is now understood as a brain circuit that regulates a sense of hopelessness and pessimism.[16] This discovery brings us back to how important it is to foster agency among the workforce as a source of hope and optimism. It was a revelation for Ahmed to learn about the scientific basis for optimism and hope. It confirmed why negativity dragged him and others down, leading to a sense of futility and hopelessness.

FEELING FULFILLED (DOING GOOD)

Psychologist Jack Bauer, whom we met in the chapter on conscious leadership, describes meaning as fulfilling our values by turning them into a desired outcome, such as raising a happy child or growing a respected company or inventing a new medical treatment.[17]

A sense of fulfillment comes from doing things that are meaningful. Here people are simply putting their values to work, whether it's enabling a customer's success, or upgrading teamwork, or celebrating a little extra prosperity for your team during the holiday season. For example, if one of your top character strengths is appreciation of beauty, the extra effort you put in to get a work product to excellence or to beautify a presentation is a meaningful, fulfilling activity.

PRACTICE

Our practice for positive leadership is simply for you to prioritize cultivating your own positive emotions and well-being as resources you'll need to navigate your challenges. Here we turn to a simple yet profound exercise using Barbara Fredrickson's positivity ratio.

You can complete the ratio assessment at positivityratio.com to find your current ratio of positive to negative emotions and track it over time. A good rule of thumb is to increase your average ratio to 3:1 and above.[18] For marriages, which are apparently more challenging than our work lives, the optimal ratio is 5:1. Ideally you have five good things to say *to* your partner for every negative one.[19]

You can keep this simple and look for ways in your daily life to do things that generate positive energy—express gratitude, do something nice for someone, learn something new, savor a small pleasure, appreciate what you have (rather than bemoan what you don't have), or schedule an hour or two for a flow-producing activity.

Or you can draw on the nine leadership capacities as durable sources of positive energy and well-being—seeing clearly, caring, flexing, helping, strengthening, resonating, sharing, serving, and transforming.

INTEGRATION—OVERUSE

It may seem counterintuitive to think that positive leadership can be overused or that too much positivity could be problematic, but in some instances it can be overdone.

Over-emphasis of an optimistic and joyful environment can obscure darker truths. It can lead to avoidance or dismissal of important negative emotions. In real life, loss, sadness, failure, and suffering are part of the journey, aspects of life's essential polarity of positive and negative, both personally and organizationally.

A leader focusing too much on positivity can fall victim to the "rose-colored glasses effect"—overfocusing on the positive while minimizing the negative.

GROWTH EMERGES FROM SUFFERING

Research on posttraumatic growth has shown that resilience after loss or trauma comes *not* from a focus on positivity at the expense of acknowledging trauma but from accepting, experiencing, and befriending the pain. This acceptance of trauma or loss enables individuals, especially with support from companions, coaches, mentors, or leaders, to shift from a victim mindset to a growth mindset.[20] The acceptance mindset improves the ability not just to bounce back but to bounce forward (grow) when things don't go well. The message? Balance positivity with realism in leadership.

LEADERSHIP EXAMPLE

Lisa, the head of research and development at a major pharmaceutical firm, modeled incredible positive energy and optimism. She believed in the importance of positivity to ignite the motivation of her team. She focused on their strengths, showed appreciation, and fortified their sense of efficacy.

Her body language sometimes revealed a deeper truth, however. Despite her positive front, Lisa was experiencing significant loss in her personal life and was unhappy with her highly critical boss. Her internal negative emotions, depression and even despair, contrasted sharply with her outward optimism, creating what is described as toxic positivity, the belief that one must remain positive and suppress negative experiences.[21]

POSITIVITY CAN BE TOXIC

Lisa's commitment to *not* showing her negative emotions led to a disconnect between her words and her demeanor. Her team's awareness of her struggles made it difficult for them to speak up when Lisa's excessive positivity left no room for discussing challenging issues. Lisa began working with a coach, who could see how deeply unhappy she was.

In feedback sessions and in confidence with colleagues in different departments, some of her direct reports shared their belief that the disconnect between Lisa's sad demeanor at times and upbeat style at other times reflected a form of denial. Unfortunately, this disconnect led to the very dynamic Lisa was committed to avoiding: distrust in her leadership.

POSITIVITY REQUIRES ALIGNMENT WITH REALITY

It was a revelation for Lisa to see that balancing optimism with acceptance of the deeper truth of her frustrations and challenges could strengthen her leadership. As she slowly let down her mask and shared small snippets of her frustrations, she came to recognize that showing vulnerability wouldn't diminish others' respect for her capability. Instead, doing so would allow her to ask for help and show her team that life's complexities require both positive energy and honesty about challenges.

This shift humanized her and allowed everyone else to relax as well—to be more transparent and honest about successes and challenges, because they experienced both. By fostering an environment where resilience, agency, competence, and positivity were balanced with an openness to facing setbacks, Lisa could maintain alignment and integrity in her positive leadership approach. She could rebuild trust in her leadership and reinforce psychological safety for her team.

LIFE IS A MIXED BAG: BALANCE IS KEY

In summary, positive leaders embrace positive energy while being open about difficulties, putting to good use the best elements of positive leadership without overusing them to the point at which positivity lacks integrity.

By being realistic, and still positive, leaders can appreciate "what works," while not denying the existence of both positive and negative experiences. Resilience and growth emerge from deploying strengths to overcome hardship, while avoiding victim energy.

Chapter Summary

- As a positive leader, you help yourself and others get stronger.

- As a positive leader, you help others develop more psychological capital, including agency, competence, positivity, optimism, and fulfillment.

- You see clearly, care, flex, help, and strengthen.

FROM SCIENCE TO IMPACT ON YOU

- What makes positive leadership valuable to you?
- What inspires you to become a more positive leader?
- What did you learn about being a positive leader?
- What did you know that was confirmed?
- What questions come up?
- Revisit your self-ratings in table I.1 in the introduction: How has this chapter
    - Confirmed your strengths as a positive leader?
    - Increased your motivation and confidence to increase positivity in appropriate ways?
    - Impacted your interest in getting better at being a positive leader?

CHAPTER 6

COMPASSIONATE
Resonate

Our human compassion binds us the one to the other—not in pity or patronizingly, but as human beings who have learnt how to turn our common suffering into hope for the future.

—NELSON MANDELA[1]

As a compassionate leader, you integrate conscious, authentic, agile, relational, and positive leadership capacities into compassion. You understand the everyday stresses and strains of organizational life. You hold space for grief and posttraumatic growth during terrible experiences such as natural disasters, terminal diseases, and the loss of life. You combine the warmth of concern with accountability—being tough on performance.

LEADERSHIP STORY

Patricia is one of the most compassionate individuals we have ever met. You might ask, why write about a leader who already demonstrates strong compassion?

Patricia's transformative journey shows how a strength in one domain can become a liability in another. Recall in our integration discussions of capacity overuse that strengths are two-sided coins. The flipside of your greatest strength in one context can be your greatest weakness in other contexts.

Patricia grew up on a farm in northern England, developing an early love for the natural world, especially animals. Even as a child, she knew she wanted to work with animals. She loved riding horses and being with the chickens, dogs, and cows, often feeling more at home with animals than with people. Patricia became a veterinarian.

Years later, as vice president of animal research at a global pharmaceutical company in a suburb of London, Patricia led a team of research scientists and support staff caring for (and experimenting on) hundreds of small rodents. Patricia and her team played a crucial role in scientific studies aimed at safely treating human diseases and extending healthy lives.

Despite the challenging nature of some studies, her team demonstrated compassion and provided excellent care. Staff kept cages clean and tended to the animals' needs 24/7, ensuring they were in the best possible health during scientific work.

Patricia and her boss, the division head of research, often clashed. She lived in a state of anxiety and fear about losing her job. Conflicts arose over budgeting, space, and her push for better animal care.

Her boss respected her credentials and goals, but was frustrated by her tendency to prioritize animal care over the ultimate goal of drug development. As the head of research, he faced pressure from the C-suite to adhere to strategic plans and budgets while navigating regulatory oversight and tight restrictions on animal use.

The scientists on his team worked under deadlines and pressure from finance and sales leaders who wanted drugs developed quickly. But drug development is a tedious and laborious process with no guaranteed results. Animal testing can take years before a compound proves safe and effective for testing on humans.

Both Patricia and her boss understood the complexities of working with animals, which is why he hired a veterinarian to lead the animal science center. However, Patricia often missed deadlines and lacked strong arguments for hiring more staff or giving raises. She appeared negative about the business side of the operation, and her boss frequently reminded her that the enterprise was not a charity.

To Patricia's surprise, her boss engaged a coach to work with her. Initially, coaching aimed to help Patricia develop accountability, reduce conflicts, and adopt a positive attitude toward colleagues and senior staff. She needed to become more strategic and savvier about the financial complexities of running an animal research center. Her boss wanted her to be a team player with an understanding of the challenges he faced.

Some scientists in another division were frustrated with Patricia, feeling that she prioritized animals over their needs. When confronted, she became defensive. The challenge was for her to extend her compassion beyond animals and her support staff to her colleagues and boss.

Patricia was at a critical point in her career. She had left private practice to have a more impactful role in a large organization involved in lifesaving science. As a scientist, she wanted humane and scientifically sound experiments on animals. She advocated for lower-level employees who worked tirelessly to care for the animals, feeling it was her duty as a compassionate leader to push for better conditions, pay, and recognition.

Patricia's frustration with her boss and his lack of interest in supporting her and her team led to her reputation as negative and condescending. She was considering returning to private practice, feeling out of place in the corporate environment. She was concerned about aligning with senior leaders focused on profit and rapid drug development. Yet her deep compassion for her staff and animals would become the catalyst for her transformation as a leader.

COMPASSION FOR THE WHOLE

Patricia believed in the vision of developing drugs to treat or even cure diseases. She wasn't against using animals for research, but wanted it done ethically and compassionately. She wanted her team to feel respected and autonomous. But she lacked compassion for her colleagues and boss, viewing them as obstacles rather than teammates.

Patricia realized that going into meetings with a negative attitude about budget cuts was counterproductive. Compassion at its best is not selective. With the help of her coach, she came to realize that she needed to demonstrate compassion toward everyone, including those she disagreed with.

As we explain in the science section, compassion in leadership enables resonating with the whole, "building shared mindfulness, hope, compassion and playfulness" across an organization.[2] This broadminded perspective on compassion is what separates close-in compassion (toward those we are closest to) from compassionate leadership, which embraces everyone.

Reflecting on her values and the organization's goals, Patricia saw the disconnect. She realized that one day she might be in her boss's role, responsible for balancing budgets and strategic goals. Initially resistant, she admitted understanding the limits of resources and the pressures scientists faced. Recognizing her boss's challenges, she began to empathize with his difficult decisions.

This shift in perspective led Patricia to align her vision with the broader organizational goals. She started to see her boss as a human being with his own struggles, leading to more productive dialogues. She reflected on how her compassion for animals could be applied to her interactions with colleagues and her boss.

FROM EMPATHY TO WHOLE-SYSTEM RESONANCE

Patricia began to approach her conversations with empathy, and ultimately with compassion. She listened to understand, paying closer attention to the challenges others faced. This change improved her relationships and transformed her reputation as a leader. As we will discuss in the science section, moving beyond empathy to compassion brought a deeper level of humanity to the entire enterprise.

Patricia's transformation led her to reconsider leaving the company. Instead, she stepped into a higher-level leadership role and increased her impact in this global pharmaceutical research organization. Her story illustrates that true compassion is widely inclusive and resonates throughout an organization.

UNDERSTANDING THE SCIENCE

The scientific study of compassion (including self-compassion) is a relatively new field, and its application in leadership is early in being defined and studied.[3]

While compassion is a complex phenomenon, we are able to simplify the complexity because compassion draws on the first five leadership capacities that you've already encountered (see table 6.1 for a quick review). A compassionate leader scores highly in all five capacities. Compassion is a synthesis of all of them.

TABLE 6.1   COMPASSION CAPACITIES

CONSCIOUS—I SEE CLEARLY	Be aware of others' values, needs, resources, well-being, and suffering.
AUTHENTIC—CARE	Demonstrate concern for others' performance and well-being.
AGILE—FLEX	Balance valuing growth/profit and human thriving.
RELATIONAL—HELP	Understand others and act to help them get better.
POSITIVE—STRENGTHEN	Act to help others improve performance and well-being.
COMPASSION—RESONATE	Cultivate resonance across vision, values, goals, strategy, and capacities.

When you act more and more in concert with the first five capacities through the day in, day out leadership work of strategizing and implementing, you can reach a place where compassion flows naturally. Your built-in, broad respect and concern for our shared humanity, values, and journey come alive. All by itself, improving on these five capacities will likely bring about more compassion.

The book on compassionate leadership written by Rasmus Hougaard (Denmark) and Jacqueline Carter (US) also simplifies compassion in leadership nicely in its title: *Compassionate Leadership: How to Do Hard Things in a Human Way.*[4]

WHAT IS COMPASSION?

In defining compassion, a British and American research team led by Clara Strauss notes that an evolutionary perspective on compassion can be traced to Darwin. He concluded that "those communities which included the greatest number of the most sympathetic members would flourish best, and rear the greatest number of offspring."[5]

The team went on to summarize that compassion, stemming from the Latin word *compati*, meaning "to suffer with," is now defined as going beyond empathy, which was defined in chapter 4 on relational leadership as cognitive and emotional resonance and understanding.

Compassion moves beyond an empathic desire to understand into engagement—doing something to make things better. It combines the *desire or motivation* to act with *acting* to alleviate suffering and promote well-being.[6] Compassion also stretches upward and outward to understanding human suffering as a shared, universal experience. It includes the ability, and the strength, to tolerate the discomfort and distress brought on by caring and action.

In some contexts, and in leadership broadly, compassion has been declared a standard for authentically good intentions and actions. Strauss and collaborators cite the American Medical Association's Principles of Medical Ethics, starting with "A physician shall be dedicated to providing competent medical services with compassion and respect for human dignity."[7]

Paul Gilbert, at the UK Center for Compassion Research and Training, describes the universality of compassion across societies, based on a shared reality of human suffering and common physiological mechanisms for caring for and sharing suffering with kin, strangers, and animals. Gilbert notes that an absence of compassion, which is environmentally and socially driven, is callousness: insensitivity to others' concerns or suffering and seeing others as resources to be exploited. Cruelty, "a deliberate cause of suffering for pleasure or sense of power," is the most extreme lack of compassion. Gilbert explains that the strongest expressions of compassion are for people we do not love or even like.[8]

We saw that Patricia came to understand that her selective approach to compassion, as an impassioned advocate for the animals and her staff, was insensitive, not compassionate, to her boss and others outside her department.

The physician authors of *Compassionomics* assert that Western societies are becoming less compassionate and more callous.[9] And according to Paul Gilbert, "Compassion turns out to be the most courageous and wise of all of our motives."[10] That means Western societies are losing courage and wisdom in our less compassionate times.

COMPASSION—BETTER THAN EMPATHY

Led by psychologists Jane Dutton, Jacoba Lilis, and others, the Center for Positive Organizational Scholarship at the University of Michigan put compassion in leadership on the map twenty years ago. They reported on benefits of compassion in the workplace: "Employees who experience compassion in times of suffering are more likely to: feel acknowledged . . . ; have a feeling of elevation . . . ; recover more quickly . . . ; feel more satisfied in their jobs and more committed to their organization . . . ; experience positive emotions while at work; direct caring and supportive behavior towards others."[11]

A Toronto team led by psychologist Gregory John Depow summarized research showing significant benefits of being compassionate:[12]

- Compassion is associated with better mental health and less worry.

- Compassionate individuals tend to be happier and physically healthier than their peers.

- Compassion training can alter structures of the brain associated with reward, enabling individuals to remain positive even in the face of the distress of others.

- Compassion is associated with reduced occupational burnout, whereas empathy is associated with increased burnout.

- Leaders who show concern and respond to the emotional cues of their followers tend to have more successful followers and to be more successful themselves.

The Toronto team highlights a revealing linguistic analysis of more than two million Facebook posts conducted by psychologist David Yaden and collaborators. This study showed that when a person is facing negative emotions, compassion is associated with other-focused writing and positive health outcomes, whereas empathy is associated with self-focused writing and negative health outcomes.[13]

The Toronto team's research further highlights the benefits of compassion as opposed to empathy (caring versus sharing) for leaders: "Leaders who tend to focus on compassion over empathy when responding to negative follower emotions report lower distress, burnout, and intention to quit. In addition, compassion-focused leaders feel more effective as leaders, report fewer negative and more positive emotions, and even report higher life satisfaction. Importantly, we show that followers who perceive their leader as having a compassion focus also have a higher quality relationship with their leader and are themselves more engaged at work and committed to their organization."[14]

Patricia "got the memo" about the benefits of compassion. She leaned in to help her boss, feeling compassion for the pressure he was under. She began to share accountability for cost-effective research. She started to grow into the global leader her boss had hoped for all along.

EXPANDING COMPASSION IN LEADERSHIP

Leadership researcher Brad Shuck and his collaborators conceptualize compassionate leadership as a much bigger deal than compassion, which is already a big deal. Their study of compassionate leaders reveals that they stand out for their presence, integrity, authenticity, and accountability. They are role models for inclusion by seeing the dignity in everyone.[15]

The team also defined compassion in leadership to include concern for everyday stresses and strains, not just notable incidents of human suffering, such as late-stage cancer or a family death. Their research shows that compassionate leaders leverage the warmth of concern—acting on their desire to make work life better, less distressing, and more rewarding—to warm up the coolness of accountability.

An example of compassionate accountability is the handling of tough conversations: "Holding an employee accountable was experienced as the most compassionate thing a leader could do, in contrast to passing an employee along, ignoring the bad behavior, or allowing bullying to manifest. Compassionate leaders stepped up, took responsibility, and held others and themselves accountable."[16]

Shuck's team reports:

Presence was reflected in the ability of a leader to stay attuned to people, and situations by focusing their attention on the present moment. The theme of presence was operationalized as a personal state of awareness and attention to the current moment, situation, and surroundings. This theme characterized a leader's ability to deeply listen to others using a kind of social intelligence and to hear what employees were not necessarily communicating through words but through body language. . . .

This [empathy] involved an awareness of other personalities, needs, goals, and motivations as well as the ability to summarize the tone and content of conversations. . . .

Evidence from our study indicates that the sum is greater than the parts in the case of compassionate leader behavior.[17]

COMPASSION TRAINING

Miia Paakkanen and a Finnish team of psychologists conducted a preliminary study of compassion training for managers who worked in diverse industries. Their article explains that people decide whether a person's or group's suffering is worthy of compassion based on three appraisals:

- Do you believe that the person suffering deserves help?

- How relevant is the sufferer or their situation to you and your experiences?

- Do you have the resources to help?

Their study demonstrated that compassion is based on emotional skills (described in chapter 1 on conscious leadership and chapter 4 on relational leadership) and that managers can be trained effectively in these skills and improve their compassion.[18]

RESONATING WITH THE WHOLE

In their book *Resonant Leadership*, Richard Boyatzis and Annie McKee describe how resonant leaders use their emotional intelligence to build shared mindfulness, hope, compassion, and playfulness in their work relationships.[19]

Now a measure of resonance has been developed and validated by Boyatzis and Kylie Rochford. They call it a relational climate survey.

It comprises twelve statements (each rated on a scale) that address shared purpose and vision, compassion, relational energy, and positive energy. We reorganized the statements, connecting resonance to five leadership capacities:

Resonant Purpose (Authentic Leadership)

1. My organization's purpose is clear.

2. Members of my organization have a shared purpose.

Resonant Vision (Transformational Leadership)

3. My organization's actions are guided by a shared vision.

4. My organization's daily work aligns with our vision.

5. Members of my organization have similar visions of the organization's future.

Resonant Humanity (Compassionate Leadership)

6. Members of my organization care about each other's well-being.

7. Members of my organization are empathetic toward each other.

8. People in my organization notice when others are in need.

9. When someone in my organization is in need, my organization takes action to assist them.

Resonant Relationships (Relational Leadership)

10. The relationships in my organization are a source of energy.

11. Interactions in my organization are lively.

Resonant Positive Energy (Positive Leadership)

12. The atmosphere in my organization is vibrant.[20]

These twelve statements capture the complexity of compassionate leadership in a nutshell. They describe what it takes for leaders and followers all to resonate together—on a shared purpose and future; in their shared humanity; in lively, energetic relationships; and in a vibrant, shared culture.

Giving Boyatzis the last words here, his book *The Science of Change* connects compassion and resonance: "Resonant relationships have three qualities. Through shared vision we experience hope. Through shared compassion we experience caring and gratitude. Through shared energy, we activate and vibrate to the same frequency as others. Through shared mindfulness, we achieve a degree of centeredness, and joy through playfulness."[21]

PRACTICE

"Oh the humanity," exclaimed Herbert Morrison in 1937, in his recorded narration of the *Hindenburg* zeppelin bursting into flames at the end of a transatlantic crossing, with ninety-seven people on board.[22] Years later his audio recording was paired with the video, which can't help but evoke compassion as you relive what Morrison witnessed.[23]

A good way to practice your built-in, genuine compassion is to pause and attune to the shared humanity of a tragedy that is crushing for many. And, to exercise your agility, feel compassion for the uplift to humanity of a collectively positive experience, such as the Olympics, the end of a war, or the safe landing of a damaged plane. Agile compassion is the ability to resonate with both the tragic loss to some and the positive uplift to others, which can sometimes happen simultaneously.

While Morrison's sentiment—*Oh the humanity*—lives on, our compassion can get lost when we are stressed and pressured. It comes back online when we are calm and objective. A good way to switch on your compassion when it is offline is to stabilize your mind and become present to our shared humanity during the unfolding of a human tragedy or a significant human achievement. Forgiveness is also a compassionate act. There is no shortage of opportunities to exercise your compassion neural networks.

Having read the first five chapters, you are primed to broaden your compassion and embrace the shared direction and humanity in your organization. You can feel self-compassion for your own leadership shadows; you can read the emotional climate at a given moment in your organization and inject the positivity that's needed.

As Paul Gilbert notes, true compassion exists when you are generous in your interpretation, defined as a positive default assumption that people are worthy of compassion even when you do not like or respect them.[24] The growth opportunity is to be inclusive and generous in your practice of compassion, to leave at the door your consideration of whether you relate to those suffering and your judgment that they are not worthy of your compassion.

So your first exercise is to make time to pause and sit with the experience of our collective humanity. You can do this as a mindfulness exercise. Take a few deep breaths. Feel the values, journey, hopes, and importance of relationships shared by humanity—first with your family, then outward to your team, organization, society, and beyond.

The second exercise is a more intimate one called "companioning," adapting Dr. Alan Wolfelt's tenets of caring for the bereaved. Here are key aspects of companioning:[25]

- Set aside your mental states of analyzing, judging, directing, and imposing order or logic.

- Let go of desire, intention, or responsibility for finding the way out, for taking away the suffering or making the bereaved one's situation better.

- Hold space for the other who is suffering—a still, safe, respectful space.

- Be present to the suffering.

- Listen with your heart, not your head.

- Be curious and learn.

- Walk alongside, not leading.

INTEGRATION—OVERUSE

The multidimensional strength of compassionate leadership improves the performance and well-being of the workforce, but it can be taken too far. Overuse of compassion can compromise the performance of a leader and their team. High-compassion leaders do *not* overserve others and neglect self-care, leading to exhaustion. Compassionate leadership requires an intentional focus on balance—mental, emotional, and physical.

LEADERSHIP EXAMPLE

Leslie, the head of the surgical residency program at a major hospital, was a highly educated, dedicated, and successful surgeon. As a capable physician and leader in a male-dominated environment, she was promoted to the position of chief of the residency program. She was recognized for her compassion, positive energy, and relational strengths. She excelled in her clinical care, educational, and leadership roles.

But Leslie constantly lived on the edge of burnout. Her dedication to her patients, residents, and family (she had young children), and often having to work overnight shifts, left her little time for exercise or sleep.

Leslie's overuse of her compassion toward others meant she neglected herself. She started to realize that as a borderline burned-out leader, she was not a good role model. In a state of perpetual exhaustion, she found it almost impossible to maintain a positive demeanor without showing signs of despair and depression. She tried desperately to stay engaged and attentive to the needs of her patients, her students, and her family. But at times, her compassion disappeared, and symptoms of burnout would trigger anger, even rage, at the smallest thing. It was crucial that she learn a key lesson for a compassionate leader: first, take care of yourself.

The critical step for Leslie was to integrate self-time into her calendar, make time for exercise, and try to get adequate sleep. Ironically, she paid close attention to the work, sleep, and exercise routines of her patients and residents. By doing the same for herself, she brought balance back into her compassionate leadership, including herself in the mix. Her compassion for others could now be balanced with compassion for herself.

Leslie also needed to reflect on when in her career she felt particularly positive, which was, in fact, most of the time over many years. She recognized that she had lost touch, in her overdrive behavior toward others, with many additional practices that had kept her in a positive flow:

- **Journaling.** By regularly reflecting in writing on her experiences, both positive and negative, Leslie gained some distance from her tendency to be self-critical and instead acknowledge accomplishments and short- and long-term successes. Seeing herself as a success helped her relax and enjoy life more.

- **Setting realistic self-care goals.** By reestablishing goal setting for herself in her personal habits—exercise, yoga, diet, creative outlets—she was able to reengage with her stronger, more confident and relaxed sense of self—reaping the benefits of self-compassion in action.

- **Prioritizing friendships and family.** By prioritizing making quality time with people she loved, Leslie focused more on what worked in her life and where she felt supported, and avoided the loneliness and sense of isolation of overwork.

In summary, by incorporating practices of self-compassion, leaders can maintain the balance of compassion toward others and their own self-care. Their compassion is replenished by their well-being.

Chapter Summary

- As a compassionate leader, you resonate with followers.

- You appreciate the everyday strains of work life and hold space for grief.

- You act to help make work life better for followers while holding them accountable.

- You cultivate resonance in organizations around vision, purpose, and values.

- As a compassionate leader, you see clearly, care, flex, help, strengthen, and resonate.

FROM SCIENCE TO IMPACT ON YOU

- What makes compassionate leadership valuable to you?
- What inspires you to become a more compassionate leader?
- What did you learn about being a compassionate leader?
- What did you know that was confirmed?
- What questions come up?
- Revisit your self-ratings in table I.1 in the introduction: How has this chapter
  - Confirmed your strengths in being compassionate with others?
  - Increased your motivation and confidence to show more compassion?
  - Impacted your interest in getting better at being compassionate?

CHAPTER 7

SHARED

Share

The leader builds dispersed and diverse leadership—distributing leadership to the outermost edges of the circle to unleash the power of shared responsibility.

—FRANCES HESSELBEIN[1]

Shared leadership, also known as collective or distributed leadership, is the capacity to shift from "I" to "We," sharing and distributing leadership capacities within teams and throughout an organization and empowering everyone to lead in their own contexts. You use an open and inclusive approach to team or organizational visioning, defining values and purpose, designing strategy, setting goals, and making decisions. You help develop the workforce capacity to contribute meaningfully to these direction-setting activities.

LEADERSHIP STORIES

The shift to shared or distributed leadership represents a significant change in mindset, intention, and action for most leaders. This transition from "I" to "We" expands the focus of a top-down leader to include and uplift others. This chapter presents two stories to illustrate different aspects of distributed leadership.

SCOTT'S INVESTMENT BANK

Scott, on the verge of becoming a partner at a boutique investment bank, worked in an environment that had been designed for distributed leadership over a decade earlier. The firm, known for its expertise in highly leveraged buyout opportunities, had minimal hierarchy. Cultural values were individual autonomy, collaboration, and teamwork.

Scott lacked self-confidence. He didn't see himself as a partner among partners, grounded in his strengths and contributions. He also needed to get better at developing and mentoring the next generation. He needed to develop in two ways: to share leadership with senior partners and to develop his team so they could share leadership with him.

The investment bank's shared leadership structure required Scott to operate with significant autonomy, making decisions that impacted the firm's strategic direction. This autonomy included navigating relationships with senior partners who had decades more experience. Scott's self-doubts stemmed from a deep respect for his senior colleagues, which sometimes translated into reluctance to speak up or share a dissenting opinion.

STEPPING UP TO THE "WE" OF DISTRIBUTED LEADERSHIP

Scott realized that his position was unusual as a young Black leader, although he trusted that his firm was committed to supporting non-White leaders. He also understood the importance of seeking support and not shouldering all responsibilities alone, which is crucial in a distributed leadership context. His firm engaged a coach to help with his self-confidence.

With his coach's urging, Scott engaged in self-reflection exercises. He traveled back to signature moments where his strengths, authenticity, and relational skills brought strategic value to the firm. He needed to internalize that his insights were valuable, particularly in the ESG (environment and social governance) space where he was a recognized expert in delivering results. His confidence and mindset improved, and he began to assert his voice in strategic discussions. Scott found that instead of experiencing pushback, as he feared, his thoughtful input was well received, putting his fears to rest.

In the science section, we distinguish the leadership "why" (purpose, vision), "what" (strategy, goals) and "how" (leadership capacities). Scott's firm encouraged his engagement in the why (ESG contributions) and what (strategy). Sharing the why and what with more-senior partners helped him feel part of the senior-level "We."

A pivotal moment was a firm-wide strategy retreat where Scott facilitated a session on ESG initiatives. He showcased his expertise and leadership by bringing home the importance of ESG in the firm's overall strategy. He shifted the perceptions senior partners had of him. They saw that he was ready to lead. This successful performance relieved his insecurities and calmed his anxious ego.

The firm's leaders modeled inclusivity, an important element of shared leadership. Scott's self-confidence grew because the senior partners shared strategic leadership with him. They were open and respectful of his insights.

He felt he belonged as a leader in the firm.

LEVELING UP RELATIONAL AND POSITIVE LEADERSHIP

Scott's development as a leader also involved developing his team by honing his coaching and mentoring skills. He recognized that empowering his team was not just about delegating tasks but also about investing time in their development. He upgraded his relational leadership (helping well, as we discussed in chapter 4). He coached his team members so as to increase their psychological capital, including agency, competence, and fulfillment (chapter 5).

Here it may help you (as it did with Scott in his coaching process) for us to distinguish among delegating, advising, mentoring, and coaching. While they are all useful forms of helping, the focus and dynamic are different in each. Here's a summary his coach helped Scott understand:

- **Delegating.** You direct, even instruct, followers to complete specific tasks within a specific timeline, aligned with the helping guidance in chapter 4: Help just in time based on followers' needs—in the right way, with the right dose.

- **Advising.** After first asking permission, you offer your own expertise and then share advice or specific knowledge. Scott played the role of expert advisor and teacher when he taught his team about ESG principles and how to apply them in their work.

- **Mentoring.** With permission, you share your knowledge and wisdom based on your own experience (what you would do in this situation) to support others' development, which they can take or leave.

- **Coaching.** This is a partnering dynamic, using open-ended questions, active listening, and perceptive reflections, in which you facilitate others' self-discovery of their deeper values, strengths, rhythms, and creative paths forward.

To be clear, Scott initially felt anxious about adding staff development to his workload. He knew that sharing his partner-level responsibilities with his junior team members would be time-consuming—holding regular one-on-one meetings, giving constructive feedback, and creating opportunities for them to take on leadership projects.

Scott discovered that regular thirty-minute development sessions using coaching were effective in empowering and upskilling his subordinates to step up and reduce his workload. He also learned to deliver coaching in short bursts, a technique called laser coaching. Beyond lightening his load, his coaching efforts fostered a team culture of continuous learning and development.

Scott's self-transformation to becoming an equal among senior partners then supported his team leadership as a role model and coach. The "We" approach was alive and thriving from top to bottom.

HOLACRACY IN A REGENERATIVE FARMING START-UP

Johannes, a Dutch agricultural engineer, founded a regenerative farming start-up in the Netherlands that was committed to a holacratic leadership model. What is a holacracy? From their qualitative study of Swiss holacratic organizations, Swiss researchers Sabrina Schell and Nicole Bischof derived this definition: "Holacracy, a self-managing design for organizations, uses the radical decentralization of authority and a lack of a manager-subordinate relationship."[2] In this start-up, the holacratic model involved a founding constitution and rotating leadership roles based on expertise and project needs.

A key scientist, Suska, became a bottleneck owing to her resistance to hiring additional scientists. Without the usual authority of a leader, she feared competition would hinder progress. Suska's breakthrough came when she recognized her strategic role in building a team and mentoring new geneticists. Johannes also realized the need for some traditional oversight in implementing a holacracy. This story highlights the importance of both flexibility and developing junior staff to share leadership.

READINESS FOR SHARED LEADERSHIP

In the science section, we explain that shared leadership, as in a holacracy, entails exercising a great deal of agility. Leaders balance when to use "I," a directive and instructional approach, and when to use "We," a shared and developmental approach. Gradually reducing the "I" and expanding the "We," as Johannes discovered, is never easy, but is the path to shared leadership.

The founder's vision for a holacratic structure was to create an agile, responsive organization that could innovate rapidly in the field of regenerative agriculture. The founding constitution outlined the principles of collaboration, role definition, and decision-making processes. Implementation of these principles required constant adaptation and a willingness to address emerging challenges.

At the outset as a new leader without a team, Suska enjoyed feeling indispensable. Her specialized knowledge in agricultural genetics was exceptional. But her feeling of self-importance was also exceptional, accompanied by a lack of self-awareness and compounded by the high stakes of her projects. The founder could see that elevating Suska to a key leadership role was a double-edged sword: she was key to the firm's technical success, but she also lacked the humility needed to be a team player in the growth of the firm.

When it came time for Suska to hire a team of scientists, she resisted holacratic principles. She was afraid that new hires would compete with her and dilute her influence. But, through a good amount of open, facilitative dialogue with the leadership team, Suska realized that her role could evolve from being the sole expert to being a mentor and strategic leader of a specialized team. She became aware that she would need to grow as a leader, quiet her ego's need to be important, and become part of the "We" solution—building the requisite scientific capabilities in a team.

In sharing her leadership and knowledge with others, Suska realized that her value would be expanded, not diminished. The firm's collective success was the end game, not her personal need to be at the center of every initiative. This transformative shift was humbling, but with the support and guidance of Johannes and colleagues who respected Suska—some of whom shared their own struggle at times with ego needs—she could relax, grow, and show up as a true team player.

AGILITY IN SHARED LEADERSHIP

In the context of Suska's struggle, Johannes also needed to exercise agile leadership—recognizing that distributed leadership would not be embraced by everyone. She wanted to employ a fully holacratic approach from the get-go, yet not all of her leaders were ready (motivated and confident) to make this leap. Shared leadership requires a level of maturity and humility that takes time to develop. The realities on the ground when human readiness, skills, and capacities were lacking, meant that Johannes needed to adapt.

Johannes practiced her agility in working through strategic discussions in real time with her team, shifting styles as needed:

- Coaching—creating a safe and energizing space for open-ended questions and team discovery

- Mentoring—sharing her wisdom and experience without dictating a strategy

- Delegating—directing experts like Suska to take on aspects of a strategic plan, in this case the direction of the firm's genetic research

Her agile approach enabled the firm to benefit from the autonomy and rapid innovation associated with a holacracy while providing the stability and guidance necessary for new team members to grow.

UNDERSTANDING THE SCIENCE

In our first six chapters, you probably noticed that the leadership capacities are focused on creating the conditions for leaders and workforces to perform well and thrive, while moving toward goals and visions and serving a meaningful purpose. Before we move on to sharing leadership and elevating others and the system, we want you to zoom out to see leadership and leadership science from above.

Zooming out, you can see that there is a *why, what,* and *how* in leadership (figure 7.1). The *why* generates motivation and includes vision, values and virtues, meaning, and purpose. The *what* is all about strategy, decisions, goals, plans, and implementing action. The *how* is about influencing others to align with the *why* and engage with the *what.* This book focuses on the *how* of leadership, presenting the science as nine capacities.

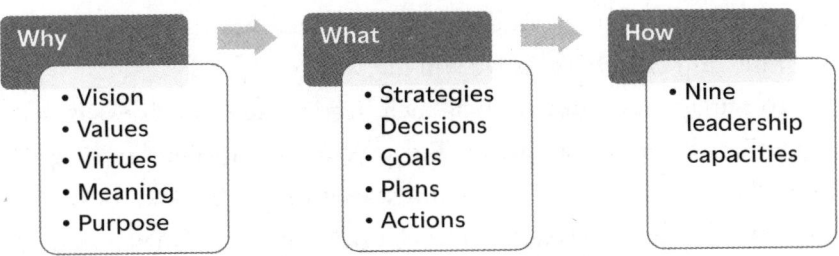

FIGURE 7.1. HOW LEADERSHIP WORKS

While business and management schools focus mainly on teaching the what, like this book, leadership science is mainly concerned with the how. To repeat: By "the how" we mean *how* leaders influence others to align fully with the why—for example, vision, purpose, mission, values, meaning—and *how* leaders influence others to engage fully with the what—strategy, goals, and so on.

Because shaping strategic direction is a primary role and purpose for leaders, strategy professor Dusya Vera and colleagues proposed that leadership researchers start collaborating with strategic management scientists to integrate strategy making into leadership science.[3]

Coming back to shared leadership, sharing the role of strategy making is important in fostering workforce engagement and alignment. And here, shifting to "We" from "I" is particularly challenging.

In Scott's case, the senior partners were mature and experienced in leading a distributed culture, which in good part enabled his growth. Johannes used an agile approach to strategic discussions with her team. She deftly moved from "I" (empowering and directing Suska) to "We" (encouraging her entire team to step up and brainstorm strategic opportunities).

When it comes to the what of setting strategic direction, there isn't an easy answer to the "We" versus "I" question. The ideal presented by leadership researchers is that high engagement, alignment, and the development of new leaders come about through collective contributions, where most everyone ("We") participates in meaningful ways in setting strategy. And the "I" approach has its place, too, for Johannes and elsewhere, as we will see.

You may have heard that such leadership capacities as self-regulation, listening, empathy, and psychological safety and capital are called soft. But the research and stories in this book show us that the how of leadership is not soft; it's hard. Alignment and engagement are not the shared, collective strengths of leaders globally, as indicated by Gallup's data showing low workforce engagement (less than 25 percent), which we discussed in chapter 5 on positive leadership.[4]

In this chapter, the science makes leadership harder, bringing the why, what, and how together at the self, other, and system levels. Leaders go beyond a shaping influence on the why and what that they figured out on their own. They empower and include people in cocreating and codeveloping the why (values, vision, purpose) and what (strategy, goals, implementation), using the how (leadership capacities).

STRATEGIC LEADERSHIP

You've likely already noticed that a polarity in shared leadership calls for agility: when to use "I" and when to use "We." When it comes to strategic leadership, setting leadership strategic direction, there isn't an easy answer. The mix of "We" and "I" depends on the collective leadership capacity available to contribute to higher-level strategy.

We already touched on the importance of "We" in our discussion of authentic leaders who care about what stakeholders need and value. Compassionate leaders also resonate with the "We" in their organizations. Caring and resonating with the "We" sets the foundation for the "We" in sharing strategy setting and decision-making.

The "We" focus of authenticity and compassion underpinned Johannes's success in designing a "We-based" holacracy. She was committed to the success not of her own career but of the team, the organization, and the stakeholders they served. Her dedication to reducing the toxic effects of industrialized agriculture powered her willingness to grow, flex, and share, and to develop others.

To better define strategic leadership, management professor Mehdi Samimi and colleagues reviewed 326 articles that connected strategic leadership to organizational outcomes. They arrived at this short description of strategic leadership: "the functions performed by individuals at the top levels of an organization that are intended to have strategic consequences for the firm." Notice the emphasis on exclusivity—individuals at the top levels. The leadership function (out of six functions the researchers identified) we are drawing out here is "making strategic decisions."[5]

Let's go now to the scholarly investigation of inclusive leadership and consider how it relates to strategic leadership. Leadership researchers in the Netherlands and South Africa, led by Ayfer Veli Korkmaz, reviewed 107 studies of inclusive leadership. A key conclusion was that in most organizations, more attention needs to be paid to inclusiveness in organization-level strategy and decision-making.[6]

Scott's firm is way out in front. Scott, a young Black leader, shifted from being a doubt-ridden leader to an empowered one because his senior colleagues committed to inclusiveness in firm-level strategy making, and committed to his development through coaching.

The *Strategic Management Journal* featured a study of "open strategy" led by Swiss strategy professor Violetta Splitter at the University of Oxford. Open strategy refers to inclusiveness in developing organizational strategy—seeking input from employees at all levels in order to integrate diverse perspectives.[7] While an inclusive strategy process is a powerful "We" approach, Splitter and collaborators explain that inclusion initiatives aren't always effective. Employees can be overwhelmed, can lack competence, can fail to engage, or can make inappropriate contributions. Therefore, emerging leaders like Scott and Suska may need training and coaching in how to conceptualize and communicate their contributions to strategy.[8]

Cynthia McCauley and Charles Palus at the Center for Creative Leadership (CCL) advocate for moving leadership *down* from the top and *out* to the collective, in effect democratizing leadership. They note:

"Leaders are not the fundamental source of leadership; leadership is an emergent property of interactions among people working together." Shifting away from leader-centricity acknowledges "the power shifts in society that elevate the role of followers."[9]

The "We" approach to arriving at strategic direction also involves what is called "complexity leadership,"[10] which starts with the premise that organizations are complex, emerging systems embedded within many other complex, emerging systems, just as we find in the natural world. None of these systems can be fully understood, predicted, or controlled in a top-down fashion. Disseminating leadership functions is vital in complex, changing systems.

To promote inclusion, Cauley and Palus propose what they refer to as the DAC framework:[11]

Direction—collective agreement on overall goals
Alignment—coordinated work toward goals
Commitment—shared responsibility for the success and
    well-being of the collective

The value of collective engagement in strategy setting starts with *alignment*. People are more engaged and aligned if they participate in the dialogue about envisioning a desired future or setting a compass in the direction of a purpose, and how to get there through strategy.[12] McKinsey's research supporting its Organizational Health Index confirms that shared vision and strategy are vital to high-performing organizations.[13]

In concert, this research from CCL and McKinsey demonstrates both the complexity and the reward that leaders can expect from sharing the strategic discussions with others who bring up-to-date expertise and fresh ideas to help shape strategy. Another point made by McCauley and Palus is that a shared, collective approach to leadership helps develop others as leaders.[14]

Now let's talk about the *quality* of strategic direction. On the one hand, the "We" or collective approach may generate a strategy of the highest quality, as Scott's firm modeled. However, that is not always the case. Business school professors Gary Hamel and Michele Zanini note in their book *Humanocracy*: "While it is true that senior leaders are ultimately accountable for strategy, it doesn't follow that they are the best ones to create it. There's only so much wisdom and experience in the executive team, and often it's not enough. Yet senior leaders are reluctant to crowdsource strategy. How can they justify their generous pay packets if they are not the ones plotting the future and making the big calls? Formal hierarchy asks too much of too few."[15]

Hamel and Zanini describe a humanocracy as a visionary form of future organizations, where organizations exist to serve humans, not the other way around, as has been common for much of human history. The people in a human-centered organization grow wealth and well-being together, rather than harm well-being to grow wealth.

THE "I" APPROACH TO STRATEGIC DIRECTION

Now let's look at the "I" approach to strategy development. Top leaders are accountable for organizational strategy and the results it produces, whether or not they have the capacity, experience, or wisdom to generate a high-quality strategic direction. But of course there is also risk in a collective approach to defining strategic direction, as noted by McCauley and Palus. It could lead the organization in a direction that is flawed, that fails or sputters. Sometimes the "I" approach fails, and sometimes the "We" approach fails.

Richard Rumelt, UCLA business school professor and former president of the Strategic Management Society, makes a strong case in his book *The Crux* for strategy to be developed by a group of well-informed senior leaders.[16] Rumelt defines a good strategy as one that crystallizes the crux out of a messy, complex situation. The crux is a key challenge that if overcome, provides a pivotal lever, propelling an organization toward healthy growth. The challenge can be internal, such as dysfunctional systems, lack of engagement or resilience, or product/service gaps. The challenge can also be external, such as changes in customer needs or market dynamics at the micro or macro levels.

Good strategy—crystallizing the crux—is then *not* vision or purpose, *not* goals, and *not* numbers and financial targets for growth and profits. In support of the exclusive "I" approach, Rumelt notes: "If a strategy is focused energy on a critical thing, then it can't be what everybody wants and everybody gets a little piece of what they do included."[17]

In Rumelt's top-down approach, of course there is room for collective engagement and contributions in strategy development—the optimal balance of "I" and "We."

BACK TO "WE"

In every moment of a leader's day, there are small and large choices to explore and decisions to be made. The "We" approach works when there are people with leadership perspectives and abilities throughout the organization, or when time and effort are invested well in building strategy-making capacity and when strategic considerations are not too complex for most to grasp.

While there is a case for the "I" approach in strategy development in some contexts, research on strategy implementation clearly advocates for the "We" approach in order to bring about full engagement, alignment, and shared responsibility. For example, a review of forty studies of shared leadership in 3,019 teams confirmed that team outcomes are improved by collaboration in defining a shared purpose and objectives, trusting relationships and mutual support, and sharing of decision-making.[18]

Our stories of an investment bank experienced in sharing leadership and an emergent, holacratic start-up show that developing the "We" approach is worthwhile, even if challenging and time-consuming. Moreover, a leader's focus on a "We" mode for strategy setting and implementation will sparkle with everything we've explored in the first six chapters that improves performance and outcomes—seeing clearly, caring, flexing, strengthening, and resonating.

As is often the case, modern-day research confirms ancient wisdom. In this case, distributed leadership scholar Charlene Tan in Cambodia brings to life the classical Chinese philosophy called Huainanzi, which integrated Daoist and Confucian thought. According to Huainanzi, an exemplary leader distributes responsibility and authority and inspires others through virtuous character, benevolence, and influence. Tan extols the leader's deep caring for all the people in an organization, modeling compassion in support of shared leadership:[18]

> The ruler of antiquity was concerned about the hardships of his subjects to the extent that if there were people starving in his state, at each meal he would have only one single dish, and if there were people freezing in winter he would not attire himself in fur garments. Only when the harvest was good and the people had plenty would he then set up the bells and drums and display the shields and axes. And with the ruler and subject, superior and subordinate, all enjoying these together, there was no sorrowful person left in the whole state.[19]

PRACTICE

Sharing and distributing leadership, moving from the top down and out, is a transformational process in which leaders shift out of authoritative styles and move into coaching, mentoring, teaching, and training others to lead better. Leaders see clearly the gaps in the leadership capacities of their followers and invest in ways to help them improve.

The "We" culture is one where in some moments leaders and followers are performing well and looking good. At other times followers are learning, are uncomfortable, even awkward, and not looking their best. Both models are welcomed and rewarded. Coaches call this a coaching culture, where everyone has a performing-well agenda and a getting-better agenda, with plenty of social support and psychological safety for the latter.

Once there is a game plan in place to adopt a shared leadership approach, then a few practices are important, none of which are new, but all of which require extra care and diligence.

- **Defined roles and responsibilities.** Clearly delineate roles and responsibilities within teams. Each member should know their specific duties and how their work contributes to the organization's goals. This prevents overlap and confusion.

- **Strong communication channels.** Foster open and transparent communication through regular meetings, updates, and feedback sessions.

- **Balanced accountability.** Implement a system of rotating accountability for different projects or functions. This ensures that responsibility is shared and that no single individual is overwhelmed. Regularly review performance and provide constructive feedback.

- **Psychological safety.** Create an environment where team members feel safe to express their ideas, ask questions, and take risks without fear of negative consequences. A key element: debriefing discussions when things go wrong—not finger-pointing or blame but a recognition and honoring that trying new things involves risk and potential failure.

- **Regular check-ins and updates.** Conduct regular check-ins and status updates to keep everyone informed about progress, challenges, and changes. This helps in identifying issues early and making necessary adjustments promptly.

Sharing leadership is an advanced approach that elevates you as a leader as you elevate others. When you practice it well, you become more relaxed and energetic—sharing strategy and goal setting, decision-making, and action plans. Spending more time coaching, mentoring, and empowering others will energize you.

INTEGRATION—OVERUSE

How might leaders overuse shared leadership? If they have integrated all the leadership capacities and committed to being strong mentors, coaches, and empowering leaders, how can they overuse this capacity?

One key to the success of shared leadership is to maintain accountability as the senior leader in charge. Fully distributed leadership systems run the risk of not having a clear sense of where the buck stops. If everyone is sharing leadership and responsibilities for functions, initiatives, programs, and strategies, and something goes well, they may all try to take credit. If something goes wrong, it may not be clear who is accountable. Recall the adage that success has a thousand mothers and fathers, but failure is an orphan.

The leader in charge needs to both maintain and distribute accountability effectively. This does not necessarily mean that you have to be accountable for all leadership outcomes and behaviors, but there should be a clear delineation of how accountability will be determined, measured, and communicated.

One approach for handling this issue might be rotating accountability for a particular initiative—such as a new product, technology, finance, or sales innovation—to improve leadership expertise and shared responsibility.

LEADERSHIP EXAMPLE

John was a highly creative, innovative, and optimistic entrepreneur, who led a nonprofit research institute dedicated to developing software in the recording, music, and film industries using artificial intelligence.

He was a firm believer in sharing and distributing leadership across different initiatives. He loved brainstorming sessions with his coleaders, which would last for hours.

John fostered an environment of strong psychological safety and respect, encouraging creativity, debate, and conflict without blame. He trusted his team leaders in various initiatives so much that he would sometimes take weeks off, telling them he was on retreat to reflect and to think of new initiatives. John's disappearing acts had negative consequences. Members of his team would often say, "John is missing in action. We've been abandoned."

While John's leadership approach created a playful, creative, and committed environment, it also led to challenges. He sometimes shared leadership to the point of losing track of who owned what initiative. Who was responsible? When projects failed to meet expectations or went over budget, there were moments of disbelief, denial, or dismissiveness among the team members. In John's absence, finger-pointing occurred. Successes were shared, but failures lacked clear accountability, undermining trust.

For John, it was a wake-up call to recognize that while sharing leadership was a strength, he needed to instill accountability in his coleaders. They needed to own responsibility for failures without feeling blamed; they needed to engage in discussions to learn and improve. John began to communicate with his team about accountability, project management, and follow through. He stayed in communication before, during, and after his retreats. This approach helped the team work through failures, reinforcing maturity and responsibility without undermining psychological safety.

As we described in the science section, "I"-focused leadership behavior is at times crucial to setting the direction and creating the conditions for the "We" phase to emerge eventually. Alignment doesn't emerge without a great deal of effort, presence, and support from leaders.

John took the feedback he received to heart and put shared leadership practices in place. The goal was not to dictate an organization chart or hierarchy but to empower his team to engage with greater awareness of one another's roles and expectations.

John pledged to be available to celebrate wins, recognize and appreciate success, and work through challenges or mishaps together, without assigning blame. Success would be shared, and so would failure. He saw that shared leadership can elevate team dynamics and individual growth, but that it must be implemented with clear guidelines in order to avoid confusion, ensure accountability, and maintain trust.

Chapter Summary

- To share leadership, you move from "I" to "We" by distributing leadership capacities throughout a team or organization.

- The shift to "We" happens when you include followers and share the processes to arrive at the *why* of vision and purpose creation, and the *what* of developing strategy, decision-making, goal setting, and action planning.

- As an inclusive leader, you see clearly, care, flex, help, strengthen, resonate, and teach and share the path to the *why*, *what*, and *how* of leadership.

FROM SCIENCE TO IMPACT ON YOU

- What makes shared leadership valuable to you?
- What inspires you to share leadership and elevate others' leadership?
- What did you learn about sharing leadership?
- What did you know that was confirmed?

- What questions come up?
- Revisit your self-ratings in table I.1 in the introduction: How has this chapter
    - Confirmed your strengths as a leader who shares leadership with others?
    - Increased your motivation and confidence in empowering the leadership of others?
    - Impacted your interest in getting better at distributing leadership to others?

CHAPTER 8

SERVANT

Serve

The servant-leader is servant first. It begins with the natural feeling that one wants to serve, to serve first. Then conscious choice brings one to aspire to lead. That person is sharply different from one who is leader first.

—ROBERT GREENLEAF[1]

As a servant leader, you put service into leadership—serving followers' well-being and development, and all of you together serving the collective good. There is an evolutionary basis for other-focused service, including the parenting role. Of course, service comes more naturally to some than to others. The pursuit of service develops with your psychological maturity, as your ego gets quieter and more stable and less dependent on the self-oriented rewards of leadership. You are a humble steward of your organization. You foster the autonomy, agency, development, and service orientation of followers, which in turn increases followers' motivation and engagement in meaningful work.

LEADERSHIP STORIES

Servant leadership expands on the values orientation of authentic leaders (to care), to integrate the virtue of service (to serve); leaders and followers all together serve some purpose greater than themselves.

Our first story revisits the regenerative agriculture start-up in the Netherlands featured in chapter 7. The second story shows how global software organizations can be led by servant leaders.

JOHANNES AND A REGENERATIVE AGRICULTURE START-UP

From the outset, the regenerative agriculture company Johannes founded was dedicated to service by improving soil and environmental health through sustainable agricultural practices. Johannes also exemplified servant leadership through her commitment to a shared governance model known as holacracy. She emphasized supporting and nurturing leadership within the organization, encouraging team members to manage projects and initiatives and to hand off leadership roles when appropriate.

Johannes viewed herself as a steward of the enterprise rather than a traditional boss. She consistently stepped back, listened, and empowered others—core principles of servant leadership, as the science section will show.

But she had room to improve. When faced with strategic decisions or team conflicts, her results-oriented approach sometimes overshadowed her servant leadership ideals. Johannes struggled to align serving the planet with serving her staff, revealing a gap in her leadership portfolio.

BECOMING HUMBLE

Johannes's strong, competent, direct nature, reflective of her Dutch culture, sometimes felt strident to her multicultural and multigenerational team. Her strong-willed nature lacked one key attribute: humility. Despite her desire to elevate others, she found it challenging to hold back her strong will, quiet her ego, and fully trust her team.

True servant leadership requires humility and a deep social awareness, not only to manifest the company's mission but also to best leverage the talent of its people. Johannes recognized the importance of humility and curiosity, but needed to practice them more consistently. By forcing herself to slow down on occasion and adopt new

habits such as acting on her reminders to stay grounded, remain curious, and seek feedback, she was able to embody the servant leader
she aspired to be.

Expanding further on Johannes's journey, there were specific instances where her servant leadership principles were tested. For example, during a critical project to develop a new sustainable farming
technology, her team faced significant technical challenges. Instead of
imposing her solutions, Johannes facilitated a series of brainstorming
sessions where team members could freely share their ideas and concerns. This approach not only fostered innovation but also strengthened the team's cohesion and commitment to the project.

BECOMING A GOOD STEWARD

Johannes's leadership style began to extend beyond the organization
to the external environment. She actively engaged with local communities, understanding that their support was crucial for the start-up's
success. Her team organized community forums and workshops to
educate farmers and residents about regenerative agriculture, listening to their feedback and incorporating their insights into the company's strategies.

Through expanding her service beyond her team to external con-
stituencies, Johannes modeled being a good steward of the company's
values and vision.

When Johannes reinforced the deeper meaning and purpose of the
firm's vision through communicating and acting on *what really matters*,
she spurred greater team engagement. The research findings described
in the science section confirm that deepening the meaning of work improves work engagement. Johannes's broad-based inclusive approach
built a collaborative and trusting environment that extended beyond
the organization and into relations with the community.

FROM CONFLICT TO COMPASSION, WITH MEANING

One pivotal moment in Johannes's journey occurred during a
major conflict within her team. Two key members had a significant

disagreement about the direction of a new project. Instead of taking sides or imposing a solution, Johannes chaired a mediation session where both parties could express their views openly.

She facilitated the conversation with empathy and encouraged mutual understanding. She showed her compassion for all concerned. The result was a compromise that resonated with everyone impacted, including the silent friends and foes at the sidelines.

The compassionate process not only resolved the conflict but also strengthened the team's ability to handle future disagreements constructively. The transparency of the process fostered trust and openness. Johannes added vulnerability and compassion to her core strengths of being an ethical, values-driven, passionate visionary. Faced with high tension, she delivered servant leadership in action.

CHRISTOPHER AND THE SOFTWARE GIANT

Our second story involves Christopher, the CEO of a globally renowned software company. Christopher had been part of the leadership team for over a decade, steering the company through exponential growth and the transition to hybrid work during the pandemic. He was visionary, creative and committed to innovation, fitting in many ways the archetype of a transformational leader that we will discuss in the next chapter.

Christopher did not initially identify as a servant leader. He believed in his vision and operated from the front, focusing on making a positive impact and growing the company. He was open to feedback and personal growth, regularly supporting leadership development workshops. Fully participating as a member of the team, he modeled self-reflection and development.

A turning point for Christopher came during a team-building workshop centered around the Enneagram, a personality assessment tool. As with other personality assessments, such as Myers-Briggs or DISC, the evidence base for the Enneagram is meager, although the Enneagram has shown preliminary alignment with the well-studied

Big Five personality theory. Small studies indicate that the Enneagram is helpful for personal growth.[2] UCLA psychiatrist Dan Siegel (who we met in chapter 1 on conscious leadership) has completed twenty years of teamwork with five scientists to create a scientific framework for Enneagram personality patterns and their development.[3] Coaches use the Enneagram in organizations to help people better understand their core drives, imbalances, and relational dynamics with others.

The HR department set up an Enneagram workshop for Christopher and his team to learn more about their individual drivers, their tendencies under stress, and how to work together to elevate everyone's best attributes. When Christopher discovered that his core personality type was a 2—the helper—out of the nine possible Enneagram types, he was a bit shocked and disappointed. He wanted to be a 3: the achiever.

HUMILITY AS A STRENGTH

At first, Christopher dismissed the result. But Christopher's team pushed back, for they recognized his helper tendencies, seeing him as a strong coach and mentor. They reminded him emphatically that these traits were important strengths. Although Christopher was a bit nonplussed at being pegged a "helper" (probably safe to say that his CEO ego took a bit of hit that day), this feedback ultimately helped him embrace his other-focused, humble, supportive nature.

In a moment of revelation, he saw a core part of his leadership identity that he couldn't deny. Christopher received nothing but positive reverberations from his colleagues about being fundamentally humble and helpful. He realized that he could be both a visionary leader, stepping up when necessary, and a servant leader, supporting and empowering others.

In the science section, we report findings that humility in a leader improves the performance and well-being of followers and teams. But researchers caution that humility in high-stakes situations isn't always ideal. Christopher was able to balance a strong, confident, decisive sense of self with a humble desire to serve others. He modeled the psychological maturity of a servant leader.

Delving deeper into Christopher's transformation, we can highlight specific actions he took to integrate servant leadership principles. He started hosting regular one-on-one meetings with employees across all levels, creating a safe space for them to voice their ideas and concerns. In his mind, if colleagues deemed him a good coach, he should leverage this strength, which he did with gusto. These sessions not only made employees feel valued but also provided Christopher with diverse perspectives that enriched the decision-making process.

Christopher wanted to reinforce the importance of every individual's role in the company's success. He championed a company culture of recognition and appreciation. He introduced initiatives to celebrate employees' achievements, both big and small, fostering inspiration and a sense of belonging.

STEWARDSHIP AND THE COMMUNITY

Christopher's commitment to servant leadership extended to his approach to corporate social responsibility. He initiated programs that encouraged employees to engage in community service and social impact projects. This both strengthened the company's reputation and aligned everyone with the servant leadership principle of serving the greater good.

Christopher serves as a model for other leaders—embracing feedback, engaging in continuous self-reflection, and adapting his leadership style to fit the moment.

||

These two stories highlight the transformative power of servant leadership. For Johannes, it involved balancing her strong, results-oriented nature with humility and social awareness. For Christopher, it meant embracing his inherent relational tendencies and recognizing the strength in humility. Servant leadership is a sophisticated and challenging framework, requiring self-awareness and continual feedback and growth. When leaders like Johannes and Christopher embrace its principles, they not only elevate their own performance but also inspire and uplift their organizations and beyond.

UNDERSTANDING THE SCIENCE

Although servant leadership is widely known and popular as a leadership framework, it is far less studied than transformational leadership, the most studied leadership topic. Robert Greenleaf, who coined *servant leadership* in a 1970 essay, made the distinction in motivation between leaders who want to serve and that's why they become leaders, and leaders who want to lead in order to achieve an ambition.[4]

Decades later, in a review of 285 articles on servant leadership led by Nathan Eva in Australia, the authors arrive at defining servant leadership as "(1) an other-oriented approach to leadership, (2) manifested through one-on-one prioritizing of followers' individual needs and interests, (3) outward reorienting of concern for self toward concern for others within the organization and the larger community."[5]

On the topic of people development, Dutch servant leadership expert Dick van Dierendonck writes: "In comparison to transformational leadership . . . servant leadership is more focused on the psychological needs of followers as a goal in itself, whereas transformational leadership places these needs secondary to the organization's goals. Transformational leaders' motive to focus on followers' needs seems to be to enable them to better achieve organizational goals (i.e., a means to an end), whereas servant leaders' is on the multidimensional development of followers (i.e., an end in itself)."[6]

On serving the evolutionary tribal need humans have for kinship and belonging, Eva et al. summarize: "Servant leadership might be able to deliver a leadership approach that can deal with challenges of the modern workplace while still delivering on our hunter-gatherer needs of belonging." Their comprehensive review concludes that servant leadership is effective: "The consistent positive relationships found between servant leadership and valued outcomes . . . at the individual level (e.g., individual citizenship behaviors, task performance, creativity), team level (e.g., team potency, team performance), and organizational level (e.g., customer satisfaction, return on investment) provide strong evidence in favor of selecting and training leaders to practice servant leadership."[7]

While Greenleaf asserts that the best leaders are servant leaders and that servant leadership is effective, we are not here to sell you on a selfless focus on others' betterment. In fact, at our developmental stages, we authors are serving both ourselves and others. When we are coaches, we are serving others first. When we are leaders, we are leading for both professional growth (self-betterment) and to serve others. We are balancing both motives, expressing them at different times in different roles.

What does the servant leadership research show? Drawing out the deeper and authentic desire you have to serve others and the greater good can improve others' engagement and performance. As your self-focused ego calms down and gets quieter, the motivation to serve comes alive. Eva et al. note that being a servant leader "requires a strong sense of self, character, and psychological maturity."

To dig in further, let's turn to the most respected survey (out of sixteen) of servant leadership, developed by van Dierendonck.[8] This survey includes eight dimensions. The good news is that we have already touched on four of those dimensions in earlier chapters (authenticity in authentic leadership, forgiveness in relational leadership, empowerment in positive leadership, and accountability in compassionate leadership). We moved courage to the next chapter on transformational leadership.

Here we focus on serving others; we cover two related dimensions. The first is humility (standing back), including giving credit, not chasing recognition, and enjoying others' success. The second is stewardship. We are also introducing some interesting research on the positive impact of servant leadership on two types of high-quality motivation—meaning-based motivation and intrinsic motivation.

Before we go there, here is an interesting study of conflict resolution and servant leaders by management researchers led by Ravinder

Jit in Delhi. Qualitative interviews of fifteen servant leaders showed that their conflict management styles were empathic and objective, and enabled an amicable solution. The researchers conclude, "The conflict-resolution approach [of servant leaders] manifests a leadership style that is cooperative and supportive, compassionate and benevolent, relational and persuasive in nature. It is proposed that such leadership orientation has the potential to give rise to a culture of civility and collaboration, cohesion and commitment and compassion and forgiveness."[9]

Recall that Johannes embodied many of these servant leadership principles in her facilitative approach to resolving a difficult conflict between two team members.

HUMILITY MATTERS

The scientific literature on humility in leadership is substantial. A review of 212 studies of humility in leadership led by management professor Jeffrey Chandler introduces key components of humility defined by researchers. At the micro level, humility is described as "(a) a manifested willingness to view oneself accurately [conscious], (b) a displayed appreciation of others' strengths and contributions [positive], and (c) teachability, or openness to new ideas and feedback [agile]." At the macro level, resonant with servant leadership, humility is, "accepting that something is greater than the self . . . low self-focus, and self-transcendent pursuit."[10]

The Chandler team's synthesis remind us of Rick Warren's words: "Humility is not thinking less of yourself; it is thinking of yourself less."[11]

Chandler and collaborators summarize the impact of leading with humility: "Humble leadership is most strongly associated with followers' satisfaction with the leader and the leaders' participative decision making. We also find humble leadership is not associated with the leader's own job performance or the performance of organizations but is significantly related to the performance of followers and teams."[12]

Unpacking the impact on followers further, the authors note: "Humble leadership is associated with increased satisfaction, affective commitment, trust, perceived psychological safety and capital, leader–member exchange [relationships], innovation, creativity, and performance among followers. Our results also find that the followers of humble leaders report less exhaustion and fewer turnover intentions compared to followers with less humble leaders."

This is a surprising finding. A leader's humility doesn't improve organizational performance (in the way it was measured in the studies), but does improve followers' performance (in the way it was measured in the studies). The authors note that more research is needed to unpack the connection between leader humility and organizational performance.

In the meantime, what should you take away about being a humble leader?

Humble leaders, and their organizations, may not perform better than those led by leaders who are not humble. However, the performance and well-being of the workforce is better when led by humble leaders. A tentative conclusion is that leaders who lead with humility do it for others' benefit, not for the sake of their own performance.

We saw this phenomenon in Christopher's story. His team pushed him to embrace his natural tendency to be humble and helpful. Christopher's being a humble servant leader had more impact on them than on him.

There is another wrinkle to share from the research on humble leaders. Chandler and team note that there may be a "too-much-of-a-good-thing effect" whereby more humility doesn't lead to more engagement and better performance.[13] In fact, too much humility can lead to perceptions of leadership weakness. Stay tuned—more about this topic is coming in the integration section.

BEING A STEWARD

Your ego may be running out of steam on servant leadership, so let's keep the discussion of stewardship simple. It's often the case that the description of a leadership framework is loftier than the simple questions asked in a research survey. In van Dierendonck's servant leadership survey, a leader's stewardship is evaluated by a follower in answering three questions, which are meant to capture a leader's motivation and efforts to be a steward, serve the organization's higher good, and stimulate others to do the same:

1. My manager emphasizes the importance of focusing on the good of the whole.

2. My manager has a long-term vision.

3. My manager emphasizes the societal responsibility of our work.[14]

Returning to the lofty, Eva and team note: "Servant leadership is a centrifugal force that moves followers from a self-serving towards other-serving orientation, empowering them to be productive and prosocial catalysts who are able to make a positive difference in others' lives and alter broken structures of the social world within which they operate."[15]

HIGH-QUALITY MOTIVATION

As we discussed in the chapters on authentic and positive leadership, meaning-based motivation that is fired up by personally meaningful work is high-quality motivation that improves workforce well-being and performance. Confirming these findings in servant leadership, a study in Pakistan led by Muhammad Mumtaz Khan concluded that employee engagement in meaningful work (serving the greater good) may explain (possibly "cause") the higher engagement of employees working for servant leaders.[16]

Over the past four decades, American psychologists Ed Deci and Rich Ryan have studied intrinsic motivation as another kind of high-quality motivation you engage when you do something that is interesting or enjoyable.[17] Meaning-based motivation is distinct from intrinsic motivation because the latter relates to doing a task that is enjoyable in and of itself—although of course you can certainly add some meaning-based motivation to further energize an enjoyable activity.

Given that intrinsically motivated employees are more likely to be creative and innovative and to perform at a higher level (as compared to employees responding to extrinsic motivation sources such as job titles and bonuses[18]), scientists began to study the role of leadership in fostering intrinsic motivation.

A review of fifty studies of leadership and intrinsic motivation led by Chinese business school professor Hanbing Xue concluded that servant leadership, with respect to employees, was associated with higher levels of intrinsic motivation than transformational leadership.[19] They surmise that servant leadership is more focused on supporting and empowering employees, which gives them more autonomy, which in turn enhances intrinsic motivation.

Our stories show that Johannes's and Christopher's intentional support for the success of others sparked intrinsic motivation and creativity in their teams.

||

This section about high-quality motivation and servant leadership is important. Said simply, employees who work for servant leaders engage more because their work is meaningful, *and* they enjoy doing their work more because they feel empowered.

Bringing us back to today's realities, we appreciate that operating as a servant leader in a real-world environment of short-term profits, competition, and globalization is anything but easy. But as Eva et al. note, servant leadership is a lifelong pursuit, and worthwhile:

> Along with the many benefits of servant leadership, practitioners must be prepared to exert tremendous effort in developing a servant leadership culture, starting with themselves as role models. Prioritizing the needs of followers is in many ways counter to humans' survival instincts that are driven by

a focus on self-interest. It takes discipline for servant leaders to minimize these instincts within themselves through role-modeling, and within their followers through encouragement of sharing and helping among followers.

Because servant leadership is difficult to master, it requires deliberate and continuous practice to maintain a servant leadership orientation. . . . however, it is worthwhile, because the benefits of developing strong bonds of mutual trust between leaders and followers pay dividends to organizations. That is, followers want to engage in the behaviors that help fellow workers, customers, and the organization.[20]

PRACTICE

Our practices for the servant leader capacity build on what you learned in chapter 4 on relational leadership and chapter 5 on positive leadership. They focus on showing respect and practicing humility. In their book *Humble Inquiry*, management professor Edgar Schein and his son Peter Schein explain that both together foster organizational success.[21] Let's look at actions you can take to reap the benefits of both of these attributes:

Showing Respect

- **Practice active listening.** Give your full attention to the speaker. Paraphrase their points to demonstrate understanding. Delve deeper with thoughtful questions, showing others that you value their perspective.

- **Provide support.** Offer guidance to team members who may be struggling. It is not a sign of weakness to ask for help—either for yourself or a colleague. Refrain from criticism and keep their humanity in mind. Encourage individuals to seek help when needed, and provide resources for emotional well-being.

- **Assume positive intent.** Lead from a place of acceptance, looking for good intentions. Rarely does an employee (or leader, for that matter) intend to do harm.

- **Practice forgiveness.** When conflicts or mistakes occur, acknowledge those who have been negatively impacted, and forgive those involved in conflicts or who made mistakes, avoiding blame and finger-pointing.

- **Rise above grudges.** Let go of resentment so that it doesn't hinder relationships and team dynamics. By forgiving past mistakes or conflicts, you can create a more positive and productive work environment.

- **Focus on solutions.** Instead of dwelling on the past, focus on moving forward. Encourage team members to work together to address issues constructively.

Practicing Humility

- **Seek to understand before being understood.** Prioritize understanding of your team members' viewpoints before sharing your own. Speak less, judge less, listen more.

- **Value others' perspectives.** Be agile in fully recognizing and appreciating the diverse perspectives, experiences, and skills of your team members.

- **Ask empowering questions.** Whenever possible, ask open-ended questions that prompt your team members to expand their horizons, think critically, problem-solve creatively, and arrive at decisions autonomously.

- **Admit your mistakes.** Humbly acknowledge your own fallibility; doing so will be viewed as a strength, not a liability. This authenticity conveys your shared humanity while also modeling accountability.

- **Actively seek feedback.** Show you are teachable. What's neglected by many leaders is to take the risk and ask for feedback. You will learn how you are perceived, what others value in your leadership, and ways you can improve that you may never have considered.

- **Show gratitude.** Publicly and privately recognize the strengths, hard work, and dedication of others. Be explicit and direct with acknowledgment; doing so builds trust, morale, and team camaraderie.

By showing respect and being humble in these ways, you will enable your team members to feel valued, empowered, and motivated to contribute their best work.

INTEGRATION—OVERUSE

Servant leadership is a sophisticated approach that elevates everyone's leadership. But can a servant leader overuse the tendency to serve? Could being a servant leader become an obstacle to organizational success?

In their desire to elevate others, servant leaders stand back in a supportive role. If they step back too far, though, leaving their staff on their own, they may create an environment of stagnation, even alienation, despite their best intentions. Servant leaders need to be aware of the necessity to step up and be directive when things get tough.

LEADERSHIP EXAMPLE

As the software engineering VP at a large tech firm, Lee fostered an environment of trust and freedom to determine areas of focus and priorities. He encouraged the team leaders to feel empowered and gave them autonomy to act in the organization's best interests. Lee trusted, trained, and coached them, and was viewed as an exemplary model of empowerment.

But Lee had a glaring weakness as a leader: During crises, such as system failures, he was often unavailable. His team felt lost without him. Although they liked and empathized with his leadership style, they felt frustrated when they had to respond to senior management directives without Lee's immediate insights and direction.

Lee's situation aligns with the results of a study of leadership humility in China led by Shengming Liu titled "Not the Time to Be Humble!" Liu's team concludes that followers are more likely to value humility when there is low time pressure, and less likely to value humility when there is high time pressure. Followers' evaluations of *satisfaction with* and *effectiveness of* humble leaders go down as stakes get higher.[22]

The feedback Lee received was a wake-up call. He recognized that solely leading from behind wouldn't suffice if he wanted his team to achieve the next level of success.

Being introverted and supportive, Lee made a practice of standing back to assess what was needed to get the best from his team. Now he needed to detect when situations required his immediate expertise and strategic thinking. He didn't need to be dictatorial, but he had to take the lead when necessary. Here's what Lee put in place to address his team's concerns, while not losing the benefits of being a servant leader:

- Check-ins with his team to understand their needs and challenges. He assessed when they required more of his involvement and expertise, and how best to help.

- Clear decision-making frameworks and protocols so that the team knew when to act autonomously versus when they needed Lee's decision-making.

- Metrics to track the team's performance and decision-making effectiveness. These data were used to identify areas needing more direct leadership.

- Open dialogue with the team to solicit feedback on his leadership style and adjust it to better support their needs.

Once Lee learned that at times his team saw him as missing in action, he vowed to adjust and ensure they could rely on his leadership when it mattered most. He was relieved to find that the good coming from his servant leadership wasn't undermined when he was a decisive visionary and strategist.

Chapter Summary

- As a servant leader, you are a humble steward, dedicated to the betterment of followers, organizations, and stakeholders.

- Your servant leadership can improve performance at the individual, team, and organization levels (customer satisfaction, ROI).

- Your service orientation can improve followers' intrinsic motivation, creativity, and engagement through meaningful work.

- Being humble improves the well-being and performance of followers.

- As a servant leader, you see clearly, care, flex, help, strengthen, resonate, share, and serve.

FROM SCIENCE TO IMPACT ON YOU

- What makes servant leadership valuable to you?
- What inspires you to serve as a leader?
- What did you learn about being a servant leader?
- What did you know that was confirmed?
- What questions come up?
- Revisit your self-ratings in table I.1 in the introduction: How has this chapter
  - Confirmed your strengths in using your leadership role to serve others and the system?
  - Increased your motivation and confidence to serve well?
  - Impacted your interest in getting better at servant leadership?

CHAPTER 9

TRANSFORMATIONAL
Transform, Including Myself

The journey to transformational leadership is self-transformation.

As a transformational leader, you are an inspirational visionary and an influential role model. You enable creativity and facilitate innovation by fostering the motivation and confidence of followers. You engage your followers in intellectual stimulation to challenge, expand, and diversify their perspectives. You model courage and self-transformation.

LEADERSHIP STORY

Unlike servant leadership, transformational leadership is not uncommon among entrepreneurs and C-suite executives, particularly those who focus on a lifelong journey of personal growth and continuous learning. These leaders sometimes have what psychologist Jack Bauer calls a transformative self—a self with an innate drive for growth.[1]

Although transformational leaders can be particularly open to feedback and interested in coaching, this does not mean that their growth process is easy or straightforward. Our leadership story is complex and multifaceted.

Joseph is a European chief operating officer (COO) with extensive experience in technology, finance, marketing, and sales at several global manufacturing and services organizations. Joseph earned an MBA from a top business school and spent his early years as a strategy consultant with a premier consulting firm. Joseph was well versed in how robotics and artificial intelligence could help automate distribution centers and analyze big data for marketing, sales, and financial functions.

These qualifications made him well equipped, at least on paper, to take on the role of COO of a fast-growing, technology-driven e-commerce company in Qatar, a country and culture vastly different from his own.

TRANSFORMATIONAL CHANGE

Joseph's new role engaged with the complex intersection of disruptive technology and global cultural shifts. Transformational change of the organization would require Joseph to embark on his own journey of self-transformation. His path to becoming a visionary and an inspiring role model models transformational leadership.

As one of the few Western C-suite executives at this global firm based in Doha, Joseph was excited about the challenge, but was immediately out of his comfort zone. Moving his family to an environment vastly different from his German homeland was a culture shock. Although he had global experience, having studied in the US, working in a Middle Eastern business culture was also a major change.

His firm and new bosses were supportive, understanding the significant transition he was making. They were committed to building a global organization that served customers beyond their geographical roots, and to building a multicultural senior team.

While adjusting to new geography and culture, Joseph was leading a complex and global transformation of infrastructure technology. He was excited by the role while concerned that the culture's strict hierarchy might conflict with his identity as a consensus-oriented leader.

Joseph started out with many of the attributes of a transformational leader, as described in the science section:

- He had a powerful vision, a commitment to innovation, and a willingness to disrupt the firm's normal operating patterns.

- He was open to coaching, often requesting feedback and taking it to heart.

- He also was a natural servant leader:

  - He was humble in learning about the local culture.
  - With a relatively quiet ego, he focused on expanding the firm's capabilities and not his power and position.

COURAGE TO CHANGE

Joseph had always viewed himself as a work in progress. One of his first steps was to join a leadership development program, which provided coaching and opportunities to build relationships and learn about the culture outside of work.

In his managerial and leadership roles earlier in his career as a consultant and finance/tech expert, Joseph had been lauded for his mastery of details. Consultants earn credibility for the depth of knowledge they bring. But in this new role, it was his vision, inspiration, and ability to create a safe space for others to shine and innovate that would put him on the path to success.

This empowering stance toward his team was somewhat alien at first. It took courage to review his style (becoming conscious, but not self-conscious) and elevate his team to a new level of engagement—role-modeling and coaching, not micromanaging.

Joseph began to see that he had a significant leadership shadow. As a highly task-driven introvert, he tended to be hands-on, tactical, and detail oriented to a level that frustrated some of his team. His passion for getting things done and proving his worth in this new role led him to be overinvolved in their work.

Joseph's challenges were compounded by the firm's hierarchical and patriarchal culture. He faced pressure from his boss to demonstrate an authoritative style, which made him uncomfortable and conflicted with his natural approach as inclusive and collaborative in his micromanaging. He was already heavily involved at the task level, as we noted, and this additional downward push to be highly directive led him into overdrive mode, putting him on a trajectory toward burnout.

CULTURAL AGILITY

Despite his visionary ideas and commitment to innovation, Joseph struggled with the new culture. His interactions were perceived as "low context" and transactional, focusing more on work than relationships. This approach did not fit well in the "high-context" culture of the Middle East, where relationships are central to building trust and credibility.

Joseph found that his attempts to integrate into the culture were challenging, and he often felt overwhelmed and disconnected from his team. His family pressured him to be available and spend time with them (they, too, were dealing with a huge adjustment). His shy nature didn't help. Often he politely skipped the coffee outings and postwork gatherings where he might have built more personal connections.

Before it was too late, Joseph decided to focus on cultivating relationships. He made it a priority to spend more time with family and colleagues. He started to slow down and be more present, positive, and personally available to his staff.

Having his own strong vision may have been vital to his getting the role, but he came to see that for his team to buy in, they needed not only to align with his vision but to cocreate it. He started to share leadership, cocreating a vision and a strategy to realize the vision with his team.

Joseph began to be more authentic, more personal and personable, less all about work. He held dialogue sessions where he did little speaking and more listening, creating an environment where people felt psychologically safe to speak up and share their concerns. A huge breakthrough for Joseph was recognizing the value of being open and transparent about his own challenges, which called for a level of vulnerability that was new for him.

When his team shared that they were anxious about the new direction and about the impact of AI on their jobs, he built trust by sharing his own fears and his awareness of his own missteps (such as being a bit of a micromanager at first). This openness not only built trust but calmed his team's fears.

MODELING TRANSFORMATION

What was key to this transformational moment in Joseph's journey? Self-reflection, courage, and a willingness to change. It was inherently risky to open his heart and share his own flaws (especially as he could not control how his openness might translate back to his boss), yet the result was palpable to everyone (and his boss was moved and impressed). He was soon respected, even revered for his presence and human touch. In a sense, he came to embody the very transformation he had been hired to oversee.

Joseph's final breakthrough came when he reflected on the deeper meaning and purpose of his role. It wasn't just about achieving goals or completing tasks. By finding meaning in technological innovation—making products and services quickly available, accessible, and more affordable, thus elevating the lives of many (that was his hope)—he was able to share a more personally driven purpose with his team.

When he brought multiple levels of staff into brainstorming sessions where they could hammer out strategies together, he leveraged a sense of meaning to improve self-efficacy. His empowering others energized their efforts.

Joseph's transformational leadership journey shows that success is often not about doing more but about *being* more—more present, more balanced in work-life dynamics, more positive, and more relational. By aligning his actions with his core purpose, he was motivated to elevate his team's capabilities and foster the collaborative environment that he desired. He started to feel more at home in his new home.

What you see in Joseph's story is all the nine capacities working together. He raised his consciousness, and he transcended his leadership shadow. He became more authentic about himself and his purpose. His agility improved. He grew more relational and positive, and compassionate for the whole of the organization. He learned to share leadership. His natural inclination to serve came alive. All together he modeled self-transformation, and, in time, he transformed his relationship with his colleagues, subordinates, and the entire ecosystem. In a word, he and those around him, despite their cultural differences, thrived.

UNDERSTANDING THE SCIENCE

As you well know by now, transformational leadership is the most studied leadership construct in leadership research.[2] The term was introduced by James McGregor Burns in his 1978 book on leadership. According to Burns, a transformational leader serves as an independent force in shifting followers' motivation in the direction of positive transformation.[3] Secil Bayraktar and Alfredo Jiménez, management researchers at French business schools, sum up transformational leadership as "the most effective and influential leadership style for an organizational change process because it helps employees change behaviors."[4]

BERNARD BASS

In 2006, Bernard Bass (founding editor of *Leadership Quarterly*) and colleagues defined and operationalized transformational leadership as including four components, which we have modified here for our purposes:

- Being an influential role model
- Inspiring others to be visionaries

- Fostering creativity and innovation (what Bass et al. called intellectual stimulation)

- Coaching followers to increase confidence[5]

Since Bass's formulation of the four components of transformational leadership, hundreds of studies of transformational leadership have been conducted. However, the field suffers from the same broad criticisms we touched on in the introduction, including reliance on survey evaluations completed by followers rather than on observed behaviors of leaders and followers, correlations rather than causal roles in producing positive outcomes, and error-prone research methods.

Management researcher Max (Nathapon) Siangchokyoo and colleagues conclude that studies of transformational leadership have *not* provided evidence for these three original propositions of Bass's model:[6]

- Leaders are responsible for relatively enduring change (i.e., transformation) in followers.

- Followers are transformed in specific ways.

- The systematic, relatively enduring change in followers explains the process through which leaders achieve positive workplace results.

Critique aside, Bass's widely known four components of transformational leadership can be supported with other scientific investigations, which we integrate next.

BEING AN INFLUENTIAL ROLE MODEL

The first component—being an influential role model others want to follow—builds on the research we shared in the chapter on relational leadership: leaders skilled in relationships are influential role models.[7] Bass noted that leaders model how to reach ambitious goals. The value of role modeling also draws on the seminal work of psychologist

Albert Bandura. Bandura showed that when you observe a role model's behaviors, your confidence in performing these behaviors improves.[8]

When a leader is an effective role model, followers are guided by the leader's example. Modeling leadership capacities, like caring, serving, and flexing, helps followers appreciate the leader's positive impact and become more confident in engaging those capacities.

INSPIRING OTHERS

Before we discuss *inspiring others to be visionaries,* we want to tell you about the science of inspiration and studies of inspirational leadership. Inspiration is a motivational state distinct from the other two forms of high-quality motivation we have already discussed—meaning based (personal importance and values) and intrinsic (for enjoyment). Psychology professors Todd Thrash and Andrew Elliot defined the inspired state as having three core qualities: evocation, transcendence, and approach motivation.[9]

Evocation refers to an internal (in our own minds) or external stimulus that triggers us to receive an uplifting illumination. Transcendence refers to receiving (not generating, as in the creative process) a sudden, vivid insight or awareness, like a flash of light appearing in the dark. The light flash illuminates new or better possibilities. Approach motivation can emerge out of the evoked flash of awareness; it refers to the resulting desire to move toward a positive outcome.

Being inspired *by* something (such as watching an Olympic runner win a gold medal) produces an uplifting flash of inspiration, a moment of evocative transcendence. Being inspired *to do* something adds approach motivation to move forward into action (such as starting to train for a 5 k race).

Joseph was inspirational when he "let his hair down," being vulnerable in front of others. He described the moment as "a sudden release of pressure, like all the air in a puffed-up, stretched tire, was allowed to escape. I felt myself relax . . . and everyone in the room seemed to sigh, all at once." Showing some vulnerability set off a chain reaction for Joseph and his team. Everyone became inspired to take new risks, such as thinking outside the box.

Yi Cui, Todd Thrash, and colleagues studied how inspiration contributes to creativity. They note that inspiration is more likely to occur on weekdays, which is good news for leaders. Inspiration can cause an upward spiral—first leading to intrinsic motivation (enjoying the work), then increasing creativity and making creativity more productive, which in turn improves confidence in moving forward. It also works hand in hand with effort; inspiration energizes persistence. Success needs far more inspiration than 1 percent to fuel the 99 percent that is perspiration, Thomas Edison's formula notwithstanding.[10]

In transformational leadership, inspiration operates as "inspired to" in ways other than role modeling. Two ways to note: a leader's inspiring vision of the future, which goes above and beyond material profit; and a leader's intellectual stimulation that inspires people to leave their comfort zone and overcome challenges on the path to the vision.

From Bernard Bass: "Envisioning a desired future and showing how to get there is a key factor of the inspirational process, which moves followers towards creativity, and thus towards innovation, by creating alternative possible solutions."[11]

The covisioning process worked well for Joseph, playing to his tendency to be introverted. He was aware that his job was to stimulate the intellectual exploration of others, not to proclaim his vision as "the answer." He put a broad vision on the table and then listened well, creating the space for the talent and creativity of his team to make his vision theirs too.

Inspiration by leaders can, but doesn't always, stimulate innovation. A study of health care teams led by management professor Rebecca Mitchell in Australia shows that inspirational leaders with the same professional identity as followers (e.g., physician leaders inspiring physicians or nurse leaders inspiring nurses) improve the positive mood of followers, which opens minds, brings greater flexibility in thinking, and stimulates innovation. The research team also found that inspiration from leaders who followers don't relate to (such as a physician inspiring a nurse) improves the followers' mood, but doesn't stimulate innovation.[12]

Inspiration is an important tool of transformational leaders, but it doesn't follow a simple formula. Joseph didn't know in advance that sharing his vulnerability would be an inspiration. He also discovered that his team was inspired by a shared vision of technological advances that enhance human well-being.

Choosing what, when, and how to generate inspiration during the change process is not straightforward, and the outcome isn't predictable. But, the uplifting impact makes it worth the effort to experiment. It's a good zone for action research.

INSPIRING OTHERS TO BE VISIONARIES

A visionary leader develops and communicates an image of an ideal or better future for a team's or organization's impact. The description of an ideal or better future state may also implicitly or explicitly express important values and/or purpose. The vision is accompanied by the intention of inspiring and influencing others to share the values and purpose inherent in the ideal state and contribute to the realization of the vision.[13]

Management professor Nüfer Yasin Ateş led a Dutch and American research team that studied visionary leadership. They concluded that strategic alignment and consensus of the C-suite with the workforce *on the vision* is vital to commitment and implementation.[14]

We suggest a higher bar.

Taking sharing and alignment even further, being a leader who *inspires followers to become visionaries themselves* is a worthy aim. That's what Joseph accomplished. Ideally, followers develop a personal vision for their own impact as well as adopt the vision for their organization's impact, on their own, or with coaching from a leader or coach.

Visions of a better future, for individuals and organizations, typically call for significant, disruptive change and are not easy to reach. They don't have a clear timeline or road map, and the path ahead is chock-full of challenges and opposing forces. In the chapter on shared leadership, we described strategy scholar Richard Rumelt's focus on designing strategies that transform key challenges into new strengths.[15] A leader's having to develop and implement new strategies to turn obstacles into strengths, over and over, is a heavy intellectual and emotional lift.

Beyond inspiration, leaders and followers all need to find deep and reliable sources of other high-quality motivation (through authentic and servant leadership) and confidence (positive leadership) to energize their engagement, perseverance, and resilience. It makes sense then that the engagement of personal and shared values, purpose, and meaning discussed in the chapters on authentic and servant leadership are high-octane motivational fuel for the journey of change toward a vision of a better future.

FOSTERING CREATIVITY AND INNOVATION

Like Joseph, transformational leaders take risks and challenge the status quo, promoting creativity, innovation, and positive change. In their research review, a team from the UK and Australia led by David Hughes describes leadership as an important force in enhancing or hindering workplace creativity and innovation.

They define creativity and innovation: "Workplace creativity concerns the cognitive and behavioral processes applied when attempting to generate novel ideas. Workplace innovation concerns the processes applied when attempting to implement new ideas.[16]

The same team, led by Allan Lee, then completed a review which shows that authentic leadership had a higher correlation to individual creativity than transformational leadership, and that servant leadership had a higher correlation to individual innovation than transformational leadership.[17] The researchers recommend the following:

- Creativity—Cultivate close relationships with high levels of autonomy, trust, and psychological safety.

- Innovation—Be less "leader-like," including role modeling, supporting, and coaching through open inquiry.

These practices resonate with Joseph's experience. He was naturally a servant leader and became a more authentic leader. He integrated these capacities into his transformational leadership—a winning combo for creativity and innovation. Now let's add agility.

A study of the agile mental processes involved in creativity and innovation, including strategy making, by strategic management researcher Chan Hyung Park in Zurich is worth mentioning. Park's experiments demonstrate that when it comes to solving novel problems, it is vital to start with a comprehensive, rational analysis of a wide variety of needs and pain points, followed by a nonlinear intuitive process (e.g., brainstorming, mind-wandering, going for a walk) from which emerges your intuitive judgment. Moving back and forth from rational attention to intuitive evaluation is key to novel problem formulations that are strategic, innovative, and valuable. Park calls this approach the informed intuition model, combining analytic attention and intuitive judgment in an agile fashion.[18]

COACHING ON CONFIDENCE

We already mentioned the importance of leaders as role models in improving followers' confidence. Now we come back to management professors Bayraktar and Jiménez, who surveyed the experiences of 298 employees going through an organizational change process. They concluded that the behaviors of leaders that improved employee confidence, or self-efficacy (a type of psychological capital we discussed in chapter 5 on positive leadership) were vital to employee commitment and readiness to change.[19]

This leadership finding aligns with research on individual behavior change in coaching (applied in our readiness exercise in the introduction). People who cultivate and sustain both high-quality motivation and self-confidence in their ability to change are more likely to be successful in making sustainable change.[20]

TRANSFORMING BEHAVIORS

Beginning to address the limitations of research on transformational leadership, a study co-led by George Stock, George Banks, and Nicole Voss validates the positive impact of six transformational leader behaviors (observed not surveyed) on followers; these are behavioral signals related to transformation.[21] We organized the six behaviors into two categories:

- Confidence

  ○ Delivering words of affirmation of competence and strengths
  ○ Teaching life lessons
  ○ Introducing followers to development opportunities

- Intellectual stimulation

  ○ Questioning critical assumptions and perspectives
  ○ Seeking different perspectives
  ○ Presenting different perspectives

You might remember that van Dierendonck and collaborators included courage in their survey of eight dimensions of servant leadership.[22] Self-transformation and transformational leadership require ongoing acts of courage in the face of significant risks to reinvent yourself and your organization. If you are acting as a servant leader and want also to embody transformational leadership—transforming yourself and others in order to serve some form of greater good—the need for courage is even greater.

Many of the leaders in our stories modeled courage: being honest, transparent, and open with their teams about their limitations and how they themselves were changing, all in service of the greater good.

Bringing forth high-quality motivation, increasing psychological capital, and applying both forces in transforming mindsets and behaviors, make for a tough road to travel. At every step there is a tension between the status quo and the new, between stability and disruption, and between the known and the unknown. Managing these tensions requires leaders to be continually agile, effortful, even courageous.

Transformational leaders embrace opportunity and empathize with and learn from those who fear change. They inspire as much as they can.

Courage feels possible when all nine capacities come into play together. *See clearly. Care. Flex. Help. Strengthen. Resonate. Share. Serve.* The courage to *transform*, at least to transform yourself as a self-transforming role model for others, may well come from a wholeness of leadership we've brought to you in this book.

PRACTICE

The two self-coaching practices for you to consider in becoming transformational are, first, envisioning your future ideal self as a leader, and, second, engaging in generative discussions and processes that shift your own, and others', perspectives, mindsets, and then behaviors. These exercises are part of the coaching process; they can come naturally to transformational leaders.

ENVISIONING YOUR IDEAL FUTURE SELF

Richard Boyatzis has studied envisioning one's ideal self as a starting point for personal transformation as a leader.[23] He asks you to imagine a picture in your mind, or one that you can draw on paper, or a written, even poetic, description. The imagining process captures your aspirations for your desired future. This vision could be a stretch—a place you've never been before. Or it could amplify or make more consistent you at your best as a leader now.

An ideal vision is one that incorporates both your current and future strengths and what's most important to you, what energizes you. You can weave in any of the nine capacities as a starting point in imagining your ideal self, now that you understand how they operate. Stay away from what Boyatzis calls your "ought" selves, versions of you that are more driven by external things—social norms and values, material possessions, titles, and pressures to look good, impress, or fit in.

Your vision guides you, helps you persist when you lose steam, and helps you self-regulate. Having a vision of your future ideal self helps you make choices in the moment that serve your future, rather than a desire for an immediate and temporary pleasure.

Zooming your mind's focus out to the bigger picture of your ideal self also activates the "relax and rejuvenate" side of your nervous system—the parasympathetic nervous system. This phenomenon was shown in a brain imaging study by Boyatzis, Tony Jack, and Angela Passarelli. Thinking about your ideal self is like a mini vacation from thinking about your real self, which activates the stress side of your nervous system—the sympathetic nervous system.[24]

Here's a simple self-coaching exercise you can do to bring your ideal self to life; then you can discuss the results with a thinking partner or coach. It's also a good team or even family exercise.

1. Get out a piece of blank paper and a marker (or a few colored markers if you are feeling creative).

2. Draw a picture of an ideal day for you as a leader.

3. Draw yourself in the picture if you haven't already.

4. Describe, name, and write down the emotions this picture evokes for you.

ENGAGING IN GENERATING CHANGE

The shortest, although not easiest, path to transforming yourself aligns with the Greek Stoic philosophy popularized in Ryan Holiday's book *The Obstacle Is the Way*.[25] Whatever is agitating your emotions right now (e.g., frustration, stress, disappointment, worry) is the obstacle that is both in your way and the way forward. Remember strategy expert Chan Hyung Park's work on novel problem formulations? (See the "Fostering Creativity and Innovation" section earlier in this chapter.) Here's how it could work for addressing your own obstacles.

Begin with a formulation of an obstacle that is agitating your inner calm. Think through a variety of perspectives that define and influence the obstacle. Let's say a member of your team failed to meet an important deadline, and you are frustrated and angry. Open your mind, be curious, and generate at least nine different perspectives on what happened, even farfetched ones. Lay them all out so that they sink in and populate your working memory, sitting in waiting for your brain to automatically turn them into new insights or patterns. (There is no magic in the number nine. It's just a large enough number to ensure you've thought about the obstacle broadly and deeply.) The broadening process will help defuse your heated frustration and cool it down to calm and accepting curiosity.

Now that your rational mind has done some good work, dial up your intuition. Take a break, sleep on it, or go for a walk. Allow your brain to integrate all the data and perspectives into a new insight, some wisdom, and a way forward. This process goes further and faster with a coach or partner.

Notice that this process is similar to the exercise we introduced in the chapter on conscious leadership: integrating your leadership shadows. You don't really have to go looking for ways to grow—your obstacles show up as your ego noise.

INTEGRATION—OVERUSE

Leaders for whom transformation comes naturally are often not mature leaders; in particular, many lack humility. When they are not humble, their self-confidence can spill over into arrogance or an inflated view of themselves. This overconfidence is common among entrepreneurs who have succeeded by being forceful, courageous, and unwilling to tolerate naysayers. They can get caught up in their success, overusing their capacity to be visionary and creative, and they can be hypercritical and judgmental of followers.

Another overuse phenomenon for transformational leaders is a lack of shared leadership, with an overemphasis on "I" and an underemphasis on "We." This manifests in claiming ownership and not appreciating others and giving them credit. Such leaders may not be open to feedback about being self-centered, arrogant, and self-aggrandizing, and may deflect criticism by emphasizing their personal contributions.

Occasionally, transformational leaders exhibit narcissistic traits. They may deny accountability, blame others for failures, and claim ownership of every idea when it's successful. They may appear inclusive initially, but can become dismissive of others' contributions. These leaders often resist coaching and may deflect negative feedback as counter to their inflated self-image. In the worst cases, they denigrate others and avoid accepting responsibility for mistakes.

LEADERSHIP EXAMPLE

A top-tier analytics and strategy consultancy led by a highly talented visionary named Josh reached the pinnacle of success. The firm developed a new modeling technique for analyzing a company's economic positioning and growth prospects. Josh exemplified transformational leadership with his creativity, risk-taking, and ability to articulate an inspiring vision. He was sought after as a top leader, quite skilled at investing in the best talent. His communication style was inspirational; he used melodic, searingly powerful language and gestures that could inspire greatness in his team and impress his clients.

But Josh's leadership had problems. In situations where clients were dissatisfied or engagements went awry, he was quick to criticize and blame others, rarely holding himself accountable for his role in the setbacks. His communication style, while inspirational, mostly used the pronoun "I," and he tended to claim ownership of all successes. He supported his team with extrinsic rewards, but rarely shared credit for the firm's overall success or showed appreciation for others' contributions.

Josh struggled to hear negative feedback, often deflecting criticism by emphasizing his role as the firm's key ambassador in the field.

His wake-up call came when a group of his team members threatened to leave if he didn't change. This painful experience led Josh to do some soul-searching. He confided his challenges to mentors and supporters, who helped him take more care in claiming responsibility for successes and to recognize the contributions others made in creating those successes.

Being vulnerable and humble, and sharing what he considered weakness, were initially difficult to stomach for Josh. But he finally realized that humility made him a better leader.

Transformational leadership can elevate the entire team to a higher level of performance. Self-transforming leaders see themselves as flawed, evolving humans, and inspire others to transform themselves too.

To overcome self-serving tendencies, transformational leaders need to increase their self-awareness and understand how others see them. This process can be painful, but it's necessary if transformational leaders are to be inclusive—recognizing and valuing everyone's contributions.

No matter how successful transformational leaders may be at one moment in time, they continue to evolve. New challenges continue to draw out flaws. Growth never abates. This moment is always a new beginning, which brings us back to where we started—being conscious.

||

We have now journeyed together through all nine capacities. Before we conclude, we turn to a final story in chapter 10—a real-life evolution of a senior leader who worked through (at her own pace and in her own order) all nine of the capacities. By sharing this CEO's journey, we encourage you not to dismiss any of the capacities. Chances are they will all come in handy.

Chapter Summary

- As a transformational leader, you are an inspirational visionary and influential role model.

- You use intellectual stimulation to support creativity and innovation: challenging, expanding, and diversifying the perspectives of followers.

- You help followers improve their motivation and confidence in overcoming obstacles on the road to a shared vision.

- You are courageous in visioning, risk-taking, and navigating oppositional forces.

- As a transformational leader, you see clearly, care, flex, help, strengthen, resonate, share, serve, and transform.

FROM SCIENCE TO IMPACT ON YOU

- What makes transformational leadership valuable to you?
- What inspires you to become a transformational leader?
- What did you learn about being a transformational leader?
- What did you know that was confirmed?
- What questions come up?
- Revisit your self-ratings in table I.1 in the introduction: How has this chapter

- Confirmed your strengths in being transformational?
- Increased your motivation and confidence to transform yourself, your team, and the organization?
- Impacted your interest in getting better at transformational leadership?

CHAPTER 10

PUTTING ALL NINE TOGETHER

You will never be lost on the path to growth.

Our final leadership story is a big one. It shows how one highly engaged leader worked through all nine science-based leadership capacities. Putting them all into practice is where the rubber meets the road. The order of the evolution described here may or may not match yours, and it doesn't match the order of the capacities in this book. The path to self-transformation, a fancy way of saying continuously growing and expanding, is yours and yours alone, and can be accomplished by coaching yourself; by working with a peer, mentor, or coach; or by the time you read this, maybe with the help of an AI bot.

What matters most is not whether you use our book as your guide or hire the most expensive and revered coach available—it's understanding that your journey toward greater impact is just that, a journey. That's why we caution that the following story tells of one leader's path among many. That said, we want to share a true story (altering some details to protect confidentiality) that demonstrates how your leadership can evolve and expand stepwise through all nine capacities, with stopping points at each of the three major junctures we outlined in the introduction: self-focus, other focus, and finally, system focus.

For you to improve all nine capacities over time, it's a reasonable strategy to move through these three phases of reflection and practice in their natural order of complexity. Aim first to become more adept at leading yourself, then an inner circle—a team or department/division. Then, ultimately, broaden your vision and capacity to include an entire ecosystem in which you operate. In stepping up to system-level leadership, whether by sharing leadership, serving others, or transforming, you can impact the broadest possible array of stakeholders, extending even to customers and communities you serve.

A LEADERSHIP JOURNEY BEGINS

The four-year-old "start-up" had reached an important inflection point. Two software engineering founders from Stanford University had devised an innovative application to minimize commuting time by providing analysis of traffic patterns and suggesting alternatives to users in real time. The app was a hit with Silicon Valley start-ups and technology firms looking to ease the burden of travel for their employees. The company had grown from ten to over one hundred employees in the first few years, as many local companies became clients. As the technology moved out of beta, the next phase would take the firm nationwide. It was time to "grow up" and put a strategy in place for broader and deeper market penetration, so the company hired Stephanie, an accomplished software sales manager, to be CEO.

When Stephanie first arrived, the company was in the midst of a huge growth spurt. Her first efforts were focused on building out a sales team, something the engineer founders had neglected due to their lack of marketing and sales expertise. Early on, word of mouth had been enough to spur sales, but that simple method of growing had petered out.

Soon enough, it became clear that beyond developing a strong sales capability, the company would need to transform, moving from start-up to full-on organization with other functions: finance, HR, client services, and consulting. The private-equity firm that owned a substantial portion of the original business recognized that even though Stephanie could fill the shoes of a top sales leader, she was not fully ready to be the CEO, so the firm hired an executive coach for her.

At first, Stephanie was resistant to coaching. She was proud of her long career (she had over twenty years of sales experience at major software firms) as a corporate leader. She thought that the young engineers twenty years her junior who had founded the firm were more in need of coaching than she was. It was true that neither of the founders had ever led a fast-growing company—and they, too, needed to grow as leaders.

In the short term, however, it was the CEO who was most overwhelmed: Stephanie's sales expertise notwithstanding, the first order of business was for her to become a broader, deeper, and more flexible leader for the entire organization.

Urged on by her boss at the private-equity firm, Stephanie soon relaxed into the coaching engagement. Eventually she discovered one clear benefit: "I have someone on the outside who I can confide in." This job would be tough. A lot needed to happen to bring a new level of maturity to the firm: They needed to expand and hire professionals in marketing, sales, finance, HR, and product development; they needed to scale up the company's engineering capabilities and expand beyond one product.

Over the next year and a half, Stephanie went on a journey as she reinvented herself as the fully capable leader that the company needed. In fits and starts, Stephanie moved through all nine stages of leadership transformation and became a high-impact leader.

So where did she start?

CONSCIOUS LEADERSHIP—FOCUSING ON YOURSELF

How did Stephanie see herself? Once Stephanie became comfortable and felt safe being coached, she started to explore her sense of identity as a leader. She came to see that she was attached to her identity as "sales executive" as a story line for her success. She saw herself, accurately, as a high achiever, focused, disciplined, and authoritative.

But sales leader was not the role for which she was brought in. She needed to become thoughtful, present, and reflective around the distinctions between CEO leadership and sales leadership.

As a fast-paced leader who tended to always be "in action," Stephanie needed to become self-aware (a key first step in conscious leadership), which was rather foreign to her at first. It would require her to slow down and to understand the science-backed practices of mindfulness and self-observation. She would need to insert contemplative practice and self-reflection into her day job—not something with which she immediately resonated. "Stopping to reflect doesn't come naturally to me," she noted, "especially to think about myself! I focus on the deal, trying to keep the client and the staff moving fast toward a result."

As the broader dimensions and responsibilities of being a CEO sank in, Stephanie came to see that being more conscious as a leader asked of her something more—and potentially painful: to consider the flipside of her strengths as a sales director. She could be triggered into overdrive, frustration, impatience, even anger. These were uncomfortable moments of reflection for Stephanie, but she tried to not be overly self-critical, and always returned to the value of self-knowledge.

It wasn't often that her shadow tripped her up, but in a firm where the cofounders were decades younger and less mature, there were strategic decision-making moments that could trigger her. Becoming aware of this tendency—on the edge where right turns into righteous—Stephanie started putting in place practices to catch herself, reflect, and re-center.

This first step on the journey of expansion, as we shared in the introduction and in chapter 1, asks you to step back and develop the ability to see clearly, to be objective—even tough—in seeing yourself. Stephanie was off to a great start.

Questions Stephanie considered:

- How did she define a leader?
- Who did she want to be as a leader?

- How did she define success?

- What are the attributes of leaders she admired? How did she stack up?

Once Stephanie came to see that she would need to expand and grow her "leadership chops" (her words), she realized that her self-definition was not a fact but a well-honed story of a professional journey that had led to success at one level but would not move her to the next. As executive coach and best-selling author Marshall Goldsmith titles his book, "What got you here won't get you there."[1]

AUTHENTIC LEADERSHIP—KNOWING YOUR VALUES

Stephanie's reflection and exploration led seamlessly into a conversation about what she would consider her authentic self as a leader. She switched gears and moved into a new theme: her values.

A deep dive into the topic of authenticity led to an interesting side trip, one that later became crucial to her future success: her interest in building a values-driven corporate culture.

At first, Stephanie's desire to build a corporate culture based on values, although well intentioned, was entirely self-focused. This makes sense according to the research, for knowing one's personal values, as we outlined in chapter 2, is key to grounding a leader with a foundation of integrity and sincerity. Hence, it wasn't a surprise that Stephanie saw herself as the "keeper of the flame," so to speak, the one who would dictate the values for the firm. But as she would learn, she would need to embody and role-model the values important to her to earn the respect of the team. Dictating the company values was not going to work.

The company had two very engaged founders and more than one hundred staff members. Having been in business for over five years, it already had a culture. It would be problematic for Stephanie to simply overlay her value system on the organization. On reflection, she ultimately realized that her values and those already in existence at the company did not differ much. Both she and the founders could summarize their purpose simply: "We are committed to providing a service that makes our clients' lives easier, less stressful, and more pleasant. If our product can add a chunk of free time to people's day—including our own people—that's a win. Life is better for our clients and for us." As CEO, Stephanie needed to ensure that this commitment was part of every employee's DNA, and that her own values-driven work life was a model for all to see and emulate.

Essential to this part of her journey was becoming awake to the intrinsic core of her motivation to succeed as CEO. Her desire to lead with impact took a big step beyond the extrinsic motivators of sales figures and revenue targets, into a deeper exploration and discovery of her personal why: Why did she want to be the CEO? What could her leadership bring to the organization that would be impactful beyond profit?

Questions Stephanie considered:

- What mattered most to her?
- Why did she want to be a CEO?
- How would she integrate her values into her interactions with others?

AGILE LEADERSHIP—LEARNING TO FLEX

Stephanie was acutely aware of the constantly shifting contexts in which her leadership decisions and behaviors were taking place. Developing flexibility and fluidity would be crucial if she was to embody the adaptive leadership required in today's rapidly changing economic and technological landscape.

In other words, Stephanie needed to be agile.

When she reflected on her journey through the first two capacities, she realized that being grounded in her purpose and her personal why would only take her so far. She faced difficult and at times competing corporate challenges. For example, she knew that the team needed to invest in expanding the capabilities of the product beyond local navigation. She also knew that she needed to invest in new geographic markets, requiring expensive new sales staff.

Which was the higher priority? The engineer founders were pushing for expansion of the product and service lines with more innovation—translating into a need for more time and tech resources. The private-equity owners of the company wanted to see market penetration across multiple geographies. Money was tight. How could the company accomplish both?

Agile leadership is most effective when it is carried out with regular feedback loops. Agile leaders strive to build comfort with polarities, recognizing that disruptions in business, teamwork, and life occur when oppositional perspectives emerge.

Stephanie was continuously faced with this dilemma in her decision-making: Should she risk investment in a new product, or spend her limited resources on add-ons to what already worked? Should she bring all the employees back to the office after COVID-19 subsided, or foster teamwork virtually? Should she emphasize growth over quality, or the other way around? When is leading with accountability her job, and when should she point to the team?

For Stephanie, the answer lay in working with her leadership team to clarify the balance between internal growth (more creative resources) and external growth (sales in new markets). Paying attention to her own attachments and opinions while relying on feedback from experts on her team, she came to see that they all could navigate the polarities together: she didn't have to know the answer. They could experiment, learn, and adapt.

Agile leading is a both/and dynamic that requires constant vigilance and awareness of one's strengths and shadows—all those elements of good leadership that she had developed over many months of personal work. The end game for Stephanie was to find balance, in business and life—for the polarities in leadership seem endless. As found by Mihaly Csikszentmihalyi, author of the seminal book *Flow*, becoming present in the moment and receptive, focused, attentive, flexible, and intentional—even playful—combines the art and science of agile leadership.[2]

Her shift toward agile leadership was one she happily took in stride. She would never again see herself as a one-trick pony enabler of sales but rather as a flexible, attuned leader capable of integrating multiple capacities of leadership into her expansive and growth-oriented mindset.

She brought her team's experts into the dialogue needed to make decisions that had conflicting options. They brought research, evidence, and opinions—and she took time to listen. Looking deeply at the potential upside and downside of each investment required Stephanie to hold back her own opinion at times, to create space for others to disagree and take a stand, and for her to bring the team to consensus. It was hard work and took time.

Yet Stephanie also reflected, "I see now that navigating the opposing forces facing my team is not unlike working through the resistance we get from potential buyers. Getting to yes with a client is not that different than working through the scenarios of what my team wants versus what they resist. I just needed to become equally adept at balance and timing internally, as I always had been with clients. Patience and listening. Seems obvious to me now."

It was also at this juncture in her leadership journey that Stephanie became aware of another crucial pivot: from self-focus to other focus. Agile leadership required a flexible, open, and receptive mindset, but didn't require Stephanie to operate alone or make all the difficult decisions herself. She could integrate the core elements of self-awareness, personal values, and a flexible mindset. She would turn more outward in her perspective—with an intentional focus on being positive, relational, and compassionate with those she led, as her move into the next three capacities demonstrates.

Questions Stephanie considered:

- How did she want to respond to a constantly shifting external landscape?

- How did she want to navigate the polarities inherent in leadership?

- How did she want to test and retest her flexibility as an agile leader?

- How did she want to integrate multiple modalities into her self-narrative as a leader?

POSITIVE LEADERSHIP—BUILDING ON STRENGTHS

Stephanie's recognition of the similarities between agility in sales and agile leading brought her back to reflecting on her strengths. What had made her a great sales leader? This exploration led her to see the importance of positive leadership. She realized that her tendency to be self-critical and critical of others was disempowering.

Seeking out what she perceived as wrong or broken and spending inordinate amounts of time fixing it brought her frustration when things didn't work out. But she knew intuitively that this tendency could lead to burnout, for her and the team. "Ha," she would chuckle. "I got stuck on another polarity—doing things right versus doing the right thing. I can be a bit of perfectionist. I see what's wrong and want to fix it. But I know sometimes my frustration shows."

She was aware that she tended to diagnose the problems her sales associates were having, complain about the immaturity of her young staff, and demand they do better. But just recognizing what wasn't working didn't by itself motivate anyone. Her identifying the challenges and obstacles to the company's growth just left her dispirited.

Stephanie's recognition that leading from a "fix this" mentality would not be enough to inspire the team to greatness revealed the key question: What *would*? Positive leadership, where leaders draw out what is working—the strengths, resilience, capacities of her team that had positioned them, thus far, for growth and success—was a far better approach than was fixating on what was wrong.

The breakthrough moment came when she recognized that the cofounders and team would be inspired by building on what was already working well by unpacking their strengths and talents. Appreciating their successes would reignite the motivation and confidence they needed to move to the next level. "I posted a sticky note on my computer screen with the words, 'What's working?' . . . to remind me to start from the positive. And that worked!"

Questions Stephanie considered:

- What has made this organization successful so far?

- What was she grateful for as the CEO?

- What were the strengths and resources exhibited by the team?

- How could she reinforce what works to elevate everyone, drawing out their best?

- How could she appreciate the team?

RELATIONAL LEADERSHIP—LEARNING TO HELP

Over many months, Stephanie had become more conscious of the variety of roles she would need to play, depending on the goal and context in which she found herself—very different as the lead rep for an important client meeting than as the champion of positive leadership in building the internal value system to engender loyalty and alignment. These nascent ways of seeing herself as a multifaceted leader led to another leap forward into relational leadership.

In an organization where all players are seen for their strengths, talents, flaws, and potential, the leader is no longer "above the fray," pushing or pulling, motivating or directing. They are engaged first in high-quality relationships that involve empathy, listening, and helping each other.

For Stephanie the breakthrough came with reflection on her role as helper. Perhaps she could relax more; rely on others more; be a mentor, advisor, and coach; and not be the lone wolf with all the answers. "It's time I stopped making all the decisions," she noted after one rather grueling strategy session with the cofounders and other leaders. "I will burn out if we don't find a way to operate more as a team."

Relationship-driven leadership enabled Stephanie to place herself "in the mix" with colleagues in a way that recognized the value of everyone's input. It also created psychological safety within the team. Stephanie had reached a pain point with her colleagues, which led to this epiphany: "I coach girls' soccer and have so much fun doing it," she reflected, "probably because I'm not the one out there making every move and taking every hit. Maybe here at work, I've got to coach more and boss less."

The relational dynamic—reinforcing alignment, interconnectedness, and support of one another—is what makes a team. Moving toward the interactive dynamic of coaching, Stephanie's guiding and supporting her team moved her toward shared leadership with a sense of "We," not just "I."

Questions Stephanie considered:

- How could she foster relationships that bring out everyone's full potential?

- What happens in relational dynamics that nurtures change, growth, and effectiveness for a team?

- How could she metabolize interpersonal conflicts into creativity and innovation?

COMPASSIONATE LEADERSHIP—RESONATING WITH THE WHOLE

For Stephanie, the revelation that she would need to communicate from a place of positivity rather than blame or finger-pointing was challenging at first. She was used to telling others what to do better, what needed to be fixed. This approach mapped to her narrative about holding herself and others accountable. But was it sufficient to just stay positive? Of course not.

Leadership is nuanced, and balance is key.

Seeing the power of positivity led her into a deeper reflection on the emotional side of leadership: humans are motivated not just by analysis and conceptual framing of problems but by feelings. Stephanie came to see that her own tendency to be tough-minded had its place—after all, this was a for-profit work environment, not a support group. Yet her tendency to be strident and critical led to stress, both for herself and those around her. In moments of extreme challenge—when an important client complained about service levels, for example—her tendency to come down hard on the staff (and herself) was counterproductive and demotivating. So, what would work?

With her coach, Stephanie discussed the science of compassionate leadership including two articles by Richard Boyatzis and collaborators on how performance feedback handled poorly activates the brain processes that generate stress.[3] Boyatzis and coauthors summarized the results of fMRI studies (brain imaging research that showed activation of brain networks) in their book *Helping People Change: Coaching with Compassion for Lifelong Learning and Growth.*[4]

The main takeaway from this research was that coaching with empathy, active listening, and a focus on the coachee's "ideal self" was more effective in stimulating motivation and action than focusing on compliance with what others want fixed.

Stephanie reflected on how she behaved as a parent with her small children. "I know that my parenting skills are much more successful when I am patient and attentive—applauding my son's attempts to learn rather than being critical," she noted. "I guess that same way of handling tough conversations might work at the office." Showing compassion toward her children when they're frustrated and struggling with developing new skills was an apt parallel to how compassion at work could shift the energy of her team and bring herself—and them—to a more grounded, present, and energized place.

Leading with compassion soon became a key element of her self-narrative as she learned to track herself and identify triggers that would take her off track or cause her to revert to blame. A return to the practices of conscious leadership—mindfulness, centering, presence—became her go-to formula for supporting her team to do their best.

We can now reflect on the outward turn Stephanie's journey has taken. Being more positive at the right moments; enhancing her role as coach, mentor, and helper; and cultivating more emotional resonance with her team—all signaled that her leadership had begun to extend outward to her impact on others. She stepped fully into her capacities to connect and attend to the needs of her people, building a focused and aligned team.

As we pointed out in chapter 6, this emergent step toward feeling and exhibiting greater compassion as a leader shows up in the real world as several capacities working synergistically. Stephanie had become adept at integrating all five of the earlier capacities: conscious, authentic, agile, positive, and relational. She would never again lead others with a focus on being right, dictating or being reactive when things didn't go as planned; instead she now showed up as a broader, deeper, more grounded, and agile CEO, one attuned to her own needs and emotions and the needs and emotions of others.

Questions Stephanie considered:

- What was the benefit to her and the organization when she showed compassion?

- How could she demonstrate compassion for others?

- How did she take care of herself and those she loved?

- What is self-acceptance? How did she experience it?

There was still more for Stephanie to learn.

TRANSFORMATIONAL LEADERSHIP—
LEADING WITH VISION AND COURAGE

With a new understanding of the power of positivity and compassion to elicit creativity and innovation, Stephanie was primed to revisit with fresh eyes her vision for the culture of the organization. She wanted to inspire the company to grow into new markets and offer new technical solutions that were less diagnostic of today's problems and more focused on future possibilities. This shift led her to reflect on the power of vision to move organizations and people forward—the province of transformational leadership.

Stephanie became energized and excited at the prospect of being a transformational leader. She worked to articulate how her values and priorities—her purpose as CEO—could inspire those around her to take risks, experiment, see past limitations, and move fearlessly into uncharted territory. It was an exciting adventure for her to integrate her earlier personal work and expand her self-narrative from sales generator to visionary.

Key to the move into transformational leadership was recognizing the value of cocreating a vision for the firm with the cofounders. After a powerful offsite brainstorming session with the cofounders and key people on her team, Stephanie reflected: "We rolled up our sleeves and debated all sorts of legitimate and maybe a few crazy ideas. It was extraordinary to experience the team come alive with creativity."

As shown in research on transformational leadership, the best visionary leaders work in concert with others to take on risky strategies and do it with courage. In fact, her team was rather astounded with how much bigger and more expansively she came to see her role—and how energetically she supported growth both in the company and in its people. She was primed for the next level: servant leadership.

Questions Stephanie considered:

- What was her long-term vision for herself?

- What was her vision for the organization?

- How could she align and integrate her vision with the vision of others?

SERVANT LEADERSHIP—LEADING FROM BEHIND

The culture Stephanie sought for her company was based on core values: innovation, risk-taking, collegiality, support, and resilience. The challenge she faced, as she described it, was that the culture she wanted to embed in the growing firm, if foisted on the team on top of what was already in place, would feel artificial and generate resistance. As Stephanie was reminded from her earlier reflections on personal values, when C-suite leaders attempt to impose their version of corporate culture on the company from the top, the result is often the opposite of what they desire.

So, how to proceed without alienating longtime employees, including the founders, who might not appreciate her well-intentioned efforts to reorient the corporate culture?

The solution lay in a core tenet of servant leadership: leading from behind. Stephanie was aware that servant leadership was about flipping the hierarchy and being in service. It was initially alien for her to take a back seat in culture discussions, but she came to see the value in listening for the nuggets of creative ideas that emerged from even the least experienced team members.

She got interested in exploring the value of the multiple perspectives on culture offered by multigenerational cohorts of employees. She enlisted a young associate from the engineering team to lead the culture-building initiative for the entire firm.

Over a three-month period, Stephanie supported this young engineer, who was energetic, creative, and well-liked by colleagues and who showed a talent for facilitation, to embark on a series of dialogue sessions with staff from all departments and levels in the organization. This process led to a beautifully articulated statement of company values, as well as an exciting vision for the future. As a servant leader, Stephanie played the role of mentor and coach. She was aware that her CEO voice would reverberate more loudly than others', so she held back, mainly listening during the few sessions she attended.

The associate who led the initiative was not only Gen Z and female but also from a non-Western culture. Stephanie was surprised and pleased to learn that this associate was celebrated for her tenacity, skills at conflict resolution, patience, and work ethic. She was viewed by the team as a role model for the future of the firm. Through this culture-building initiative, Stephanie also discovered the importance of creating an environment where talents like this young associate could emerge.

In stepping into the role of servant leader and supporting, from behind, the team-driven effort to articulate and promote an emerging company culture around diversity, quality, creativity, and respect, Stephanie shifted gears in her leadership journey once again. She focused her role as leader on the entire system.

Company culture, as she came to see, would emerge over time as a deeper reflection of what was most important to the entire firm, not just to her. Her role in promoting the culture would be key, but in stepping back and supporting her team to articulate *their* values, she was now fully engaged in leading the system, growing her impact in ways seen and unseen that would reverberate positively far into the future.

Questions Stephanie considered:

- How would she serve the well-being of others in service to the organization?
- How would she listen more and speak less as a leader?
- How would she identify and nurture key talent?

SHARED LEADERSHIP—ELEVATING OTHERS

The success of the culture initiative led to deeper reflection—Stephanie's return to her earliest exploration of the role of leader. It was not a huge leap for Stephanie to engage with the potential of shared leadership once she had become more comfortable—conscious and authentic—with her role as, in her words, the "gardener of the flowerbed" of talent. Implementing a distributed framework for leading multiple projects was a natural outgrowth of her evolution as a leader.

She found that she was able to step back and identify where leadership roles could be shared, distributed, and literally given away to others.

To some extent Stephanie was already doing this, by empowering her colleagues to own their initiatives and be accountable for their contributions and the contributions of their teams. Her breakthrough in distributing leadership came out of her reflecting on how to expand diversity.

It is typical for leaders to be drawn to people like themselves, and to hire and promote them. Yet Stephanie was a firm believer that diversity of gender, culture, race, and demographics would improve the odds of organizational success. Her belief in the power of diversity was key, but not always easy for her to put into action. It required that she hire, train, and elevate team members who were quite different from her in both obvious and subtle ways.

Demographics came to the fore as her opportunity to expand diversity. Millennials and Gen Z workers held values and even work habits (especially in the current hybridization of workplaces post-COVID) that were different than what baby boomer Stephanie was comfortable with. That said, she understood that distributing work required a willingness to diversify the work style—and to look for the creativity and energy of younger generations to bring new ideas to the table and spark innovation.

Questions Stephanie considered:

- How would she nurture leadership capacities in others?
- What aspects of leadership could she hand over to someone else, based on their capability but also as a growth opportunity?
- How would she empower others to lead?

- How would she track accountabilities when she distributed leadership roles?

||

In closing, we only need to jump a year or two closer to the present
to see that Stephanie and her expanding team continue to grow and
adapt to changes in the marketplace. The only constant is change.

It's not a linear path upward. In the face of failures, setbacks, and
adversity, Stephanie can relax, knowing they are growth opportunities. She can always revisit and expand her own leadership capacities
to meet these challenges. More important, her focus on elevating and
empowering a growing team of leaders by her side means she now has
a leader-full ecosystem on which she can rely.

In taking the advanced steps into shared, servant, and transformational leadership, in her own ways and in alignment with the needs
of her organization, Stephanie has fully embraced the capacities she
needs to lead the system.

The future is unknown, yet bright.

MOVING INTO ACTION

Play a symphony, not a solo.

Our tour of the science of leadership has come to an end. You may be feeling good about the capacities that you are using well—good work. Perhaps you're celebrating because you're already doing well with respect to all nine capacities—great work. We close our book with two options for action, some recapping of the capacities and leadership stories, and our last words.

TWO OPTIONS

A first option is immediately available—dial up any capacity in any moment. This is agility in action. Mindfully adjust your approach in the moment by popping yourself out of your automatic mode to pause, read the moment, and ask yourself: Which capacity is called for, or what do others or the system need from me, or where do I need to lean in more right now? See clearly? Care? Flex? Help? Strengthen? Resonate? Share? Serve? Transform?

You could practice pausing several times a day or week and making a mindful, intentional choice to dial up one or more capacities and perhaps dial down others. These small adjustments can increase your impact in any situation.

A good example is to get agile quickly in a heated conversation: reflecting on what matters to others, quieting your ego noise with some deep breaths, remembering to encourage others' autonomy, or challenging your and others' thinking with compassion.

A second option is the one-at-a-time approach, where you pick one capacity to improve first. Recall that we laid out this option in the introduction. You can think of this path as your own action research—improving one capacity at a time, over time, based on your readiness to improve.

You may want to revisit table I.1 in the introduction and repeat your self-ratings one more time. Going back to figure I.1 in the introduction can help you update your motivation and confidence scores on any of the nine capacities. Remember that having scores of 6/10 on both motivation and confidence is vital so that you have enough resources to be successful.

If your motivational energy and confidence are robust across the board, you might decide to follow the natural order of complexity, where each capacity builds on the previous ones. Begin with conscious leadership, as Stephanie modeled in chapter 10.

Here is how you can move into action:

1. Make a decision about which capacity (or level) to improve first.

2. Recruit a friend, colleague, family member, or a book group. When you are improving yourself, it's easier to stay on track with social support, with your own cheering squad.

3. If the pressure or stakes are high, you may want to find a skilled coach to help you both see yourself more clearly and go further and faster.

4. Imagine yourself at your ideal level of impact—a 10/10

score on your chosen capacity. Describe the ideal impact—how you're influencing others, how you're advancing the interests of your organization. Consider what you are thinking, feeling, and doing at your 10/10 ideal. Set your mental compass on this ideal vision for your impact and your ideal self.

5. Score your current state out of 10.

6. Identify something you can experiment with next week that could increase your current score by one point.

7. After your weekly experiment, unpack what you learned and whether it worked or not, and decide on your next experiment.

8. Repeat steps 1–7 over and over until you discover your formula—the right mindset and practices that produce the impact you want, getting closer and closer to your 10/10 vision.

As you focus on improving a particular capacity, you may start to see it everywhere in others and in systems—clarity, purpose, agility, relationships, well-being, compassion, elevating, service, and innovation. Over time the new habits will become second nature—your nature.

RECAP OF THE NINE CAPACITIES

Recapping the nine capacities can deepen your reflection on where best to start. The lists in the box that follows will help you take stock with sets of reflection questions. More simply put, the self-oriented level includes clarity, purpose, and agility. The other-oriented level includes helping, strengthening, and resonating with others. The system-oriented level includes elevating, serving, and transforming others and the system.

REFLECT ON NINE CAPACITIES—SELF, OTHERS, SYSTEM

SELF-ORIENTED CAPACITIES

- Conscious: What enables you to be calm, stable, and objective?
- Authentic: What matters most to you and those you serve?
- Agile: How will you be flexible when things change, and inclusive of diverse, opposing interests?

OTHER-ORIENTED CAPACITIES

- Relational: How will you help others do their best work?
- Positive: How will you help others leverage and expand their strengths?
- Compassionate: How will you generate resonance with others on a vision, purpose, and action?

SYSTEM-ORIENTED CAPACITIES (ORGANIZATION/TEAM ORIENTATION)

- Shared: How will you elevate leadership capacities across your team/organization?
- Servant: How will you best serve followers, customers, and other stakeholders?
- Transformational: How will you cocreate and manifest a vision that positively impacts all stakeholders?

Now that the capacities are familiar, look at them all together. Over the next six to twelve months, which capacity or leadership level, or combination of two or three capacities in more than one level, might be most impactful? You could also begin to think about strengths and weaknesses in these capacities in others you lead, and across your system. You all could engage together with the book as a team or organization, using the reflection questions in each chapter or the group discussion guide at the end of the book.

RECAP OF THE LEADERSHIP STORIES

Now for a quick recap of our leadership stories to help you reflect even further. Our first two chapters were on conscious and authentic capacities because these two ground you in clarity, values, and purpose. The ability to regulate your emotions, quiet your ego, and align with what matters most right now gives you a reset whenever you need it.

Recall that Sidney had a major wake-up call when he connected the dots between his childhood relationship with his harsh and critical father and his tendency to be short and dismissive with his colleagues. We all have triggers that disconnect us, momentarily, from being our best, thoughtful selves.

Jennifer got sidetracked from what was truly important to her by personal ambition. Ultimately, she acted on her values, positively impacting the people around her. When you ground yourself in what is virtuous and express it with sincerity, you become an authentic leader walking your why.

Walking our talk matters to followers—particularly the rising generation of leaders who have inherited what leadership scholars call our grand challenges,[1] including social and global instabilities and the rapid depletion of the earth's resources. This brings us to agility, balancing the optimism needed to forge ahead with clear-eyed objectivity about what is realistic.

Most leaders are dealing with some degree of ego noise. We all need to take note of any tendencies we may have to be strident, attached, or stubborn. These are signals to become open and accepting, flexing in the face of challenges and fears.

As we learned with Anita's story of action without empathy, it is all too easy to push for results at all costs. The price paid is dear: You may win in the short run and lose the game. Empathize, listen, coach, and take time to build a psychologically safe environment. Organizations run on high-quality relationships.

Anita shifted her orientation toward others; she became more relational, positive, and compassionate. As a relational leader, you focus on your role as coach and mentor—listening, understanding, and respecting others' contributions in ways that make them feel valued, safe, and supported. An organization in which leaders appreciate others' strengths is one that people want to be part of.

As we saw with Ahmed, Lisa, Patricia, and Leslie, the right mix of meaning, gratitude, appreciation, and compassion creates an environment where people do their best work—*and* it can all be overdone, leading to burnout. Your personal self-care regimen needs to bring you into balance. Start at home—practice self-care, self-compassion, and self-appreciation.

These first six capacities are oriented toward yourself and your relationships with others. Now on to the last three, which are more system oriented. Competence in these capacities is one of the things that distinguishes senior leaders from junior ones. The system complexity and demands are higher for leaders with a wide span of responsibility in large organizations, in comparison to leaders of small organizations.

Shared leadership and servant leadership ask you to step up in ways that are somewhat foreign to many leaders. Many leaders struggle, as did John and Lee, to find the optimum balance between leading from the front and supporting autonomy.

As Peter's and Bob's stories showed, you will regularly be tested by disruption and opposition. Enlisting others' participation and feedback is vital to rising above turmoil.

As Scott, Johannes, and Christopher learned, empowering the leadership of others, while maintaining a reliable presence and a steady focus on accountability, can relieve you from the overwhelm and sense of isolation, the "lonely at the top" experience. Does loneliness have to be a given? It does not, when we consider the impact of shared leadership. Moreover, you leave a positive legacy when you empower others. High-performing cultures can outlast your time at the helm.

LAST WORDS

Before we say goodbye, here are our last words on leadership research, our grand challenges, and our next edition.

SOME RESEARCH FINDINGS EXPIRE

There is a challenge with the science of leadership—and all research, for that matter—that we haven't mentioned yet: Research findings can expire. They can become quickly out of date. To quote cardiology researcher Christopher Labos's author bio, "He [Christopher] realizes that half of his research findings will be disproved in five years; he just doesn't know which half."[2]

In fact, your experience on today's front lines of organizational life may even break new ground and open up new research directions. Thus it is all the more important for you to consider yourself an action researcher using scientific methods: conducting an objective self-assessment (with others' input), forming a hypothesis about what might be impactful, testing the hypothesis (experimenting), then observing, learning, and adjusting your approach based on the results.

The good news is that we aren't expecting the fundamental nature of the nine capacities to change. Cognitive agility, visioning, compassion, relationships, and character in leadership aren't going anywhere. The fact that leadership, well-being, and coaching share a common scientific foundation helps with scientific longevity. We can, however, expect lots of new findings on the why, what, and how of applying many elements that contribute to leadership capacities and their impact on others' performance and well-being.

GRAND CHALLENGES

The second thing for us to talk about has to do with how leaders can address the grand challenges of our times, including AI, wars, and our depleted and polluted planet. This is the next frontier of leadership and the science of leadership.

Crossan, Crossan, Newstead, and Sturm, a global team of researchers focused on leadership character, advise that these grand challenges "require a strength of character that appears to exceed current capacity."[3]

It's hard to overstate the magnitude of what's needed to lead at the macro level. For example, philosophers of science are talking about super-sized integrations of the best of modernism (capitalism as the "I") and the best of postmodernism (liberalism as the "We") to produce metamodernism, a healthy balance of societal "I" and "We."[4]

This sounds like we are headed, eventually, toward a quiet ego for all of humanity, a collective state of balanced concern for the well-being of self and others. Whether we like it or not, whether we are reactive or proactive, the way forward for humanity is our collective integration of our collective ego noise.

While resolving these grand challenges is still well beyond the reach of even the best leaders, upgrading this book's nine capacities is a place to begin—by first transforming ourselves and the people and organizations we lead.

THE NEXT EDITION

From here forward we can meet up at the book's web home—scienceofleadership.com. There you can access the latest resources. You can share your leadership stories—your own action research—and ask questions, all of which will help with the next edition. You will be able to find news on emerging research and the timing of our next edition.

Our vision is of a collaborative effort among leaders, researchers, coaches, trainers, and everyone else who cares about expanding the positive impact of leaders by applying good science.

Let's do it together—see clearly, care, flex, help, strengthen, resonate, share, serve, and transform.

Discussion and Study Guide

OBJECTIVE

Explore how nine leadership capacities, supported by research, can help leaders and leadership teams improve the performance and well-being of their teams and organizations.

SESSION DURATION

1.0 hour per chapter/capacity and 1.0 hour wrap-up = 10 hours total group time

Note: This is a basic guide. You can also add advanced discussion questions—for example, on how each capacity supports and is supported by any other or even all of the other eight capacities.

CHAPTER 1—SESSION 1

Introduction: Warm-Up Discussion (10 minutes)
Goal: Set the stage, engage participants, and conduct initial assessment.

Begin with the following questions:

- Think of a leader who you consider great. What made them stand out?

- When you think of leaders who could improve their performance, what qualities come to mind for them to focus on?

- What makes science-based leadership capacities important for you and your organization?

Provide a brief overview of *The Science of Leadership*:

> The authors assembled research conducted by more than seven hundred researchers, who in turn analyzed more than fifteen thousand research studies and articles. They organized the body of leadership research that demonstrated improvements in individual, team, and organizational performance into nine capacities. This group program will help you review the capacities (leadership skill/behavior domains), the book's synopses of the science, and real-life stories of how leaders can work with a coach or mentor or self-coach to develop these capacities.

Ask participants to complete the self-assessment in the book's introduction—where they reflect on strengths and potential areas for capacity expansion.

Chapter 1: Capacity 1 and Discussion Questions (20 minutes)
Capacity 1: Conscious Leadership Defined

See clearly, including myself.

As a conscious leader, you are calm, stable, and objective. As a result, you see things clearly, including yourself. You are fully present to each moment. You have a high level of self-awareness. You reflect on your emotional states and are able to set them aside to be fully present in each moment. You see yourself and others objectively and without judgment—strengths, limitations, and growth opportunities. You recognize your leadership shadows, which are agitated, fear-based states in which you overuse strengths or avoid taking action, particularly under stress. By taking time to feel self-compassion and then process and transcend your shadow states, you transform them into new strength and calm.

Using the science section as a guide, briefly review the following concepts from chapter 1:

- Self-awareness and self-regulation
- Seeing clearly—becoming conscious of reality
- Mindsight
- Leadership shadow
- Integration
- The quiet ego

DISCUSSION QUESTIONS

- What does it mean to "see clearly, including yourself"?
- What is your personal definition of being present and self-aware?
- What is a leadership shadow? Why is this important to understand?

Practical Application Activity (20 minutes)
Activity: How to Become More Conscious

Read Sidney's story and reflect together on your own leadership challenges with being conscious.

- **Leadership challenge:** Identify a current example of how being more conscious would improve your impact.
- **Leadership opportunity:** Describe how you, as a leader, could address this challenge with a specific practice.

- **Action step:** Write down one action you will take this week to apply a principle of conscious leadership.

Reflection and Wrap-Up (10 minutes)

1. **Group sharing:**

   - Invite participants to share their action plans or key takeaways from the discussion.

2. **Closing question:**

   - What's one behavior you think would help any leader to become more conscious?

3. **Next step:**

   - Suggest that participants continue reflecting on their leadership style and revisit their action plans and review progress in a follow-up session.

Additional Tips for Facilitators

- Bring in additional real-world examples or case studies to illustrate key points.

- Encourage participants to share personal leadership experiences.

- Keep the discussion focused on practical, actionable insights.

CHAPTER 2—SESSION 2

Introduction: Warm-Up Discussion (10 minutes)
Goal: Set the stage and engage participants.

Begin with a question:

- Think of a leader who you consider to be authentic—what behavior(s) demonstrate that quality?

- What do you believe to be the key qualities exhibited by authentic leaders?

- What makes authenticity important and valuable in today's organizational context?

Provide additional context for the framework in *The Science of Leadership*:

> The authors developed a framework of nine capacities that summarize leadership impact in three essential domains: self, other, and system. This framing is important, as leaders begin their development "close in" with themselves, then move out to their followers, and then move further out to team dynamics and ultimately to the organization, community, and system.

Chapter 2: Capacity 2 and Discussion Questions (20 minutes)
Capacity 2: Authentic Leadership Defined

Care.

As an authentic leader, you model character with integrity, walking the talk in communication, action, and decisions. Self-awareness includes reflecting on your personal values—what you care about; what's important about your leadership role; and what positive contribution you want to make to new leaders, the workforce, the organization, other stakeholders, and beyond. You think about what excellence means, both personally and collectively. You help a team or organization align around a shared purpose that fulfills shared values. By being open and sincere, an authentic leader creates high-quality work relationships and inspires the workforce to fulfill the organization's purpose.

Using the science section as a guide, briefly review the following concepts from chapter 2:

Values and virtues

Character

Meaning and purpose

DISCUSSION QUESTIONS

- What does it mean to walk the "values" talk in communication, actions, and decisions?

- What are your most personal values?

- Why are shared values important for relationships and organizational purpose?

Practical Application Activity (20 minutes)
Activity: How to Become More Authentic

Read Jennifer's story and reflect together on your own leadership challenges with being authentic.

- **Leadership challenge:** Identify a current example of when being more authentic would improve your impact.

- **Leadership opportunity:** Describe how you, as a leader, could address this challenge with a specific practice that incorporates your values.

- **Action step:** Write down one action you will take this week to apply the principle of authentic leadership.

Reflection and Wrap-Up (10 minutes)

1. **Group sharing:**

   - Invite participants to share their action plans or key takeaways from the discussion.

2. **Closing question:**

   - What's one behavior you think would help any leader to become more authentic?

3. **Next step:**

   - Suggest that participants continue reflecting on their leadership style and revisit their action plans and review progress in a follow-up session.

CHAPTER 3—SESSION 3

Introduction: Warm-Up Discussion (10 minutes)
Goal: Set the stage and engage participants.

Begin with a question:

- Think of a leader who you consider to be agile—what behavior(s) demonstrate that quality?

- What do you believe to be the key qualities exhibited by agile leaders?

- What makes agility important and valuable in today's organizational context?

Provide additional context for the framework in *The Science of Leadership*:

Conscious, authentic, and agile leadership capacities are particularly focused on the self and internal aspects of being a leader. Leaders work close in with themselves to develop self-awareness and objectivity, attune to their core values and virtues as leaders, and cultivate an agile mindset able to lead positive change in the face of inevitable polarities and disruptions.

Chapter 3: Capacity 3 and Discussion Questions (20 minutes)
Capacity 3: Agile Leadership Defined

Flex.

As an agile leader, you move flexibly and fluidly across many tasks, perspectives, emotional states, polarities, and conflicts. You zoom in and out, zipping up and down from detail to big picture, from adversity to opportunity, from knowing to not knowing, from deep focus to mind-wandering, from rest to driving forward, from the stable status quo to disruptive change, and on and on.

Using the science section as a guide, briefly review the following concepts from chapter 3:

Agile mind

Psychological flexibility

Resilience and well-being

Creativity and innovation as agile processes

Polarities

Agile leadership models

DISCUSSION QUESTIONS

- What does it mean to move flexibly and fluidly in leadership contexts?

- What are the most challenging polarities for you as a leader?

- How would you begin to think about balancing stability and disruptive change?

Practical Application Activity (20 minutes)
Activity: How to Become More Agile

Read Peter's story and reflect together on your own leadership challenges with being agile.

- **Leadership challenge:** Identify a current example of when being more agile would improve your impact.

- **Leadership opportunity:** Describe how you, as a leader, could address this challenge with a specific practice that incorporates a new level of flexibility.

- **Action step:** Write down one action you will take this week to apply the principle of agile leadership.

Reflection and Wrap-Up (10 minutes)

1. **Group sharing:**

   - Invite participants to share their action plans or key takeaways from the discussion.

2. **Closing question:**

   - What's one behavior you think would help any leader to become more agile?

3. **Next step:**

- Suggest that participants continue reflecting on their leadership style and revisit their action plans and review progress in a follow-up session.

CHAPTER 4—SESSION 4

Introduction: Warm-Up Discussion (10 minutes)
Goal: Set the stage and engage participants.

Begin with a question:

- Think of a leader who you consider to be relational—what behavior(s) demonstrate that quality?

- What do you believe to be the key qualities exhibited by relational leaders?

- What makes helping relationships important in today's organizational context?

Provide additional context for the framework in *The Science of Leadership*:

> The next three chapters will move the leadership capacities outward into follower and team support dynamics. Relational leadership shifts a leader into an outward focus on helping others, ideally with consciousness, authenticity, and agility.

Chapter 4: Capacity 4 and Discussion Questions (20 minutes)
Capacity 4: Relational Leadership Defined

Help.

As a relational leader, you focus on cultivating strong, high-quality relationships. With high self-awareness and sincere respect, you build rapport and trust by empathizing with others' experiences through high-quality listening. You seek to understand others' thoughts and emotions, and what is meaningful and important. You accept and forgive others' limitations and mistakes. Then you find out the best way to help others, without self-interest in impressing, dominating, or controlling relationships.

Using the science section as a guide, briefly review the following concepts from chapter 4:

Relationship management

Empathy

Listening

Trust

Forgiveness

Psychological safety

Helping

DISCUSSION QUESTIONS

- What does it mean to build rapport and trust in leadership contexts?

- What are the most challenging helping behaviors for you as a leader?

- How would you begin to think about the best way to create psychological safety in your team?

Practical Application Activity (20 minutes)
Activity: How to Become More Relational

Read Anita's story and reflect together on your own leadership challenges with being relational.

- **Leadership challenge:** Identify a current example of when being more relational would improve your impact.

- **Leadership opportunity:** Describe how you, as a leader, could address this challenge with a specific practice that incorporates a new level of relationship focus.

- **Action step:** Write down one action you will take this week to apply the principle of relational leadership.

Reflection and Wrap-Up (10 minutes)

1. **Group sharing:**

   - Invite participants to share their action plans or key takeaways from the discussion.

2. **Closing question:**

   - What's one behavior you think would help any leader to become more relational?

3. **Next step:**

   - Suggest that participants continue reflecting on their leadership style and revisit their action plans and review progress in a follow-up session.

CHAPTER 5—SESSION 5

Introduction: Warm-Up Discussion (10 minutes)
Goal: Set the stage and engage participants.

Begin with a question:

- Think of a leader who you consider to be positive—what behavior(s) demonstrate that quality?

- What do you believe to be the key qualities exhibited by positive leaders?

- What makes a positive outlook important and valuable in today's organizational context?

Provide additional context for the framework in *The Science of Leadership*:

> Chapters 4–6 move the leadership capacities outward into follower and team support dynamics. Positive leaders maintain a balance between being realistic and optimistic, remembering that focusing on the positive is important for their own resilience and well-being as well as for the motivation, health, and performance of those who follow them.

Chapter 5: Capacity 5 and Discussion Questions (20 minutes)
Capacity 5: Positive Leadership Defined

Strengthen.

As a positive leader, you leverage the key drivers of human well-being and performance at work that have been identified by researchers. You help followers cultivate sources of psychological capital and well-being as foundational resources that motivate and energize work engagement, productivity, perseverance, resilience, and growth. Five key sources of psychological capital are autonomy (feeling a sense of agency), confidence (feeling competent), positive emotions (feeling good), optimism (feeling optimistic), and meaning or fulfillment of values (feeling fulfilled by doing good).

Using the science section as a guide, briefly review the following concepts from chapter 5:

Psychological well-being

Psychological capital

Autonomy and agency

Competence

Feeling good (positive states)

Optimism

Fulfillment (doing good)

DISCUSSION QUESTIONS

- What does it mean to focus on the positive in leadership contexts?

- What are the most challenging aspects of staying positive as a leader?

- How would you begin to think about creating positivity in the workplace?

Practical Application Activity (20 minutes)
Activity: How to Become More Positive

Read Ahmed's story and reflect together on your own leadership challenges with being positive.

- **Leadership challenge:** Identify a current example of when being more positive would improve your impact.

- **Leadership opportunity:** Describe how you, as a leader, could address this challenge with a specific practice that incorporates a new level of positivity.

- **Action step:** Write down one action you will take this week to apply the principle of positive leadership.

Reflection and Wrap-Up (10 minutes)

1. **Group sharing:**

- Invite participants to share their action plans or key takeaways from the discussion.

2. **Closing question:**

- What's one behavior you think would help any leader to become more positive?

3. **Next step:**

- Suggest that participants continue reflecting on their leadership style and revisit their action plans and review progress in a follow-up session.

CHAPTER 6—SESSION 6

Introduction: Warm-Up Discussion (10 minutes)
Goal: Set the stage and engage participants.

Begin with a question:

- Think of a leader who you consider to be compassionate—what behavior(s) demonstrate that quality?

- What do you believe to be the key qualities exhibited by compassionate leaders?

- What makes compassion an important and valuable capacity in today's organizational context?

Provide additional context for the framework in *The Science of Leadership*:

> The relational, positive, and compassionate leadership chapters move the capacities outward toward a focus on the broader team and group. Together these qualities (including conscious and authentic) bring a strong sense of resonance

and caring that elevates everyone involved, including the leader, to a higher level of performance and well-being.

Chapter 6: Capacity 6 and Discussion Questions (20 minutes)
Capacity 6: Compassionate Leadership Defined

Resonate.

As a compassionate leader, you integrate conscious, authentic, agile, relational, and positive leadership capacities into compassion. You understand the everyday stresses and strains of organizational life. You hold space for grief and posttraumatic growth during terrible experiences such as natural disasters, terminal diseases, and the loss of life. You combine the warmth of concern with accountability—being tough on performance.

Using the science section as a guide, briefly review the following concepts from chapter 6:

Compassion beyond empathy

Expanding compassion in leadership

Resonating with the whole

DISCUSSION QUESTIONS

- What does it mean to move beyond empathy to compassion in leadership contexts?

- What are the most challenging aspects of expressing compassion as a leader?

- Why is compassion viewed by the authors as a synthesis of the first five capacities?

Practical Application Activity (20 minutes)
Activity: How to Become More Compassionate

Read Patricia's story and reflect together on your own leadership challenges with being compassionate.

- **Leadership challenge:** Identify a current example of when being more compassionate would improve your impact.

- **Leadership opportunity:** Describe how you, as a leader, could address this challenge with a specific practice that incorporates a new level of compassion.

- **Action step:** Write down one action you will take this week to apply the principle of compassionate leadership.

Reflection and Wrap-Up (10 minutes)

1. **Group sharing:**

   - Invite participants to share their action plans or key takeaways from the discussion.

2. **Closing question:**

   - What's one behavior you think would help any leader to become more compassionate?

3. **Next step:**

   - Suggest that participants continue reflecting on their leadership style and revisit their action plans and review progress in a follow-up session.

CHAPTER 7—SESSION 7

Introduction: Warm-Up Discussion (10 minutes)
Goal: Set the stage and engage participants.

Begin with a question:

- Think of a leader who you consider to be good at sharing leadership—what behavior(s) demonstrate that quality?

- What do you believe to be the key qualities exhibited by sharing leaders?

- What makes shared or distributed leadership an important capacity in today's organizational context?

Provide additional context for the framework in *The Science of Leadership*:

> The ability to share and distribute leadership is an important capacity that broadens impact beyond supporting close-in followers. Distributing leadership is inclusive, welcoming diverse perspectives and inviting others to step up and lead with accountability.

Chapter 7: Capacity 7 and Discussion Questions (20 minutes)
Capacity 7: Shared Leadership Defined

Share.

Shared leadership, also known as collective or distributed leadership, is the capacity to shift from "I" to "We," sharing and distributing leadership capacities within teams and throughout an organization and empowering everyone to lead in their own contexts. You use an open and inclusive approach to team or organizational visioning, defining values and purpose, designing strategy, setting goals, and making decisions.

You help develop the workforce capacity to contribute meaningfully to these direction-setting activities.

Using the science section as a guide, briefly review the following concepts from chapter 7:

The why, what, and how of leadership

Strategic leadership

The "I" approach to strategic direction

"We" in strategy implementation

DISCUSSION QUESTIONS

- What does it mean to share in leadership contexts?

- What are the most challenging aspects of distributing leadership as a leader?

- What makes directive ("I") versus shared ("We") strategy making a challenge for leaders?

Practical Application Activity (20 minutes)
Activity: How to Become a Sharing Leader

Read Scott's and Johannes's stories and reflect together on your own leadership challenges with sharing leadership.

- **Leadership challenge:** Identify a current example of when sharing a leadership responsibility with another or others would improve your impact.

- **Leadership opportunity:** Describe how you, as a leader, could address this challenge with a specific practice that incorporates a new level of sharing in your approach to developing strategy, goals, and implementation.

Action step: Write down one action you will take this week to apply the principle of shared leadership.

Reflection and Wrap-Up (10 minutes)

1. **Group sharing:**

   - Invite participants to share their action plans or key takeaways from the discussion.

2. **Closing question:**

   - What's one behavior you think would help you become more adept at sharing or distributing your leadership?

3. **Next step:**

   - Suggest that participants continue reflecting on their leadership style and revisit their action plans and review progress in a follow-up session.

CHAPTER 8—SESSION 8

Introduction: Warm-Up Discussion (10 minutes)
Goal: Set the stage and engage participants.

Begin with the following questions:

- Think of a leader who you consider to be a servant leader—what behavior(s) demonstrate that quality?

- What do you believe to be the key qualities exhibited by servant leaders?

- What makes the capacity to serve important and valuable in today's organizational context?

Provide additional context for the framework in *The Science of Leadership*:

> The final three chapters explore the more advanced capacities of leaders. These capacities expand a leader's impact into the wider context of an entire organizational culture and potentially beyond—with attributes that can impact a community of stakeholders or an ecosystem. Servant leadership is an important step into this broader domain as the emphasis shifts from leading at the front to leading from behind.

Chapter 8: Capacity 8 and Discussion Questions (20 minutes)
Capacity 8: Servant Leadership Defined

Serve.

As a servant leader, you put service into leadership—serving followers' well-being and development, and all of you together serve the collective good. There is an evolutionary basis for other-focused service, including the parenting role. Of course, service comes more naturally to some than to others. The pursuit of service develops with your psychological maturity, as your ego gets quieter and more stable and less dependent on the self-oriented rewards of leadership. You are a humble steward of your organization. You foster the autonomy, agency, development, and service orientation of followers, which in turn increases followers' motivation and engagement in meaningful work.

Using the science section as a guide, briefly review the following concepts from chapter 8:

Humility

Being a steward

Meaning-based motivation

Intrinsic motivation

DISCUSSION QUESTIONS

- Why is humility key for servant leadership to be successful?

- What are the most challenging aspects of serving others as a leader?

- How would acting as a servant leader impact the motivation of others in cultural or systemic dynamics?

Practical Application Activity (20 minutes)
Activity: How to Become More of a Servant Leader

Read Johannes's and Christopher's stories and reflect together on your own leadership challenges with leading from behind.

- **Leadership challenge:** Identify a current example of when being more of a servant would improve your impact.

- **Leadership opportunity:** Describe how you, as a leader, could address this challenge with a specific practice that incorporates a new level of service or stewardship.

- **Action step:** Write down one action you will take this week to apply the principle of servant leadership.

Reflection and Wrap-Up (10 minutes)

1. **Group sharing:**

   - Invite participants to share their action plans or key takeaways from the discussion.

2. **Closing question:**

   - What's one behavior you think would help a leader to become more servant oriented?

3. **Next step:**

- Suggest that participants continue reflecting on their leadership style and revisit their action plans and review progress in a follow-up session.

CHAPTER 9—SESSION 9

Introduction: Warm-Up Discussion (10 minutes)
Goal: Set the stage and engage participants.

Begin with a question:

- Think of a leader who you consider to be transformational—what behavior(s) demonstrate that quality?

- What do you believe to be the key qualities exhibited by transformational leaders?

- What makes the vision, courage, and innovation of transformational leadership particularly important in today's organizational context?

Provide additional context for the framework in *The Science of Leadership*:

> The capacity to be transformational is the most studied leadership capacity and a capstone level of leading that incorporates all the previous eight capacities. Transformational leaders build on sharing and servant qualities (and all six of the other capacities as well) to cocreate vision and strategic capabilities in team or an organization that aims to have innovative and transformational impact on customers, shareholders, stakeholders, and the entire ecosystem in which the organization is embedded.

Chapter 9: Capacity 9 and Discussion Questions (20 minutes)
Capacity 9: Transformational Leadership Defined

Transform.

As a transformational leader, you are an inspirational visionary and an influential role model. You enable creativity and facilitate innovation by fostering the motivation and confidence of followers on a path toward an organizational vision. You engage your followers in intellectual stimulation to challenge, expand, and diversify their perspectives. You model courage, in particular through intellectual self-stimulation and self-transformation, to increase your wisdom and impact.

Using the science section as a guide, briefly review the following concepts from chapter 9:

Influential role model

Inspirational visionary

Fostering creativity and innovation

Self-efficacy

Courage

DISCUSSION QUESTIONS

- Why is vision key for transformational leadership to be successful? How is vision different from strategy?

- What are the most challenging aspects of transformational leadership?

- Why are inspiration and courage so important for transformational leadership?

Practical Application Activity (20 minutes)
Activity: How to Become More Transformational

Read Joseph's story and reflect together on your own leadership challenges with becoming transformational.

- **Leadership challenge:** Identify a current example of when being more transformational would improve your impact.

- **Leadership opportunity:** Describe how you, as a leader, could address this challenge with a specific practice that incorporates a new level of transformational attributes.

- **Action step:** Write down one action you will take this week to apply the principle of transformational leadership.

Reflection and Wrap-Up (10 minutes)

1. **Group sharing:**

   - Invite participants to share their action plans or key takeaways from the discussion.

2. **Closing question:**

   - What's one behavior you think would help any leader to become more transformational?

3. **Next step:**

   - Suggest that participants continue reflecting on their leadership style and revisit their action plans and review progress in a follow-up session.

CONCLUDING SESSION:
CHAPTER 10 AND CONCLUDING ACTIVITY

Introduction: Warm-Up Discussion (10 minutes)
Goal: Set the stage and engage participants.

Begin with the following questions:

- What has been the most interesting and provocative aspect of the nine capacities for you?

- Have you experienced a leader who exemplifies all nine capacities in action?

- What did they do that encompassed this totality?

- How might the science of leadership evolve in the future?

- What capacities for leaders will become important as the science evolves?

Chapter 10: Case Study, Conclusion, and Discussion (20 Minutes)

Review Stephanie's story and her journey through all nine capacities in a multicultural, international leadership role.

DISCUSSION QUESTIONS

- Why did Stephanie's experience and evolution as a leader not follow the prescribed order in the book?

- Which of the nine capacities were the most difficult and challenging for Stephanie? Why?

- Which order might you have followed through all nine capacities in a similar leadership journey?

Practical Application Activity (20 minutes)

Review the conclusion on how to move into action with the nine capacities and expand your leadership impact. Discuss the two options provided in the conclusion:

- **Mindfully dial up a capacity.** Choose to bring the capacities into your daily practice by actively reflecting on the following questions:

  - Which capacity is called for at this moment?

  - What do others or the system need from me?

  - Where do I need to lean in more right now? See clearly? Care? Flex? Help? Strengthen? Resonate? Share? Serve? Transform?

- **Improve one capacity at a time.** Think of this path as your own action research—improving one at a time, over time, based on your readiness to improve. Where will you begin? What excites and motivates you to move forward?

Final Action Plan (20 minutes)

In small groups, reflect on Stephanie's story (chapter 10) and your own leadership journey and build a plan for your future leadership impact:

- Return to the readiness assessment (figure I.1) in the introduction and review your personal choices for improvement (from table I.1) and your level of motivation and confidence.

- As a final reflection, go back to the 0–10 scale and consider those capacities for which your level of motivation to grow and improve is 6/10 or higher. Finally, imagine yourself at your ideal impact—a 10/10 score on your chosen capacity.

- In group sharing, describe the impact you notice: how are you influencing others? How are you advancing the interests of your organization? Consider what you are thinking, feeling, and doing at your 10/10 ideal. Set your mental compass on this ideal vision for your impact and yourself.

- Build an action plan based on all the work you have completed that will keep you engaged with the capacities for days, weeks, and months into the future.

Reflection and Wrap-Up (10 minutes)

1. **Group sharing:**

   - Invite participants to share their action plans or key takeaways from the discussion.

2. **Closing question:**

   - What's the most valuable lesson for you from this group discussion/learning experience? Why?

3. **Next step:**

   - Suggest that participants continue reflecting on their leadership style and revisiting their action plans to monitor progress in a community network of colleagues via ongoing emails, texts, or discussions.

Notes

INTRODUCTION

1. S. Alexander Haslam, Mats Alvesson, and Stephen D. Reicher, "Zombie Leadership: Dead Ideas That Still Walk among Us," *Leadership Quarterly* 35, no. 3 (June 2024): 101770, https://doi.org/10.1016/j.leaqua.2023.101770.

2. Edward L. Deci, Anja H. Olafsen, and Richard M. Ryan, "Self-Determination Theory in Work Organizations: The State of a Science," *Annual Review of Organizational Psychology and Organizational Behavior* 4, no. 1 (2017): 19–43, https://doi.org/ 10.1146/annurev-orgpsych-032516-113108.

3. Mary Uhl-Bien and Melissa Carsten, "Reversing the Lens in Leadership: Positioning Followership in the Leadership Construct," in *Leadership Now: Reflections on the Legacy of Boas Shamir*, ed. Israel Katz, Galit Eilam-Shamir, Ronit Kark, and Yair Berson, 195–222 (Bingley, UK: Emerald Publishing, 2018).

4. Joe Bolger, "Capacity Development: Why, What and How," *Capacity Development Occasional Series* 1, no. 1 (2000): 1–8.

5. Yingting Wu and Oliver Crocco, "Critical Reflection in Leadership Development," *Industrial and Commercial Training* 51, no. 7/8 (2019): 409–20.

6. Margaret Moore, "Ground Zero in Lifestyle Medicine: Changing Mindsets to Change Behavior," *American Journal of Lifestyle Medicine* 17, no. 5 (2023): 632–38.

7. Heidi Grant Halvorson, *Succeed: How We Can Reach Our Goals* (London: Penguin, 2011).

8. Thomas Fischer, Donald C. Hambrick, Gwendolin B. Sajons, and Niels Van Quaquebeke, "Leadership Science beyond Questionnaires," *Leadership Quarterly* 34, no. 6 (2023): 101752, https://doi.org/10.1016/j.leaqua.2023.101752.

9. Mats Alvesson and Katja Einola, "Warning for Excessive Positivity: Authentic Leadership and Other Traps in Leadership Studies," *Leadership Quarterly* 30, no. 4 (2019): 383–95.

10. Annika F. Schowalter and Judith Volmer, "Are the Effects of Servant Leadership Only Spurious? The State of Research on the Causal Effects of Servant Leadership, Recommendations, and an Illustrative Experiment," *Leadership Quarterly* 34, no. 6 (December 2023): 101722, https://doi.org/10.1016/j.leaqua.2023.101722.

11. Marie T. Dasborough, Neal M. Ashkanasy, Ronald H. Humphrey, Peter D. Harms, Marcus Credé, and Dustin Wood, "Does Leadership Still Not Need

Emotional Intelligence? Continuing 'The Great EI Debate,'" *Leadership Quarterly* 33, no. 6 (2022): 101539, https://doi.org/10.1016/j.leaqua.2021.101539.

12. Aaron D. Hill, Scott G. Johnson, Lindsey M. Greco, Ernest H. O'Boyle, and Sheryl L. Walter, "Endogeneity: A Review and Agenda for the Methodology-Practice Divide Affecting Micro and Macro Research," *Journal of Management* 47, no. 1 (2021): 105–43.

13. Clem Adelman, "Kurt Lewin and the Origins of Action Research," *Educational Action Research* 1, no. 1 (1993): 7–24.

14. Hao Zhao and Chaoping Li, "A Computerized Approach to Understanding Leadership Research," *Leadership Quarterly* 30, no. 4 (2019): 396–416.

15. Jeremy D. Mackey, B. Parker Ellen III, Charn P. McAllister, and Katherine C. Alexander, "The Dark Side of Leadership: A Systematic Literature Review and Meta-Analysis of Destructive Leadership Research," *Journal of Business Research* 132 (August 2021): 705–18.

16. Peter G. Northouse, *Leadership: Theory and Practice* (Thousand Oaks, CA: Sage, 2025).

17. Jeffrey Hull, *Flex: The Art and Science of Leadership in a Changing World* (New York: TarcherPerigee, 2019).

18. Margaret Moore, Edward Phillips, and John Hanc, *Organize Your Emotions, Optimize Your Life* (New York: William Morrow, 2016).

19. Margaret Moore, Bob Tschannen-Moran, and Erika Jackson, *Coaching Psychology Manual* (Philadelphia: Wolters Kluwer, 2015).

CHAPTER 1

1. Carol S. Dweck, *Mindset: The New Psychology of Success* (Random House, 2006); Carol S. Dweck, "What Having a 'Growth Mindset' Actually Means," *Harvard Business Review* 13, no. 2 (2016): 2–5.

2. *APA Dictionary of Psychology*, s.v. "integration," updated April 19, 2018, https://dictionary.apa.org/integration.

3. John Mackey, Steve McIntosh, and Carter Phipps, *Conscious Leadership: Elevating Humanity through Business* (London: Penguin, 2020).

4. Jaroslava Kubátová and Ondřej Kročil, "A Conscious Leadership Competency Framework for Leadership Training," *Industrial and Commercial Training* 54, no. 2 (2022): 279–92.

5. Isaac Chotiner, "The Whole Foods C.E.O. John Mackey's 'Conscious Capitalism,'" *New Yorker*, February 22, 2021, https://www.newyorker.com/news/q-and-a/whole-foods-ceo-john-mackeys-conscious-capitalism.

6. Daniel Goleman, *Leadership: The Power of Emotional Intelligence* (Northampton, MA: More Than Sound LLC, 2021), 28–29, 32, 33, 34.

7. Gina Görgens-Ekermans and Chene Roux, "Revisiting the Emotional Intelligence and Transformational Leadership Debate: (How) Does Emotional Intelligence Matter to Effective Leadership?" *SA Journal of Human Resource Management* 19 (2021): 1–13.

8. Eva M. Bracht, Fong T. Keng-Highberger, Bruce J. Avolio, and Yiming Huang,

"Take a 'Selfie': Examining How Leaders Emerge from Leader Self-Awareness, Self-Leadership, and Self-Efficacy," *Frontiers in Psychology* 12 (March 24, 2021): 635085, https://doi.org/10.3389/fpsyg.2021.635085.

9. Lisa Feldman Barrett, *How Emotions Are Made: The Secret Life of the Brain* (New York: Mariner Books, 2017).

10. Margaret Moore and Shelley Carson, "Organize Your Mind for Coaching," *Coaching World*, November 13, 2014, https://viewer.joomag.com/coaching-world-issue-11-august-2014/0311374001407443858/p26?short.

11. Daniel J. Siegel, *Mindsight: The New Science of Personal Transformation* (New York: Bantam, 2010).

12. Joseph K. Carpenter, Kristina Conroy, Angelina F. Gomez, Laura C. Curren, and Stefan G. Hofmann, "The Relationship between Trait Mindfulness and Affective Symptoms: A Meta-Analysis of the Five Facet Mindfulness Questionnaire (FFMQ)," *Clinical Psychology Review* 74 (2019): 101785, https://doi.org/10.1016/j.cpr.2019.101785.

13. Manfred Kets de Vries and Katharina Balazs, "The Shadow Side of Leadership," in *The Handbook of Top Management Teams*, ed. Frank Bournois, Jérome Duval-Hamel, Sylvie Roussillon, and Joan-Louis Scaringella, 183–90 (London: Palgrave Macmillan UK, 2010); Erik de Haan, "The Leadership Shadow: How to Recognise and Avoid Derailment, Hubris and Overdrive," *Leadership* 12, no. 4 (2016): 504–12.

14. Daniel J. Siegel, "Interpersonal Connection, Compassion, and Well-Being: The Science and Art of Healing Relationships," in *Advances in Contemplative Psychotherapy*, ed. Joseph Loizzo, Fiona Brandon, Emily J. Wolf, and Miles Neale, 181–96 (New York: Routledge, 2023); Netta Weinstein, Edward L. Deci, and Richard M. Ryan, "Motivational Determinants of Integrating Positive and Negative Past Identities," *Journal of Personality and Social Psychology* 100, no. 3 (2011): 527–44.

15. Daniel J. Siegel, and the PDP Group, *Personality and Wholeness in Therapy: Integrating Nine Patterns of Developmental Pathways in Clinical Practice* (New York: Norton, 2024).

16. Jack J. Bauer, "From Insight to Growth: How the Quiet Ego Facilitates Decision Crystallization and the Transformative Self Turns It into Flourishing," in *The Routledge International Handbook of Changes in Human Perceptions and Behaviors*, ed. Kanako Taku and Todd K. Shackleford, 171–86 (New York: Routledge, 2024); Heidi A. Wayment and Jack J. Bauer, *Transcending Self-Interest: Psychological Explorations of the Quiet Ego* (Washington, DC: American Psychological Association, 2008).

17. Jonathan Ross Gilbert, Michael T. Krush, Kevin J. Trainor, and Heidi A. Wayment, "The (Quiet) Ego and Sales: Transcending Self-Interest and Its Relationship with Adaptive Selling," *Journal of Business Research* 150 (2022): 326–38.

18. David R. Vago and David A. Silbersweig, "Self-Awareness, Self-Regulation, and Self-Transcendence (S-ART): A Framework for Understanding the Neurobiological Mechanisms of Mindfulness," *Frontiers in Human Neuroscience* 6 (2012): 1–30.

CHAPTER 2

1. Martin E. P. Seligman, *Authentic Happiness: Using the New Positive Psychology to Realize Your Potential for Lasting Fulfillment* (New York: Simon & Schuster, 2004), 17.

2. Toby Newstead, Sarah Dawkins, Rob Macklin, and Angela Martin, "We Don't Need More Leaders—We Need More *Good* Leaders. Advancing a Virtues-Based Approach to Leader(Ship) Development," *Leadership Quarterly* 32, no. 5 (2021): 101312, https://doi.org/10.1016/j.leaqua.2019.101312.

3. Toby Newstead, Rob Macklin, Sarah Dawkins, and Angela Martin, "What Is Virtue? Advancing the Conceptualization of Virtue to Inform Positive Organizational Inquiry," *Academy of Management Perspectives* 32, no. 4 (2018): 443–57.

4. Mary Kay Copeland, "The Emerging Significance of Values Based Leadership: A Literature Review," *International Journal of Leadership Studies* 8, no. 2 (2014): 105–35.

5. Linda Klebe Treviño, Laura Pincus Hartman, and Michael Brown, "Moral Person and Moral Manager: How Executives Develop a Reputation for Ethical Leadership," *California Management Review* 42, no. 4 (2000): 128–42.

6. Joseph A. Crawford, Sarah Dawkins, Angela Martin, and Gemma Lewis, "Putting the Leader Back into Authentic Leadership: Reconceptualising and Rethinking Leaders," *Australian Journal of Management* 45, no. 1 (2020): 114–33.

7. Mary Crossan, Gerard Seijts, and Jeffrey Gandz, "Leader Character Framework," Ivey Business School, accessed December 2, 2024, https://www.ivey.uwo.ca/leadership/research-resources/leader-character-framework/.

8. George C. Banks, Kelly Davis McCauley, William L. Gardner, and Courtney E. Guler, "A Meta-Analytic Review of Authentic and Transformational Leadership: A Test for Redundancy," *Leadership Quarterly* 27, no. 4 (2016): 634–52.

9. Niklas K. Steffens, Nathan Wolyniec, Tyler G. Okimoto, Frank Mols, S. Alexander Haslam, and Adam A. Kay, "Knowing Me, Knowing Us: Personal and Collective Self-Awareness Enhances Authentic Leadership and Leader Endorsement," *Leadership Quarterly* 32, no. 6 (January 2021): 101498, http://dx.doi.org/10.31234/osf.io/z2r7f.

10. Shalom H. Schwartz, "An Overview of the Schwartz Theory of Basic Values," *Online Readings in Psychology and Culture* 2, no. 1 (2012): 11–20.

11. Christopher Peterson and Martin E. P. Seligman, *Character Strengths and Virtues: A Handbook and Classification*, vol. 1 (Oxford: Oxford University Press, 2004); David S. Bright, Bradley A. Winn, and Jason Kanov, "Reconsidering Virtue: Differences of Perspective in Virtue Ethics and the Positive Social Sciences," *Journal of Business Ethics* 119 (2014): 445–60.

12. "The 24 Character Strengths," VIA Institute on Character, accessed December 2, 2024, https://www.viacharacter.org/character-strengths.

13. Peterson and Seligman, *Character Strengths*.

14. "VIA Adult Survey Translations," VIA Institute on Character, accessed December 2, 2024, https://www.viacharacter.org/about/translations/via-adult-survey-translations; Ryan M. Niemiec and Danielle Casioppo, "Coaching and Character

Strengths—An Essential, Inextricable Interconnection: Core Practices and New Science," *Journal of Positive Psychology Coaching* 1 (2024): 1–24.

15. "Positive Organizational Scholarship," Center for Positive Organizations, University of Michigan, accessed December 2, 2024, https://positiveorgs.bus.umich.edu/an-introduction/.

16. Bright et al., "Reconsidering Virtue."

17. Bright et al.

18. Mary Crossan, Gerard Seijts, and Jeffrey Gandz, *Developing Leadership Character* (New York: Routledge, 2015); Crossan et al., "Leader Character Framework."

19. Mary Crossan and Bill Furlong, "Society Needs a Leadership Paradigm Shift," *LeadingBlog*, Leadership Now, December 4, 2023, https://www.leadershipnow.com/leadingblog/2023/12/society_needs_a_leadership_par.html.

20. Crossan and Furlong, "Society Needs a Leadership Paradigm Shift."

21. Rune Todnem By, "Leadership: In Pursuit of Purpose," *Journal of Change Management* 21, no. 1 (2021): 30–44.

22. Daan van Knippenberg, "Meaning-Based Leadership," *Organizational Psychology Review* 10, no. 1 (2020): 6–28.

23. Bill George and Zach Clayton, *True North, Emerging Leader Edition: Leading Authentically in Today's Workplace* (Hoboken, NJ: Wiley, 2022); Bill George and Rick Tetzeli, "Author Talks: Bill George Sets a Course for 'True North,'" McKinsey & Company, September 15, 2022, https://www.mckinsey.com/featured-insights/mckinsey-on-books/author-talks-bill-george-sets-a-course-for-true-north.

24. Carolyn Dewar, Scott Keller, and Vikram Malhotra, *CEO Excellence: The Six Mindsets That Distinguish the Best Leaders from the Rest* (New York: Simon & Schuster, 2022).

25. The VIA Character Strengths Survey, accessed February 4, 2025. https://www.viacharacter.org/account/register

26. "Get Started on Your Character Development Journey," accessed December 2, 2024. https://virtuositycharacter.ca.

CHAPTER 3

1. Henry Mintzberg, "The Strategy Concept II: Another Look at Why Organizations Need Strategies," *California Management Review* 30, no. 1 (Fall 1987): 26.

2. Martin Fowler and Jim Highsmith, "The Agile Manifesto." *Software Development* 9, no. 8 (2001): 28–35; Mike Beedle, Arie van Bennekum, Alistair Cockburn, Ward Cunningham, Martin Fowler, Jim Highsmith, Andrew Hunt, et al., "Manifesto for Agile Software Development," accessed December 2, 2024, https://agilemanifesto.org.

3. Viktoria Stray, Bakhtawar Memon, and Lucas Paruch, "A Systematic Literature Review on Agile Coaching and the Role of the Agile Coach," in *Product-Focused Software Process Improvement: 21st International Conference, PROFES 2020, Turin, Italy, November 25–27, 2020, Proceedings*, ed. Maurizio Morisio, Marco Torchiano, and Andreas Jedlitschka, 3–19 (Cham, Switzerland: Springer International, 2020).

4. Dina R. Dajani and Lucina Q. Uddin, "Demystifying Cognitive Flexibility: Implications for Clinical and Developmental Neuroscience," *Trends in Neurosciences* 38, no. 9 (2015): 571–78.

5. Margaret Moore and Paul Hammerness with John Hanc, *Train Your Brain: Get More Done in Less Time* (New York: Hanover Square Press, 2020).

6. Wilma Koutstaal, *The Agile Mind* (Oxford: Oxford University Press, 2012), 8–10.

7. Lance M. McCracken, "Psychological Flexibility, Chronic Pain, and Health," *Annual Review of Psychology* 75, no. 1 (2024): 601–24.

8. Susan David, *Emotional Agility: Get Unstuck, Embrace Change, and Thrive in Work and Life* (London: Penguin, 2016).

9. Büşra Müceldili, Berivan Tatar, and Oya Erdil, "Can Curious Employees Be More Agile? The Role of Cognitive Style and Creative Process Engagement in Agility Performance," *Global Business and Organizational Excellence* 39, no. 6 (2020): 39–52.

10. Mihaly Csikszentmihalyi, *Creativity: The Work and Lives of 91 Eminent People* (New York: HarperCollins, 1996); Gabrielle Donnelly, "Leading Change: The Theory and Practice of Integrative Polarity Work," *World Futures* 76, no. 8 (2020): 497–518.

11. Mary Uhl-Bien and Michael Arena, "Leadership for Organizational Adaptability: A Theoretical Synthesis and Integrative Framework," *Leadership Quarterly* 29, no. 1 (2018): 89–104.

12. Mengye Yu, Jie Wen, Simon M. Smith, and Peter Stokes, "Building-up Resilience and Being Effective Leaders in the Workplace: A Systematic Review and Synthesis Model," *Leadership & Organization Development Journal* 43, no. 7 (2022): 1098–117.

13. Lawrence G. Calhoun and Richard G. Tedeschi, eds., *Handbook of Posttraumatic Growth: Research and Practice* (Abingdon, UK: Routledge, 2014).

14. Moore and Hammerness, *Train Your Brain.*

15. Azuka Mordi and Mareike Schoop, "Making It Tangible—Creating a Definition of Agile Mindset." Twenty-Eighth European Conference on Information Systems (ECIS2020), Morocco.

16. Koutstaal, *Agile Mind*, 462.

17. Jeffrey Hull, *Flex: The Art and Science of Leadership in a Changing World* (New York: TarcherPerigee, 2019).

18. Wendy Smith and Marianne Lewis, *Both/And Thinking: Embracing Creative Tensions to Solve Your Toughest Problems* (Brighton, MA: Harvard Business Press, 2022), Chapter 1.

19. Joseph P. Folger, Marshall Scott Poole, and Randall K. Stutman, *Working through Conflict: Strategies for Relationships, Groups, and Organizations*, 10th ed. (New York: Routledge, 2025).

20. Marco Brand, Victor Tiberius, Peter M. Bican, and Alexander Brem, "Agility as an Innovation Driver: Towards an Agile Front End of Innovation Framework," *Review of Managerial Science* 15, no. 1 (2021): 157–87.

21. Mary Uhl-Bien, "Complexity Leadership and Followership: Changed Leadership in a Changed World," *Journal of Change Management* 21, no. 2 (2021): 144–62.

22. *Leading with Humanity: The Future of Leadership and Coaching*, Institute of Coaching, September 2021, accessed February 4, 2025, https://instituteof coaching.org/sites/default/files/downloads/IOC-Digital-Report-leading _humanity.pdf.

23. Uhl-Bien, "Complexity Leadership."

24. Ronald Abadian Heifetz, Alexander Grashow, and Martin Linsky, *The Practice of Adaptive Leadership: Tools and Tactics for Changing Your Organization and the World* (Brighton, MA: Harvard Business Press, 2009).

25. Alex Edmans, *May Contain Lies: How Stories, Statistics, and Studies Exploit Our Biases—And What We Can Do about It* (Berkeley: University of California Press, 2024).

26. Barry Johnson, *Polarity Management: Identifying and Managing Unsolvable Problems* (Amherst, MA: HRD Press, 1992).

CHAPTER 4

1. Richard E. Boyatzis, *The Science of Change: Discovering Sustained, Desired Change from Individuals to Organizations and Communities* (Oxford: Oxford University Press, 2024), chapter 1.

2. Amy C. Edmondson and Derrick P. Bransby, "Psychological Safety Comes of Age: Observed Themes in an Established Literature," *Annual Review of Organizational Psychology and Organizational Behavior* 10, no. 1 (2023): 55–78.

3. Cynthia D. McCauley and Charles J. Palus, "Developing the Theory and Practice of Leadership Development: A Relational View," *Leadership Quarterly* 32, no. 5 (2021): 101456, https://doi.org/10.1016/j.leaqua.2020.101456.

4. Ryan K. Gottfredson, Sarah L. Wright, and Emily D. Heaphy, "A Critique of the Leader–Member Exchange Construct: Back to Square One," *Leadership Quarterly* 31, no. 6 (2020): 101385, https://doi.org/10.1016/j.leaqua.2020.101385.

5. Daniel Goleman, *Leadership: The Power of Emotional Intelligence* (Northampton, MA: More Than Sound, 2011). 37–38.

6. Gina Görgens-Ekermans and Chene Roux, "Revisiting the Emotional Intelligence and Transformational Leadership Debate: (How) Does Emotional Intelligence Matter to Effective Leadership?" *SA Journal of Human Resource Management* 19 (2021): 1–13.

7. Helen Riess, "The Science of Empathy," *Journal of Patient Experience* 4, no. 2 (2017): 74–77.

8. Jean Decety and Philip L. Jackson, "The Functional Architecture of Human Empathy," *Behavioral and Cognitive Neuroscience Reviews* 3, no. 2 (2004): 71–100, https://doi.org/10.1177/1534582304267187.

9. Guowei Jian, "From Empathic Leader to Empathic Leadership Practice: An Extension to Relational Leadership Theory," *Human Relations* 75, no. 5 (2022): 931–55.

10. Jian, "Empathic Leader."

11. Margaret Moore, Bob Tschannen-Moran, and Erika Jackson, *Coaching Psychology Manual* (Philadelphia: Wolters Kluwer, 2015).

12. Jeffrey Yip and Colin M. Fisher, "Listening in Organizations: A Synthesis and Future Agenda," *Academy of Management Annals* 16, no. 2 (2022): 657–79.

13. Herminia Ibarra and Anne Scoular, "The Leader as Coach," *Harvard Business Review* 97, no. 6 (2019): 110–19.

14. Yip and Fisher, "Listening in Organizations."

15. Avraham N. Kluger and Guy Itzchakov, "The Power of Listening at Work," *Annual Review of Organizational Psychology and Organizational Behavior* 9 (2022): 121–46.

16. Kluger and Itzchakov, "Power of Listening," 138.

17. Paul J. Zak, "The Neuroscience of High-Trust Organizations," *Consulting Psychology Journal: Practice and Research* 70, no. 1 (2018): 45–58.

18. Zak, "Neuroscience."

19. Julianne Holt-Lunstad, "Fostering Social Connection in the Workplace," *American Journal of Health Promotion* 32, no. 5 (2018): 1307–12.

20. Alison Legood, Lisa van der Werff, Allan Lee, and Deanne Den Hartog, "A Meta-Analysis of the Role of Trust in the Leadership-Performance Relationship," *European Journal of Work and Organizational Psychology* 30, no. 1 (2021): 1–22.

21. Megan Tschannen-Moran, *Trust Matters: Leadership for Successful Schools* (Hoboken, NJ : Wiley, 2014).

22. Wenrui Cao, Reine C. van der Wal, and Toon W. Taris, "When Work Relationships Matter: Interpersonal Forgiveness and Work Outcomes," *International Journal of Stress Management* 28, no. 4 (2021): 266–82.

23. Cao et al., "When Work Relationships Matter."

24. Dirk van Dierendonck and Inge Nuijten, "The Servant Leadership Survey: Development and Validation of a Multidimensional Measure," *Journal of Business and Psychology* 26 (2011): 249–67.

25. Edmondson and Bransby, "Psychological Safety."

26. Mary Crossan and Bill Furlong, "Society Needs a Leadership Paradigm Shift," *LeadingBlog*, Leadership Now, December 4, 2023, https://www.leadershipnow.com/leadingblog/2023/12/society_needs_a_leadership_par.html.

27. Blaine Landis, Colin M. Fisher, and Jochen I. Menges, "How Employees React to Unsolicited and Solicited Advice in the Workplace: Implications for Using Advice, Learning, and Performance," *Journal of Applied Psychology* 107, no. 3 (2022): 408–24.

28. Colin M. Fisher, Julianna Pillemer, and Teresa M. Amabile, "Deep Help In Complex Project Work: Guiding and Path-Clearing across Difficult Terrain," *Academy of Management Journal* 61, no. 4 (2018): 1524–53.

29. M. Ghufran Ahmad and Christoph Loch, "What Do the Followers Want? The Core Functions of Leadership," *Leadership Quarterly* 31, no. 2 (2020): 101293, https://doi.org/10.1016/j.leaqua.2019.04.003.

30. Colin M. Fisher, Teresa M. Amabile, and Julianna Pillemer, "How to Help (Without Micromanaging)," *Harvard Business Review* 99, no. 1 (January-February 2021): 123–27.

CHAPTER 5

1. Ayatakshee Sarkar, Naval Garg, D. K. Srivastava, and B. K. Punia, "Can Gratitude Counter Workplace Toxicity? Exploring the Mediating Role of Psychological Capital (PsyCap)," *Business Perspectives and Research* 12, no. 2 (2024): 261–76.

2. Valesca Y. Tobias, Marianne van Woerkom, Maria Christina Meyers, and Robin Bauwens, "Coaching Based on Signature Strengths or Lesser Strengths? The Effects of Two Strengths Spotting Interventions on Managerial Coaching Behavior," *Journal of Happiness Studies* 25, no. 5 (May 2024), http://dx.doi.org/10.1007/s10902-024-00756-5.

3. Paul Fairlie, "Work Engagement and Employee Well-Being," in *Research Handbook on Work and Well-Being*, ed. Ronald J. Burke and Kathryn M. Page, 1307–12 (Cheltenham, UK: Edward Elgar Publishing, 2017).

4. *State of the Global Workplace*, Gallup.com, accessed December 2, 2024, https://www.gallup.com/workplace/349484/state-of-the-global-workplace.aspx.

5. Kim Cameron, *Positively Energizing Leadership: Virtuous Actions and Relationships That Create High Performance* (Oakland, CA: Berrett-Koehler, 2021).

6. Fred Luthans and Carolyn M. Youssef-Morgan, "Psychological Capital: An Evidence-Based Positive Approach," *Annual Review of Organizational Psychology and Organizational Behavior* 4, no. 1 (2017): 33–66.

7. Hao Zhao and Chaoping Li, "A Computerized Approach to Understanding Leadership Research," *Leadership Quarterly* 30, no. 4 (2019): 396–416.

8. "Self-Determination Theory Overview," Center for Self-Determination Theory, accessed December 2, 2024, https://selfdeterminationtheory.org/the-theory/.

9. Mehdi Hassanzade Daloee, Mina AkbariRad, Sahar Rajabzadeh Kkarizi, and Mehrdad Sarabi, "Physician Burnout: A Brief Review of Its Definition, Causes, and Consequences," *Reviews in Clinical Medicine* 7, no. 4 (December 2020): 150–56, https://doi.org/10.22038/rcm.2020.51483.1335.

10. Gavin R. Slemp, Margaret L. Kern, Kent J. Patrick, and Richard M. Ryan, "Leader Autonomy Support in the Workplace: A Meta-Analytic Review," *Motivation and Emotion* 42, no. 5 (2018): 706–24.

11. "Self-Determination Theory Overview."

12. Richard M. Ryan and Edward L. Deci, "Intrinsic and Extrinsic Motivations: Classic Definitions and New Directions," *Contemporary Educational Psychology* 25, no. 1 (2000): 54–67, https://doi.org/10.1006/ceps.1999.1020.

13. Barbara Fredrickson, "Updated Thinking on Positivity Ratios," *American Psychologist* 68, no. 9. (2013): 814–22; Rebecca Alexander, Oriana R. Aragón, Jamila Bookwala, Nicholas Cherbuin, Justine M. Gatt, Ian J. Kahrilas, Nichlas Kästner, et al., "The Neuroscience of Positive Emotions and Affect: Implications for Cultivating Happiness and Wellbeing," *Neuroscience & Biobehavioral Reviews* 121 (2021): 220–49.

14. Ed Diener, Stuti Thapa, and Louis Tay, "Positive Emotions at Work," *Annual Review of Organizational Psychology and Organizational Behavior* 7 (January 2020): 451–77, https://doi.org/10.1146/annurev-orgpsych-012119-044908.

15. Martin E. P. Seligman, *Learned Optimism: How to Change Your Mind and Your Life* (New York: Vintage Books, 2006), chapter 1.

16. Martin E. P. Seligman, *The Hope Circuit: A Psychologist's Journey from Helplessness to Optimism* (London: Hachette UK, 2018).

17. Jack J. Bauer, *The Transformative Self: Personal Growth, Narrative Identity, and the Good Life* (Oxford: Oxford University Press, 2021).

18. Barbara L. Fredrickson, "Updated Thinking on Positivity Ratios," *American Psychologist* 68, no. 9 (2013): 814–22.

19. John Mordechai Gottman and Robert Wayne Levenson, "What Predicts Change in Marital Interaction over Time? A Study of Alternative Models," *Family Process* 38, no. 2 (1999): 143–58.

20. Charlotte Henson, Didier Truchot, and Amy Canevello, "What Promotes Post Traumatic Growth? A Systematic Review," *European Journal of Trauma & Dissociation* 5, no. 4 (2021): 100195, https://doi.org/10.1016/j.ejtd.2020.100195.

21. Anishka Jain, Rameshbabu Tamarana, Uvashree Santosh, and Ritik Singh, "Relationship between Dominating Personalities and Toxic Positivity: Mediating Roles of Intrapersonal and Interpersonal Control," *Journal of the Indian Academy of Applied Psychology* 50, no. 1 (2024): 186–95.

CHAPTER 6

1. Nelson Mandela, "Message by Nelson Mandela at Healing & Reconciliation Service Dedicated to HIV/AIDS Sufferers & 'The Healing of our Land,'" Johannesburg, December 6, 2000, http://www.mandela.gov.za/mandela_speeches/2000/001206_healing.htm.

2. Richard E. Boyatzis and Kylie Rochford, "Relational Climate in the Workplace: Dimensions, Measurement, and Validation," *Frontiers in Psychology* 11 (2020): 1–15.

3. Brad Shuck, Meera Alagaraja, Jason Immekus, Denise Cumberland, and Maryanne Honeycutt-Elliott, "Does Compassion Matter in Leadership? A Two-Stage Sequential Equal Status Mixed Method Exploratory Study of Compassionate Leader Behavior and Connections to Performance in Human Resource Development," *Human Resource Development Quarterly* 30, no. 4 (2019): 537–64.

4. Rasmus Hougaard and Jacqueline Carter, *Compassionate Leadership: How to Do Hard Things in a Human Way* (Brighton, MA: Harvard Business Press, 2022).

5. Clara Strauss, Billie Lever Taylor, Jenny Gu, Willem Kuyken, Ruth Baer, Fergal Jones, and Kate Cavanagh, "What Is Compassion and How Can We Measure It? A Review of Definitions and Measures," *Clinical Psychology Review* 47 (2016): 15–27.

6. Jennifer S. Mascaro, Marianne P. Florian, Marcia J. Ash, Patricia K. Palmer, Tyralynn Frazier, Paul Condon, and Charles Raison, "Ways of Knowing Compassion: How Do We Come to Know, Understand, and Measure Compassion When We See It?" *Frontiers in Psychology* 11 (October 2020): 547241, https://doi.org/10.3389/fpsyg.2020.547241.

7. Strauss et al., "What Is Compassion?"
8. Paul Gilbert, "Creating a Compassionate World: Addressing the Conflicts between *Sharing and Caring* versus *Controlling and Holding* Evolved Strategies," *Frontiers in Psychology* 11 (February 2021): 582090 https://doi.org/10.3389/fpsyg.2020.582090.
9. Stephen Trzeciak, Anthony Mazzarelli, and Cory Booker, *Compassionomics: The Revolutionary Scientific Evidence That Caring Makes a Difference* (New York: Studer Group, 2019).
10. Gilbert, "Creating a Compassionate World."
11. Jacoba M. Lilius, Jason Kanov, Jane E. Dutton, Monica C. Worline, and Sally Maitlis, "Compassion Revealed," 2013, Ross Thought in Action, Executive White Paper Series, Center for Positive Organizational Scholarship, https://positiveorgs.bus.umich.edu/wp-content/uploads/Dutton-CompassionRevealed.pdf.
12. Gregory John Depow, Nicholas Hobson, Jason Beck, Michael Inzlicht, and Rasmus Hougaard, *The Compassion Advantage: Leaders Who Care Outperform Leaders Who Share Followers' Emotions* (2023), 7. https//doi.org/10.31234/osf.io/md2g8.
13. David B. Yaden, Salvatore Giorgi, Matthew Jordan, Anneke Buffone, Johannes C. Eichstaedt, H. Andrew Schwartz, Lyle Ungar, and Paul Bloom, "Characterizing Empathy and Compassion Using Computational Linguistic Analysis," *Emotion* 24, no. 1 (2024): 106–15.
14. Depow et al., *Compassion Advantage*, 42.
15. Shuck et al., "Does Compassion Matter?"
16. Shuck et al.
17. Shuck et al.
18. Miia Paakkanen, Frank Martela, Jari Hakanen, Lotta Uusitalo, and Anne Pessi, "Awakening Compassion in Managers—A New Emotional Skills Intervention to Improve Managerial Compassion," *Journal of Business and Psychology* 36, no. 6 (2021): 1095–108.
19. Richard E. Boyatzis and Annie McKee, *Resonant Leadership: Renewing Yourself and Connecting with Others through Mindfulness, Hope, and Compassion* (Brighton, MA: Harvard Business Press, 2005).
20. Richard E. Boyatzis and Kylie Rochford, "Relational Climate in the Workplace: Dimensions, Measurement, and Validation," *Frontiers in Psychology* 11 (2020): 1–15.
21. Richard E. Boyatzis, *The Science of Change: Discovering Sustained, Desired Change from Individuals to Organizations and Communities* (Oxford: Oxford University Press, 2024), chapter 7.
22. "Scenes from Hell: Herb Morrison - Hindenburg Disaster, 1937," *Eyewitness: American Originals from the National Archives*, accessed December 2, 2024, https://www.archives.gov/exhibits/eyewitness/html.php?section=5.
23. "'Hindenburg' Disaster Film," YouTube, accessed December 2, 2024, https://www.youtube.com/watch?v=dJ2-oCxA2rM.

24. Gilbert, "Creating a Compassionate World."
25. Alan D. Wolfelt, "Eleven Tenets of Companioning the Bereaved," Center for Loss & Life Transition, December 30, 2019, https://www.centerforloss .com/2019/12/eleven-tenets-of-companioning/.

CHAPTER 7

1. Frances Hesselbein, *Hesselbein on Leadership* (Hoboken, NJ: Wiley, 2002), 8.
2. Sabrina Schell and Nicole Bischof, "Change the Way of Working. Ways into Self-Organization with the Use of Holacracy: An Empirical Investigation," *European Management Review* 19, no. 1 (May 2022): 123–37.
3. Dusya Vera, Jean-Phillipe Bonardi, Michael A. Hitt, and Michael C. Withers, "Extending the Boundaries of Strategic Leadership Research," *Leadership Quarterly* 33, no. 3 (June 2022): 101617, https://doi.org/10.1016/j.leaqua.2022.1 01617.
4. *State of the Global Workplace*, Gallup.com, accessed December 2, 2024, https:// www.gallup.com/workplace/349484/state-of-the-global-workplace.aspx.
5. Mehdi Samimi, Andres Felipe Cortes, Marc H. Anderson, and Pol Herrmann, "What Is Strategic Leadership? Developing a Framework for Future Research," *Leadership Quarterly* 33, no. 3 (June 2022): 101353, https://doi.org/10.1016/j .leaqua.2019.101353.
6. Ayfer Veli Korkmaz, Marloes L. van Engen, Lena Knappert, and René Schalk, "About and beyond Leading Uniqueness and Belongingness: A Systematic Review of Inclusive Leadership Research," *Human Resource Management Review* 32, no. 4 (2022): 100894, https://doi.org/10.1016/j.hrmr.2022.100894.
7. "Cultivating Inclusion: The Road to Effective Open Strategy in Modern Organizations," Strategic Management Society, May 10, 2024, https://www.stra tegicmanagement.net/publications-resources/strategic-management-explorer /cultivating-inclusion-the-road-to-effective-open-strategy-in-modern-organi zations/.
8. Violetta Splitter, David Seidl, and Richard Whittington, "Getting Heard? How Employees Learn to Gain Senior Management Attention in Inclusive Strategy Processes," *Strategic Management Journal* 45, no. 10 (October 2024): 1877–1925, https://doi.org/10.1002/smj.3602.
9. Cynthia D. McCauley and Charles J. Palus, "Developing the Theory and Practice of Leadership Development: A Relational View," *Leadership Quarterly* 32, no. 5 (2021): 101456, https://doi.org/10.1016/j.leaqua.2020.101456.
10. Mary Uhl-Bien, "Complexity Leadership and Followership: Changed Leadership in a Changed World," *Journal of Change Management* 21, no. 2 (2021): 144–62.
11. McCauley and Palus, "Developing the Theory."
12. Nüfer Yasin Ateş, Murat Tarakci, Jeanine Pieternel Porck, Daan van Knippenberg, and Patrick J. F. Groenen, "The Dark Side of Visionary Leadership in Strategy Implementation: Strategic Alignment, Strategic Consensus, and Commitment," *Journal of Management* 46, no. 5 (2020): 637–65.

13. Chris Gagnon, Elizabeth John, and Rob Theunissen, "Organizational Health: A Fast Track to Performance Improvement," *McKinsey Quarterly* 4 (2017): 76–87.

14. McCauley and Palus, "Developing the Theory."

15. Gary Hamel and Michele Zanini, *Humanocracy: Creating Organizations as Amazing as the People inside Them* (Brighton, MA: Harvard Business Press, 2020).

16. Richard Rumelt, *The Crux: How Leaders Become Strategists* (London: Profile Books, 2022); Brian Leavy, "Richard Rumelt: A 'Challenge-Led' Approach to Creating Effective Strategy," *Strategy & Leadership* 50, no. 5 (2022): 3–8.

17. Yuval Atsmon, "Why Bad Strategy Is a 'Social Contagion.'" McKinsey Podcast (2022), https://www.mckinsey.com/capabilities/strategy-and-corporate-finance /our-insights/why-bad-strategy-is-a-social-contagion.

18. Qiong Wu, Kathryn Cormican, and Guoquan Chen, "A Meta-Analysis of Shared Leadership: Antecedents, Consequences, and Moderators," *Journal of Leadership & Organizational Studies* 27, no. 1 (2020): 49–64.

19. Charlene Tan, "An Ancient Chinese Interpretation of Distributed Leadership," *Asian Philosophy* 34, no. 3 (2024): 220–34, https://doi.org/10.1080/095 52367.2024.2309773.

CHAPTER 8

1. Robert K. Greenleaf, "What Is Servant Leadership?" Center for Servant Leadership, accessed December 2, 2024, https://www.greenleaf.org/what-is-servant -leadership/.

2. Joshua N. Hook, Todd W. Hall, Don E. Davis, Daryl R. Van Tongeren, and Mackenzie Conner, "The Enneagram: A Systematic Review of the Literature and Directions for Future Research," *Journal of Clinical Psychology* 77, no. 4 (2021): 865–83.

3. Daniel J. Siegel and the PDP Group, *Personality and Wholeness in Therapy: Integrating Nine Patterns of Developmental Pathways in Clinical Practice* (New York: Norton, 2024).

4. Greenleaf, "What Is Servant Leadership?"

5. Nathan Eva, Mulyadi Robin, Sen Sendjaya, Dirk van Dierendonck, and Robert C. Liden, "Servant Leadership: A Systematic Review and Call for Future Research," *Leadership Quarterly* 30, no. 1 (2019): 111–32.

6. Dirk van Dierendonck, "Servant Leadership: A Review and Synthesis," *Journal of Management* 37, no. 4 (2011): 1228–61.

7. Eva et al., "Servant Leadership."

8. Dirk van Dierendonck and Inge Nuijten, "The Servant Leadership Survey: Development and Validation of a Multidimensional Measure," *Journal of Business and Psychology* 26 (2011): 249–67.

9. Ravinder Jit, Chandra Shekhar Sharma, and Mona Kawatra, "Servant Leadership and Conflict Resolution: A Qualitative Study," *International Journal of Conflict Management* 27, no. 4 (2016): 591–612.

10. Jeffrey A. Chandler, Nicholas E. Johnson, Samantha L. Jordan, and Jeremy C.

Short, "A Meta-Analysis of Humble Leadership: Reviewing Individual, Team, and Organizational Outcomes of Leader Humility," *Leadership Quarterly* 34, no. 1 (2023): 101660, https://doi.org/10.1016/j.leaqua.2022.101660.

11. Rick Warren, *The Purpose Driven Life: What on Earth Am I Here For?* (Grand Rapids, MI: Zondervan, 2012).

12. Chandler et al., "Meta-Analysis of Humble Leadership."

13. Chandler et al.

14. van Dierendonck and Nuijten, "Servant Leadership Survey."

15. Eva et al., "Servant Leadership."

16. Muhammad Mumtaz Khan, Muhammad Shujaat Mubarik, Syed Saad Ahmed, Tahir Islam, Essa Khan, Asif Rehman, and Farhan Sohail, "My Meaning Is My Engagement: Exploring the Mediating Role of Meaning between Servant Leadership and Work Engagement," *Leadership & Organization Development Journal* 42, no. 6 (2021): 926–41.

17. Richard M. Ryan and Edward L. Deci, "Intrinsic and Extrinsic Motivations: Classic Definitions and New Directions," *Contemporary Educational Psychology* 25, no. 1 (2000): 54–67, https://doi.org/10.1006/ceps.1999.1020.

18. Edward L. Deci, Anja H. Olafsen, and Richard M. Ryan, "Self-Determination Theory in Work Organizations: The State of a Science," *Annual Review of Organizational Psychology and Organizational Behavior* 4, no. 1 (2017): 19–43, https://doi.org/10.1146/annurev-orgpsych-032516-113108.

19. Hanbing Xue, Yifei Luo, Yuxiang Luan, and Nan Wang, "A Meta-Analysis of Leadership and Intrinsic Motivation: Examining Relative Importance and Moderators," *Frontiers in Psychology* 13 (August 2022): 941161, https://doi.org/10.3389/fpsyg.2022.941161.

20. Eva et al., "Servant Leadership."

21. Edgar H. Schein, and Peter A. Schein, *Humble Inquiry: The Gentle Art of Asking Instead of Telling* (Oakland, CA: Berrett-Koehler, 2021).

22. Shengming Liu, Jih-Yu Mao, Ning Li, and Zhang Yue, "Not the Time to Be Humble! When and Why Leader Humility Enhances and Deteriorates Evaluations on Leader Effectiveness and Satisfaction with Leader," *Journal of Management Studies* (September 20, 2024).

CHAPTER 9

1. Jack J. Bauer, *The Transformative Self: Personal Growth, Narrative Identity, and the Good Life* (Oxford: Oxford University Press, 2021).

2. Hao Zhao and Chaoping Li, "A Computerized Approach to Understanding Leadership Research," *Leadership Quarterly* 30, no. 4 (2019): 396–416.

3. James MacGregor Burns, *Leadership* (New York: Harper and Row, 1978); James Bailey and Ruth H. Axelrod, "Leadership Lessons from Mount Rushmore: An Interview with James MacGregor Burns," *Leadership Quarterly* 12 (2001): 113–27, http://lessonsonleadership.org/wp-content/uploads/2014/08/Bailey-2001-LQ.pdf; George C. Banks, Kelly Davis McCauley, William L.

Gardner, and Courtney E. Guler, "A Meta-Analytic Review of Authentic and Transformational Leadership: A Test for Redundancy," *Leadership Quarterly* 27, no. 4 (2016): 634–52.

4. Secil Bayraktar and Alfredo Jiménez, "Self-Efficacy as a Resource: A Moderated Mediation Model of Transformational Leadership, Extent of Change and Reactions to Change," *Journal of Organizational Change Management* 33, no. 2 (2020): 301–17.

5. Bernard M. Bass and Ronald E. Riggio, *Transformational Leadership* (New York: Psychology Press, 2006).

6. Nathapon Siangchokyoo, Ryan L. Klinger, and Emily D. Campion, "Follower Transformation as the Linchpin of Transformational Leadership Theory: A Systematic Review and Future Research Agenda," *Leadership Quarterly* 31, no. 1 (February 2020): 101341, https://doi.org/10.1016/j.leaqua.2019.101341.

7. Julianne Holt-Lunstad, "Fostering Social Connection in the Workplace," *American Journal of Health Promotion* 32, no. 5 (2018): 1307–12.

8. Albert Bandura, "Self-Efficacy: Toward a Unifying Theory of Behavioral Change," *Advances in Behaviour Research and Therapy* 1, no. 4 (1978): 139–61.

9. Todd M. Thrash and Andrew J. Elliot, "Inspiration as a Psychological Construct," *Journal of Personality and Social Psychology* 84, no. 4 (2003): 871–89.

10. Yi Cui, Todd M. Thrash, Rebecca Shkeyrov, and Peter J. Varga, "Inspiration in the Creative Process," *Encyclopedia of Creativity* 1, no. 3 (2020): 660–66.

11. Bass and Riggio, *Transformational Leadership.*

12. Rebecca Mitchell and Brendan Boyle, "Inspirational Leadership, Positive Mood, and Team Innovation: A Moderated Mediation Investigation into the Pivotal Role of Professional Salience," *Human Resource Management* 58, no. 3 (2019): 269–83.

13. Nüfer Yasin Ateş, Murat Tarakci, Jeanine Pieternel Porck, Daan van Knippenberg, and Patrick J. F. Groenen, "The Dark Side of Visionary Leadership in Strategy Implementation: Strategic Alignment, Strategic Consensus, and Commitment," *Journal of Management* 46, no. 5 (2020): 637–65.

14. Ateş et al., "Dark Side."

15. Richard Rumelt, *The Crux: How Leaders Become Strategists* (London: Profile Books, 2022).

16. David J. Hughes, Allan Lee, Amy Wei Tian, Alex Newman, and Alison Legood, "Leadership, Creativity, and Innovation: A Critical Review and Practical Recommendations," *Leadership Quarterly* 29, no. 5 (2018): 549–69.

17. Allan Lee, Alison Legood, David Hughes, Amy Wei Tian, Alexander Newman, and Caroline Knight, "Leadership, Creativity and Innovation: A Meta-Analytic Review," *European Journal of Work and Organizational Psychology* 29, no. 1 (2020): 1–35.

18. Chan Hyung Park, "Finding a Road Less Traveled: Combining Analysis and Intuition to Develop Novel Problem Formulations," *Strategic Management Journal* 45, no. 11 (2024): 2368–92.

19. Bayraktar and Jiménez, "Self-Efficacy as a Resource."

20. Margaret Moore, "Ground Zero in Lifestyle Medicine: Changing Mindsets to Change Behavior," *American Journal of Lifestyle Medicine* 17, no. 5 (2023): 632–38.

21. George Stock, George C. Banks, E. Nicole Voss, Scott Tonidandel, and Haley Woznyj, "Putting Leader (Follower) Behavior Back into Transformational Leadership: A Theoretical and Empirical Course Correction," *Leadership Quarterly* 34, no. 6 (December 2023): 101632, https://doi.org/10.1016/j.leaqua.2022.101632.

22. Dirk van Dierendonck and Inge Nuijten, "The Servant Leadership Survey: Development and Validation of a Multidimensional Measure," *Journal of Business and Psychology* 26 (2011): 249–67.

23. Richard E. Boyatzis and Udayan Dhar, "Dynamics of the Ideal Self," *Journal of Management Development* 41, no. 1 (2021): 1–9.

24. Anthony Ian Jack, Angela M. Passarelli, and Richard E. Boyatzis, "When Fixing Problems Kills Personal Development: fMRI Reveals Conflict between Real and Ideal Selves," *Frontiers in Human Neuroscience* 17 (August 2023): 1128209, https://doi.org/10.3389/fnhum.2023.1128209.

25. Ryan Holiday, *The Obstacle Is the Way: The Timeless Art of Turning Trials into Triumph* (London: Penguin, 2014).

CHAPTER 10

1. Marshall Goldsmith with Mark Reiter, *What Got You Here Won't Get You There: How Successful People Become Even More Successful* (New York: Hachette Books, 2007).

2. Mihaly Csikszentmihalyi, *Flow: The Psychology of Happiness* (New York: Random House, 2013).

3. Richard E. Boyatzis and Anthony I. Jack, "The Neuroscience of Coaching," *Consulting Psychology Journal: Practice and Research* 70, no. 1 (2018): 11–27; Richard E. Boyatzis, Angela M. Passarelli, Katherine Koenig, Mark Lowe, Blessy Mathew, James K. Stoller, and Michael Phillips, "Examination of the Neural Substrates Activated in Memories of Experiences with Resonant and Dissonant Leaders," *Leadership Quarterly* 23, no. 2 (2012): 259–72.

4. Richard E. Boyatzis, Melvin L. Smith, and Ellen Van Oosten, *Helping People Change: Coaching with Compassion for Lifelong Learning and Growth* (Brighton, MA: Harvard Business Press, 2019).

CONCLUSION

1. Christian Seelos, Johanna Mair, and Charlotte Traeger, "The Future of Grand Challenges Research: Retiring a Hopeful Concept and Endorsing Research Principles," *International Journal of Management Reviews* 25, no. 2 (2023): 251–69, https://doi.org/10.1111/ijmr.12324.

2. Christopher Labos, "Too Much of a Good Thing: Can Endurance Exercise Be

Harmful?" *Medscape*, August 30, 2024, https://www.medscape.com/viewarticle/too-much-good-thing-can-endurance-exercise-be-harmful-2024a1000fhx?form=fpf.

3. Mary Crossan, Corey Crossan, Toby Newstead, and Rachel E. Sturm, "Developing Leader Character: Finding a Way Forward," *Academy of Management Learning & Education* 23, no. 4 (2024), https://doi.org/10.5465/amle.2023.0520.

4. Anita Pipere and Kristīne Mārtinsone, "Metamodernism and Social Sciences: Scoping the Future," *Social Sciences* 11, no. 10 (2022): 1–20.

Acknowledgments

RESEARCHERS

Our first and deepest gratitude goes to the thousands of researchers who have dedicated their intellect and work lives to the study of leadership and the workplace over the past fifty years. Throughout the book we named many researchers, from twenty-two countries, when we cited their scientific studies and articles. We encourage you to thank them directly online (most have LinkedIn profiles) for work that inspires you or is important to you. We encourage researchers to let us know what we might have missed or misunderstood or misrepresented, and to keep us posted on new research that can guide us all to leading better.

COACHING CLIENTS

Second, we dearly thank our coaching client leaders whose real names and identities are disguised in the book. It was their commitment to being coached and increasing their impact that brought the science to life through the lived experiences of leaders. Beyond this group of twenty leaders, our work with hundreds of leaders has taught us how to blend the emergent process of coaching with the sharing of scientific findings to inspire leaders to try new things. With their adventurous experiments, they enable us to separate the signals of effective leadership from the noise.

BERRETT-KOEHLER

Third, we thank the entire Berrett-Koehler team, dedicated to publishing books on leadership science and practice, for their belief in the potential of this book. We owe a huge debt of gratitude to our editor,

Steve Piersanti, for being patient with Jeff through three rounds of proposals and then magically suggesting that Margaret and Jeff would make a great team as coauthors. We had been friends and leaders together at the Institute of Coaching for over a decade, but had not considered writing a book together. With Steve's steady and wise guidance (he's not only a superb publisher and editor but also an amazing coach!), this book took shape quickly, and our friendship has not only remained intact but flourished. With the surefooted guidance of Jeevan Sivasubramanian, Christy Kirk, Katelyn Keating, Ashley Ingram, Alexis Woodcock, Susan Geraghty, and the entire production team at BK, we could not have felt more supported throughout the writing and publishing journey.

We also thank our thoughtful and thorough BK reviewers, who provided invaluable feedback on our draft manuscript and helped us make the final book sing. To Jennifer Hoover, Mary Kay Chess, and Leslie Gale, we are eternally grateful. A hearty thank you to Michele Jones for her world-class copyediting. And for extraordinary support and feedback at just the right time, we thank our dear friend, colleague, and cofounder of the Institute of Coaching, Carol Kauffman. Her insights into making a coauthored book flow well between two writers were extremely helpful.

A special thank you to Rosie Hunter for her eagle eye in sourcing research and editing the book's prose and citations.

INSTITUTE OF COACHING

Speaking of the Institute of Coaching (IOC), a few years ago we set a vision for coaches to step up as leaders, bringing leadership science to leaders through coaching. This led to the formation of a passionate group of forty-five leadership coaches who have been dear friends and colleagues in the IOC global community for many years. They worked tirelessly to produce a rich coaching guide on current leadership models. Many enriching conversations inspired our collective engagement with the science of leadership over the past three years. We thank this team of coaches for their dedication to elevating the coaching profession and their commitment to reviewing and organizing leadership research, which is now a valuable handbook for coaches and leaders, available on the IOC website.

A special thank you to Jaspal Bajwa, who convened and led the team over three years. We also appreciate the team's fearless coleaders: Greg Pawlson, Patricia Hinton Walker, Loretta Donovan, John Lazar, and David Bright. We call out to Celia Sikorski, whose introduction to Jack Bauer's book on the transformative self was, well, transformative. The team of coaches includes Aidan McCormack, Alan Graham, Alexandra Fabiola Pallamar Azua, Andrea-Leven-Marcon, Adeboye Martins, Betsy Cox, Bernhard Schaller, Carmen Qadir, Celia Sikorski, Cindi Acree, Dudun Peterside, Henry Kahn, James Lamberti, Jodi Kohut, Jean Johnson, Kate Anderson Foley, Kay Peterson, Kemia Sarraf, Kevin Dunal, Krishna Kumar, Laura Berenstain, Lili Shalev Shawn, Marderé Birkill, Michele Weston, Monique Valcour, Murali Krishna Jayaprakash, Nancy Pettigrew, Paul Butler, Phillip Brooks, Raman Nanda, Randi Brosterman, Rhonda Foster, Sophia Petrides, Steve Longan, Steve Scanlon, Susan Johnson, Tanya Kleindienst, Teresa Ramos, and Yasmina Suleyman.

We thank our amazing IOC team, who keep the engines running at IOC. We are particularly grateful for our wonderful leaders and scholars: David Rosmarin, Angela Passarelli, Pamela Larde, and David Bright; and our extraordinary small and mighty team of associates who support more than four thousand members and professional fellows of the IOC worldwide: Emily Terrani, Tiffany Dally, Michael Kalygin, Austin Matzelle, Dana Deek, Janet Durfee, Sue Brennick, Darnell Bradley, Jessie Carpenter, Chelsea Tirone, Taruna Aggarwal, and Kevin Dunal.

JEFFREY'S PERSONAL ACKNOWLEDGMENTS

No book comes into being without a great many shoulders to lean on. I have been fortunate to have had many friends who were ready to listen, coach, and raise a glass (or two) with me when the project felt intense or stressful. With gratitude for Steve Mendelsohn, Barbara Phillips, Maura Conlon-McIvor, Rick Rudolph, Christian van Seeters, Joel Monk, Laurens van Aarle, Antonie Knoppers, Tim Odenkirchen, Katherina Norden, Ben Preston, David Frechter, and Polly Howells.

I also thank special friends in my worldwide coaching community, whose expertise and wisdom are formidable. You teach me how to be a better coach and leader, every day: Haesun Moon, Andreas Bernhardt, Hetty Brand-Boswijk, Rolf Pfeiffer, Ramon Estrada, Eileen Fracchia, David Bishop, Eric Kaufmann, Jan Rybeck, Alison Whitmire, Allison Davis, David Drake, Pam Marcheski, and Amii Barnard-Bahn.

I look back fondly on my decision to transition from therapist to coach, and the fateful day in 2013 when my dear friend Pascal Scemama introduced me to Carol and Margaret, cofounders of IOC. That meeting changed my life. My interest in helping coaching become a credible profession led to a passion for translating the growing evidence base into education programs, conferences, and community building that has taken me across the globe and back. For their partnership and encouragement (along with that of Susan David, the third cofounder) as I stepped forward to lead, I am eternally grateful.

Most of all, I make a bow of special thanks to my partner of fifteen years, Jason Kim, who has provided unending support through the ups and downs of years of proposal writing and the completion of three books. It is always a joy to have the final toast of the day with you and Pinot.

My interest in what makes a leader effective began in the halls of Booz Allen Hamilton over thirty years ago. I may have thought it culminated in my PhD thesis on the leadership of healing groups, but I was wrong—and my passion for the subject continues to thrive. Working on this book has reinvigorated my belief in the potential for good leaders to help build a sustainable future for the human and nonhuman beings that share this tiny planet. What I'm most grateful for: being a small part of the journey to get us there.

MARGARET'S PERSONAL ACKNOWLEDGMENTS

I'm starting close in with my dear husband of twenty-four years, Paul Clark (retired biotechnology patent attorney and industry leader). Paul is my top thinking partner and writing coach, who shares my love of science and scientists. His editing and polishing of our book, forgoing our 2024 summer vacation and relaxation, were essential to its impact on all of us.

My deepest thanks go to our early Wellcoaches team for our energetic and creative collaboration from 2000 to 2009 to integrate science into coaching, making this book possible—Bob Tschannen-Moran, Erika Jackson, Kate Larsen, Christina Lombardo, Pam Schmid, Gloria Silverio, Jessica Wolfson, Gabe Highstein, and Julie Compton.

I am eternally grateful for my brain-expanding conversations about coaching practice, life, and leading, with close collaborators Carol Kauffman, David Drake, and Eric Kaufmann. I can count on their counsel in existential moments.

Thanks to Carol for recommending that I complete training in internal family systems (IFS) practice. I was fortunate that IFS Institute founder Dick Schwartz was our instructor for all three levels of IFS training.

During the first IFS training, in meditative states I identified nine personality "voices" or "parts" in my own inner world, described in a hypothesis paper and Harvard Health book. Meeting psychiatrist Dan Siegel, who presented at our IOC conference, led me to his work on integration and personality patterns (establishing a scientific framework for the Enneagram nine-part model). If not for Dick's and Dan's work, I would not have become the leader and coach I am today. I could not have seen a path through the leadership literature in terms of nine capacities, which are likely the leadership expressions of nine universal personality parts.

I look back now to being in my midtwenties, graduating with an MBA from Ivey Business School in 1983, and remembering how much I loved Michael Porter's book on competitive strategy. That was our leadership guide forty years ago, before the field of leadership research got rolling. Leadership was strategy, and thanks to Ivey, my MBA degree made me a strategic leader.

All the threads of my work life since the MBA degree come together in this book, as if I had a grand strategy. But I didn't see it coming. I'm eternally grateful to Jeff and Steve at Berrett-Koehler for the invitation to coauthor this book. In gratitude, I will do my part in bending the arc of leadership upward.

Index

Page numbers followed by *fig* refer to a figure on that page. Page numbers followed by *t* refer to a table on that page.

acceptance, 32, 81, 101
accountability
  in compassionate leadership, 7, 112
  as leadership character dimension, 46
  in servant leadership, 152
  in shared leadership, 134, 135, 136
  in transformational leadership, 172, 173
action research, 14
action steps, 67
actions, 58, 58*fig*, 109
active listening. *See* listening
adaptive leadership, 65
advising, 123
affective trust. *See* trust
agency, 96–97
agile compassion, 115
agile leadership, 53–70
  compassionate leadership and, 108*t*
  cultural agility in, 50, 51–52, 157, 158, 159–60
  leadership stories on, 53–56, 68–69, 181–84
  overuse of, 67–69
  overview of, 6
  practicing of, 65–67
  relational leadership and, 76, 82, 84
  science behind, 56–65, 58*fig*
  self-rating of, 9*t*
  shared leadership and, 125–26

Agile Manifesto, 56
agile mind, 57–58, 58fig
The Agile Mind (Koutstaal), 57–58, 58fig
agile mindset, 61
Ahmad, Ghufran, 83
Ahmed (cardiac surgeon), 91–94
alignment, 126–27, 130, 165
Amabile, Teresa M., 83, 85
American Medical Association, 110
animal care, 104–8
Anita (pharmacy saleswoman), 71–75, 80
approach motivation, 163
Arena, Michael, 60
Ateş, Nüfer Yasin, 165
attention, 31
authentic leadership, 37–52
  agile leadership and, 64
  compassionate leadership and, 40, 46, 108*t*, 114
  leadership stories on, 36–41, 50–52, 179–80
  overuse of, 49–52
  overview of, 6
  polarities in, 62
  practicing of, 48–49
  relational leadership and, 46, 78, 82, 84
  science behind, 41–48
  self-rating of, 9*t*

authentic leadership (*cont.*)
    shared leadership and, 46, 128
    transformational leadership and,
        42–43, 166–67
autonomy, 7, 96–97, 167

bad listening behaviors, 79
Bandura, Albert, 163
Banks, George, 42–43, 168
Barbara (pharmaceutical leader), 86–88
Barrett, Lisa Feldman, 26
Bass, Bernard, 161–62, 164
Bauer, Jack, 29, 99, 156
Bayraktar, Secil, 161, 167
beliefs, 50
Bernhardt, Andreas, 83–84
bias, 66
Bischof, Nicole, 124
Bob (IT security head), 68–69
Both/And Thinking (Smith & Lewis),
        62–63
Boyatzis, Richard, 71, 113–14, 115,
        169, 170, 187
Bracht, Eva, 26
brain, 26–27, 29, 30–33, 78, 80, 187
Brand, Marco, 63
Bransby, Derrick, 82
Bright, David, 45
Buber, Martin, 77
burnout, 117–18
Burns, James McGregor, 161

callousness, 110
Cameron, Kim, 44–45
Cao, Wenrui, 81
capacities of leadership, 4–8, 16
    See also specific capacities of leadership
care. *See* authentic leadership
Carter, Jacqueline, 108
causation, 14
Center for Creative Leadership (CCL),
        75, 129–30
Center for Positive Organizational
        Scholarship, 110–11
Chandler, Jeffrey, 147–48

change
    in agile leadership, 54–56, 63–64
    in authentic leadership, 44
    theories of, 11
    in transformational leadership,
        157–59, 162, 167–68, 170–71
character assessments, 48–49
character dimensions, 46–47
check-ins, 56, 134, 154
Christopher (software company CEO),
        142–45
coaching
    in agile leadership, 53
    in authentic leadership, 37–39
    benefits of, 178
    in compassionate leadership, 106,
        107, 186, 187
    conscious leadership and, 20, 22, 29
    core capacities of, 16
    definition of, 123
    Enneagram in, 143
    leadership behaviors commonly
        targeted in, 62
    in relational leadership, 72, 78–79,
        83–84
    in shared leadership, 121–22, 123,
        126, 134
    in transformational leadership, 158,
        162, 167–68
Coaching Psychology Manual (Moore et
        al.), 16
collaboration, 38–39, 46, 62, 132
collective leadership. *See* shared
        leadership
commitment, 130
communication
    in agile leadership, 56, 62
    in compassionate leadership, 186–87
    dialing up leadership capacities in,
        195
    feedback in (*see* feedback)
    listening in (*see* listening)
    in shared leadership, 134, 136
    in transformational leadership,
        172–73

community engagement, 141, 144

companioning, 116–17

compassion capacities, 108, 108*t*

compassionate leadership, 104–19

    authentic leadership and, 40, 46,
        108*t*, 114

    conscious leadership and, 32, 108*t*,
        187

    leadership stories on, 104–8,
        117–18, 186–88

    overuse of, 117–18

    overview of, 7

    practicing of, 115–17

    science behind, 108–15, 108*t*

    self-rating of, 10*fig*

    servant leadership and, 141–42, 147

    shared leadership and, 128, 133

Compassionate Leadership (Hougaard &
    Carter), 108

Compassionomics (Trzeciak et al.), 110

competence, 97

complexity leadership, 130

concepts, 58, 58*fig*

concern, 7, 112

confidence

    as high-quality motivation source,
        166

    in improvement in leadership
        capacities, 11–12, 12*fig*

    as psychological capital, 7

    in shared leadership, 121–22

    in transformational leadership, 8,
        163, 167–68, 171–72

    See also efficacy

confirmation bias, 66

conflict, 63, 86–88, 141–42, 147, 152

conscious leadership, 19–36

    agile leadership and, 64

    authentic leadership and, 41, 46

    compassionate leadership and, 32,
        108*t*, 187

    leadership stories on, 19–24, 33–34,
        178–80

    overview of, 5–6

    practicing of, 30–33

    relational leadership and, 82, 84

    science behind, 24–30

    self-rating of, 9*t*

    transformational leadership and, 158

    underuse of, 33–35

conservation, 43–44

control, 57–58, 58*fig*

corporate culture, 190–91

correlations, 14

courage, 8, 44, 46, 158–59, 168–69, 187

COVID-19 pandemic, 54–56, 192

Crawford, Joseph, 42

creativity, 7–8, 59–60, 87, 162, 164,
    166–67

critical behavior, 20, 21, 23, 28

Crocco, Oliver, 8

Crossan, Corey, 201

Crossan, Mary, 46–47, 201

cruelty, 110

the crux, 131–32

The Crux (Rumelt), 131–32

Csikszentmihalyi, Mihaly, 59–60,
    182–83

Cui, Yi, 164

cultural differences, 50, 51–52, 157,
    158, 159–60

culture, corporate, 190–91

curiosity, 59, 84, 140–41

Darwin, Charles, 109

David, Susan, 59

de Haan, Erik, 28

Deci, Edward, 96, 149

decision-making, 62, 68, 154, 182

delegating, 123, 126

Depow, Gregory John, 111–12

Dewar, Carolyn, 47–48

dialing emotions, 30–33

differences

    in agile leadership, 64

    in authentic leadership, 50, 51–52

    in relational leadership, 86–88

    in servant leadership, 141–42, 152

    in shared leadership, 192

direction, 130

directive leadership, 54, 55–56, 124, 159

disagreement, 63, 86–88, 141–42, 147, 152

distributed leadership. *See* shared leadership

doing, 58, 58*fig*, 109

drive, 46

Dutton, Jane, 110–11

Dweck, Carol, 20

Edmans, Alex, 66

Edmondson, Amy, 74, 81–82

efficacy, 26, 93, 95, 97, 167

See also confidence

ego

in authentic leadership, 43

in conscious leadership, 5–6, 23, 29–33

in facing grand challenges, 201

in servant leadership, 146

in shared leadership, 125

in transformational leadership, 158

einfühlung, 77

Elliot, Andrew, 163

emotional agility, 59, 62

Emotional Agility (David), 59

emotional intelligence, 15, 21–23, 25–26, 77, 113

emotions

in agile leadership, 58, 58*fig*, 59, 64

in compassionate leadership, 111, 117–18, 187

in conscious leadership, 5–6, 26–29, 30–33, 179

in positive leadership, 98, 99, 101–2

as psychological capital, 7

in relational leadership, 72–73

in transformational leadership, 170–71

empathy

in authentic leadership, 40

in compassionate leadership, 107–8, 109, 111, 113, 114, 187

in conscious leadership, 22

in relational leadership, 6, 72–73, 77–78, 79, 80

in servant leadership, 142, 147

employee engagement gap, 94

empowerment, 56

endogeneity, 14

enforcing leadership, 83

engagement, 7, 62, 109, 128, 141

See also motivation

Enneagram, 142–43

Enron, 42

envisioning. *See* vision

ethics, 24, 41–42

Eva, Nathan, 145–46, 149, 150–51

evocation, 163

extraversion, 54, 55, 60

extrinsic motivation, 150

facilitative leadership, 83

failure. *See* mistakes and failure

feedback

in agile leadership, 182

in authentic leadership, 39, 49

in compassionate leadership, 187

in conscious leadership, 20, 22, 33, 34

in positive leadership, 92–93

in relational leadership, 72, 73, 185

in servant leadership, 141, 144, 152–53, 154

in shared leadership, 134, 136

in transformational leadership, 158, 172, 173

feelings. *See* emotions

Fisher, Colin M., 78, 83, 85

Flex (Hull), 16, 62

flexibility. *See* agile leadership

Flow (Csikszentmihalyi), 182–83

followers, in definitions of leadership, 3–4

forgiveness, 6, 45, 81, 152

Fredrickson, Barbara, 98, 99

fulfillment, 7, 99

Gallup, 94, 128

Gandz, Jeffrey, 46–47

generosity, 78, 116
George, Bill, 47
Gilbert, Paul, 110, 116
goal posts, 68, 69
Goldsmith, Marshall, 180
Goleman, Daniel, 25, 77, 79
good listening behaviors, 79, 84
Görgens-Ekermans, Gina, 25–26, 77
Gottfredson, Ryan, 75–76
grand challenges, 200–201
gratitude, 92–94, 99, 153
Greenleaf, Robert, 139, 145, 146
groupthink, 86
growth mindset, 20, 101

Hamel, Gary, 131
Haslam, Alexander, 3
Heifetz, Ronald, 65
"helper" personality type, 143
helping others. *See* relational leadership
Helping People Change (Boyatzis), 187
HERO (hope, efficacy, resilience,
        optimism), 95
Hesselbein, Frances, 120
"high context" cultures, 159
higher-level values, 44
high-quality motivation, 149–50, 166
holacracy, 124–26
Holiday, Ryan, 170–71
hope, 95, 99
The Hope Circuit (Seligman), 99
Hougaard, Rasmus, 108
"how" in leadership, 126, 127, 127*fig*,
        128, 181
Huainanzi, 133
Hughes, David, 166
Hull, Jeffrey, 16, 62, 83–84
human capital, 95–96
humanity, 44, 46, 114, 115–16
humanocracy, 131
Humanocracy (Hamel & Zanini), 131
Humble Inquiry (Schein & Schein),
        151–53
humility
    in agile leadership, 56, 60

    as leadership character dimension,
        46
    in servant leadership, 140–41,
        143–44, 146, 147–48, 152–53,
        154
    in shared leadership, 125
    in transformational leadership, 158,
        173

"I" approach
    in facing grand challenges, 201
    in relational leadership, 186
    in shared leadership, 124, 127–28,
        131–32, 136
    in transformational leadership, 172,
        173
ideal self, 169–70, 187
improvement, 11–13, 12*fig*
inclusivity, 7, 122, 129–30, 141
individual performance, 43
informed intuition model, 167
innovation
    in agile leadership, 60, 67, 68–69
    in relational leadership, 87
    in transformational leadership, 8,
        158, 162, 165, 166–67
inspirational leadership, 163–66,
        172–73
Institute of Coaching, 64
integration, 23–24, 28–29
integrity, 6, 46, 47
intellectual stimulation, 8, 32, 43, 162,
        164, 168
intentions, 85, 116, 152
interdependence, 66–67
interpersonal acceptance, 81
intrinsic motivation, 149–50, 164
introversion, 53–56, 60, 158–59
intuition, 167, 171
Itzchakov, Guy, 79–80

Jack, Tony, 170
Jennifer (saleswoman), 37–41
Jian, Guowei, 78
Jiménez, Alfredo, 161, 167

Jit, Ravinder, 146–47
Johannes (agricultural engineer),
    124–26, 140–42
John (nonprofit research leader), 135–37
Johnson, Barry, 66–67
Joseph (chief operating officer),
    156–61, 163–64
Josh (analytics and strategy consultant),
    172–73
journaling, 118
judgment, 46
justice, 44, 46

Kaluza, Antonia, 95
Keller, Scott, 47–48
Khan, Muhammad Mumtaz, 149
Kluger, Avraham N., 79–80
Korkmaz, Ayfer Veli, 129
Koutstaal, Wilma, 57–58, 58*fig*, 61
Kročil, Ondřej, 24
Kubátová, Jaroslava, 24
Kumbaya effect, 86

Labos, Christopher, 200
Landis, Blaine, 83
laser coaching, 123
leader character assessment, 48–49
leader-member exchange, 185
leadership
    definitions of, 3–4
    in grand challenges, 200–201
    nine capacities of, 4–8, 16 (*see also*
        specific capacities of leadership)
    overview of research on, 1–3, 13–16
    readiness to improve in, 11–13, 12*fig*
    self-rating of, 8–9, 9*t*–10*t*, 195–96
Leadership (Goleman), 25
Leadership (Northouse), 15
leadership shadows, 23–24, 28–29,
    30–33
leadership stories
    on agile leadership, 53–55, 68–69,
        181–84
    on authentic leadership, 36–41,
        50–52, 179–80
    combining all nine leadership
        capacities in (*see* Stephanie
        (software company CEO))
    on compassionate leadership, 104–8,
        117–18, 186–88
    on conscious leadership, 19–24,
        33–34, 178–80
    on positive leadership, 90–94,
        101–2, 184–85
    on relational leadership, 71–75,
        86–88, 185–86
    on servant leadership, 139–45,
        153–55, 190–91
    on shared leadership, 120–26,
        135–37, 191–93
    on transformational leadership,
        156–61, 172–73, 189–90
Lee (software engineering VP), 153–55
Lee, Allan, 166–67
Leslie (surgical residency program
    head), 117–18
Lewin, Kurt, 14
Lewis, Marianne, 62–63
Li, Chaoping, 15
Lilis, Jacoba, 110–11
Lipps, Theodore, 77
Lisa (pharmaceutical leader), 101–2
listening
    in agile leadership, 183
    in compassionate leadership, 113
    in conscious leadership, 22
    in relational leadership, 6, 72, 73,
        78–80, 84
    in servant leadership, 151, 190
    in transformational leadership, 160,
        164
Liu, Shengming, 154
LMX theory, 75–76
Loch, Christoph, 83
loneliness, 199
"low context" cultures, 159

Mackey, John, 24
Malhotra, Vikram, 47–48
Mandela, Nelson, 104

Mary (nonprofit operating officer), 50–52

May Contain Lies (Edmans), 66

McCauley, Cynthia, 129–30

McKee, Annie, 113

McKinsey partners, 47–48, 130

meaning, 47–48, 126, 127*fig*, 149–50, 160, 166

mediation, 142

mental dial, 30–33

mentoring, 123, 126

   See also coaching

metamodernism, 201

Mike (travel services CEO), 33–34

mindfulness, 21–22, 27, 30–33, 35, 179

Mindset (Dweck), 20

mindsight, 27–28

Mintzberg, Henry, 53

mistakes and failure

   accountability for (*see* accountability)

   forgiveness of, 6, 45, 81, 152

   psychological safety and, 74

Mitchell, Rebecca, 164–65

modeling. *See* role modeling

modernism, 201

Moore, Margaret, 16, 30

morals, 41–42

Mordi, Azuka, 61

Morrison, Herbert, 115

motivation

   in authentic leadership, 181

   in compassionate leadership, 109

   in conscious leadership, 25, 27

   in definitions of leadership, 3

   in forgiveness, 81

   in improvement in leadership capacities, 11–12, 12*fig*

   in positive leadership, 184, 185, 187

   in servant leadership, 7, 149–50

   in transformational leadership, 8, 163, 164, 166

   See also engagement

Müceldili, Büsra, 59

multitasking, 57

Nadella, Satya, 79

needs, 85

nervous system, 170

Newstead, Toby, 41, 201

nine capacities of leadership, 4–8, 16

   See also specific capacities of leadership

North Star, 48

Northouse, Peter, 15

The Obstacle is the Way (Holiday), 170–71

obstacles, 170–71

open strategy, 129

openness to change, 44

opposite perspectives, 66

optimism, 7, 45, 95, 98–99, 100–101, 102

Organizational Health Index, 130

Organize Your Emotions, Optimize Your Life (Moore et al.), 16

other-oriented capacities, 6–7

   See also compassionate leadership; positive leadership; relational leadership

"ought" selves, 170

oxytocin, 80

Paakkanen, Miia, 113

Palus, Charles, 129–30

paradoxes. *See* polarities/paradoxes

parasympathetic nervous system, 170

Park, Chan Hyung, 167

Passarelli, Angela, 170

path clearing, 85

Patricia (veterinary pharmaceutical leader), 104–8

perceptions, 58, 58*fig*, 64

performance, 94

personal values, 48–49, 180

perspectives

   in agile leadership, 66, 84

   in conscious leadership, 32

   in relational leadership, 6, 84, 86–88

   in servant leadership, 152

   in transformational leadership, 8, 168, 171

pessimism, 99
Peter (nonprofit director), 53–56, 62, 64
Peterson, Christopher, 44, 46, 48
physical energy, 59, 61
Pillemer, Julianna, 83, 85
polarities/paradoxes
    in agile leadership, 6, 56, 61–64, 65, 66–67, 182
    in positive leadership, 184
Polarity Management (Johnson), 66–67
polarity mapping, 66–67
positive leadership, 90–103
    authentic leadership and, 46
    compassionate leadership and, 108*t*, 114
    leadership stories on, 90–94, 101–2, 184–86
    overuse of, 100–102
    overview of, 6–7
    practicing of, 100
    science behind, 94–99
    self-rating of, 9*t*
    shared leadership and, 122–23
    transformational leadership and, 166
positivity ratio, 99
postmodernism, 201
posttraumatic growth, 101
presence, 84, 112–13, 116–17
Principles of Medical Ethics, 110
productivity, 67
professional identity, 164–65, 178–79
psychological capital (PsyCap), 6–7, 91, 92–93, 95–96
psychological flexibility, 58–59
psychological safety
    in agile leadership, 64
    in positive leadership, 92, 93, 102
    in relational leadership, 74–75, 80, 81–82, 85, 87–88, 185
    in servant leadership, 142
    in shared leadership, 134, 136
    in transformational leadership, 160, 167
    See also trust; vulnerability

purpose
    in authentic leadership, 47–48, 84
    in relational climate survey, 114
    in transformational leadership, 160–61, 165, 166
    in "why" in leadership, 126, 127*fig*

quiet ego. *See* ego

reactive behavior, 23
readiness to improve, 11–13, 12*fig*
realism, 101, 102
relational climate survey, 113–15
relational leadership, 71–89
    authentic leadership and, 46, 78, 82, 84
    compassionate leadership and, 108*t*, 114
    in cultural agility, 159
    in definitions of leadership, 3
    leadership stories on, 71–75, 86–88, 185–86
    overuse of, 85–88
    overview of, 6
    positive leadership and, 95
    practicing of, 83–85
    science behind, 75–83
    self-rating of, 9*t*
    shared leadership and, 122–23
religious beliefs, 50, 51
remote work, 54–56, 192
resilience, 60–61, 95
resonance, 77–78, 107–8, 113–15
resonant leadership. *See* compassionate leadership
Resonant Leadership (Boyatzis & McKee), 113
respect, 151–52
responsibility, 78, 116, 134, 135, 136, 149
    See also accountability
Rochford, Kylie, 113–14
role modeling
    in authentic leadership, 6, 42, 49
    in compassionate leadership, 112

in relational leadership, 75, 77
in transformational leadership, 7–8,
   160–61, 162–63, 167
roles, 84, 85, 134
Roux, Chene, 25–26, 77
Rumelt, Richard, 131–32, 166
Ryan, Richard, 28, 96, 149

Samimi, Mehdi, 129
S-ART framework, 30–33
Schein, Edgar, 151–53
Schein, Peter, 151–53
Schell, Sabrina, 124
Schoop, Mareike, 61
Schwartz, Shalom, 43–44
The Science of Change (Boyatzis), 115
Scott (investment bank partner),
   121–23
Seijts, Gerard, 46–47
self-awareness
   in authentic leadership, 42, 43
   in conscious leadership, 21–22,
      25–26, 31, 33, 34–35, 179
   in shared leadership, 125
self-care, 117–18
self-compassion, 32
self-confidence. *See* confidence; self-
   efficacy
self-determination theory (SDT), 3, 11,
   96, 97
self-efficacy, 26, 93, 95, 97, 167
   See also confidence
self-enhancement, 43
self-oriented capacities, 5–6
   See also agile leadership; authentic
      leadership; conscious leadership
self-oriented values, 43–44
self-rating of leadership, 8–9, 9*t*–10*t*,
   195–96
self-regulation, 15, 21–22, 25–26, 32,
   34–35
self-transcendence, 32–33, 34–35, 44,
   59
Seligman, Martin, 37, 44, 46, 99
servant leadership, 139–55

authentic leadership and, 46
leadership stories on, 139–45,
   153–55, 190–91
overuse of, 153–55
overview of, 7
practicing of, 151–53
science behind, 145–51
self-rating of, 10*fig*
transformational leadership and,
   145, 158, 166–67
set-shifting, 57
shadows, 23–24, 28–29, 30–33
shared leadership, 120–38
   authentic leadership and, 46, 128
   in facing grand challenges, 201
   leadership stories on, 120–26,
      135–37, 191–93
   overuse of, 135–37
   overview of, 7
   practicing of, 133–35
   science behind, 126–33, 127*fig*
   self-rating of, 10*fig*
Shuck, Brad, 112–13
Siangchokyoo, Max (Nathapon), 162
Sidney (HR director), 19–24, 25–26,
   27, 28, 29, 44
Siegel, Dan, 27, 28–29, 143
Silbersweig, David, 30
single-tasking, 57
Slemp, Gavin, 97
Smith, Wendy, 62–63
social connections, 80, 87, 118, 159
specificity, 57–58, 58*fig*
Splitter, Violetta, 129
staff development, 122–23
Steffens, Niklas, 43
Stephanie (software company CEO)
   agile leadership by, 181–84
   authentic leadership by, 179–80
   background on, 177–78
   compassionate leadership by,
      186–88
   conscious leadership by, 178–80
   positive leadership by, 184–85
   relational leadership by, 185–86

Stephanie (*cont.*)
  servant leadership by, 190–91
  shared leadership by, 191–93
  transformational leadership by,
    189–90
stewardship, 141, 144, 146, 148–49
stimulating environments, 61
Stock, George, 168
strategy, 68, 127–33, 127*fig*
Strauss, Clara, 109, 110
strengthening others. *See* positive
  leadership
strengths-spotting, 93, 184–85
stress, 80, 170, 187
Sturm, Rachel E., 201
success
  in authentic leadership, 38, 39
  in conscious leadership, 20, 180
  in shared leadership, 137
  in transformational leadership, 164,
    173
suffering
  in compassionate leadership,
    104, 110–11, 112, 113, 115,
    116–17
  in positive leadership, 101
Suska (agricultural geneticist), 124,
  125, 126
sympathetic nervous system, 170
system-oriented capacities, 7–8
  See also servant leadership; shared
    leadership; transformational
    leadership

Tan, Charlene, 133
temperance, 44, 46
thinking, 58, 58*fig*
Thrash, Todd, 163, 164
thriving, 94
timing, 85
Todnem, Rune, 47
touchstones, 21–22
transcendence, 32–33, 34–35, 44, 46,
  59, 163

transformational leadership, 156–75
  authentic leadership and, 42–43,
    166–67
  in character dimensions, 46
  compassionate leadership and, 114
  leadership stories on, 156–61,
    172–73, 189–90
  overuse of, 171–74
  overview of, 7–8
  practicing of, 169–71
  science behind, 161–68
  self-rating of, 10*fig*
  servant leadership and, 145, 158,
    166–67
  in well-being, 95
transformative self, 156
transparency, 42
transtheoretical theory of change, 11
trauma. *See* suffering
True North, 47
trust
  in agile leadership, 56
  in conscious leadership, 22, 33
  in positive leadership, 102
  in relational leadership, 74–75,
    80–81, 82, 86
  in servant leadership, 141, 142
  in transformational leadership, 160,
    167
  See also psychological safety;
    vulnerability

Uhl-Bien, Mary, 60
UK Center for Compassion Research
  and Training, 110
understanding, 152
  See also perspectives

Vago, David, 30
values
  in agile leadership, 64
  in authentic leadership, 39–40,
    43–44, 48–52, 180–81
  in conscious leadership, 21, 24–25

in positive leadership, 91, 99
in servant leadership, 191
in transformational leadership, 165, 166
in "why" in leadership, 126, 127*fig*
van Dierendonck, Dick, 145, 146, 149, 168
van Knippenberg, Daan, 47
venting, 78–79
Vera, Dusya, 127
VIA (values-in-action) Character Strengths assessment, 48
virtual work, 54–56, 192
virtues
    in authentic leadership, 40, 41–42, 43–47
    in conscious leadership, 24–25, 37
    in "why" in leadership, 126, 127*fig*
Virtuosity app, 49
vision
    in agile leadership, 68
    in compassionate leadership, 114
    in servant leadership, 149
    in transformational leadership, 158, 161, 164, 165–66, 169–70, 187–88
    in "why" in leadership, 126, 127*fig*
Voss, Nicole, 168
vulnerability
    in agile leadership, 64
    in conscious leadership, 22

in positive leadership, 102
in relational leadership, 74–75, 80, 82
in servant leadership, 142
in transformational leadership, 160, 163–64, 173
See also psychological safety; trust

Warren, Rick, 147
Wayment, Heidi, 29–30
"We" approach. *See* shared leadership
well-being, 16, 37, 60–61, 94–95, 114
"what" in leadership, 126, 127*fig*, 181
whole-system resonance, 107–8, 113–15
"why" in leadership, 126, 127, 127*fig*, 181
Wolfelt, Alan, 116–17
WorldCom, 42
Wu, Yingting, 8

Xue, Hanbing, 150

Yaden, David, 111
Yip, Jeffrey, 78
Yu, Mengye, 60

Zak, Paul, 80
Zanini, Michele, 131
Zhao, Hao, 15
Zuckerberg, Mark, 71

About the Authors

JEFFREY W. HULL, PHD, BCC

Jeff has been fascinated with leaders and leadership for over thirty years—an interest that began soon after his undergraduate work in psychology at Bowdoin College. His career has included multiyear stints as a corporate leader, leadership development consultant, therapist to leaders, professor of leadership, leadership coach, and leader of a global nonprofit institute.

CORPORATE EXPERIENCE

Beginning his career in HR at Electronic Data Systems (EDS), where he wrote his master's thesis at the University of Maryland on the leadership of Ross Perot and his firm's merger with General Motors, Jeff spent a decade in tech and consulting. After six years as a director of HR for strategy consulting firm Booz Allen Hamilton, he became an entrepreneur, cofounding TGE (The Global Edge) Associates, a leadership development consultancy in New York City, where he worked with teams in finance and technology.

PSYCHOLOGY DOCTORATE AND TEACHING

Jeff's interest in understanding the psychology of effective leaders led him to graduate work in organizational psychology at Columbia

University, and a PhD program in analytical/depth psychology at Pacifica Graduate Institute. For his doctoral thesis, *The Wilderness of Belonging: The Transformative Power of Healing Community*, Jeff studied the leadership dynamics of Alcoholics Anonymous, Bion's group therapy, and T-groups, among others.

Armed with a PhD in psychology, Jeff worked for three years as a psychotherapist with leaders going through major life transitions, which led to his first published book from Globe Pequot (2010), *Shift: Let Go of Fear and Get Your Life in Gear.* In this book, he outlined a framework for working through the anxieties of major life and organizational change with leaders in crisis. His therapeutic practice with leaders led him back into organizations, specifically counseling teams dealing with conflict and communication challenges. His teaching career also began at this time with a multiyear stint as an adjunct professor at NYU, teaching master's-level courses in entrepreneurship and C-suite leadership.

LEADERSHIP COACHING

Having begun his career in the corporate world, it was a homecoming of sorts in 2006 when he started an executive coaching business, Leadershift, Inc. Since then, Jeff has worked with C-suite leaders of Fortune 50 companies, start-ups, and everything in between, in finance, pharmaceuticals, health care, software, and manufacturing. He has coached hundreds of leaders across the globe and published numerous articles on effective leadership strategies for *Harvard Business Review* and other publications. He was profiled in the *New York Times* and *Investor's Business Daily* as a top coach during the financial crisis of 2008–2009 and joined Marshall Goldsmith's 100 Coaches in 2020.

In 2018 and 2019, he undertook qualitative research in the coaching space that led to his second book, *Flex: The Art and Science of Leadership in a Changing World* (TarcherPerigee, 2019), which has been published in English, Portuguese, Korean, Mandarin, and Japanese.

INSTITUTE OF COACHING

In 2013, Jeff sought to connect with the Institute of Coaching, founded in 2009 by his coauthor, Margaret Moore, along with Carol Kauffman and Susan David to help build the scientific base for the nascent coaching profession. He became the organization's first director of education and business development and in 2021 the executive director, as well as earning a faculty appointment as an instructor in psychology at Harvard Medical School.

As executive director of the IOC, Jeff has returned to his roots as a leader, where, along with a dedicated team, he is responsible for serving over four thousand members across the globe with webinars, seminars, live events, and roundtables. He regularly keynotes and facilitates team programs for corporate boards and multinational organizations around the world, virtually and in person.

As a passionate servant leader, he views his role as a *coach to coaches* and a *leader as coach*. In writing this book, he is excited to see his chosen professions—leadership and coaching—getting the scientific attention and application they deserve.

Jeff makes his home in Amsterdam, Netherlands, where he and his partner pride themselves on learning to navigate the bike lanes, stroll along the beautiful canals, and venture into neighboring cities for art museums, dance, music, and cultural experiences across Europe and beyond.

MARGARET MOORE, MBA

For the past forty years, Margaret has worked at the intersection of science with entrepreneurial business, non-profits, leadership, and coaching.

LEADERSHIP

At the top of her MBA class at Canada's Ivey School of Business, Margaret earned an international scholarship for her last term at London Business School. She started a seventeen-year biotechnology career at the UK's Imperial Chemical Industries, which employed 110,000 people worldwide. Back in Canada at Connaught Laboratories, she led the largest vaccines market launch in Europe up until then, in Germany: a vaccine for infant bacterial meningitis, which was an overnight market success and immediately saved lives.

At the age of thirty-five, she was appointed CEO of a US vaccines biotech company (Virogenetics, owned by a French multinational vaccines company, later integrated into Sanofi Vaccines). In Vancouver, she was the start-up COO of a Canadian biotech company, NeuroVir, developing a treatment platform for glioblastoma and other cancers, and later purchased by German biotech company Medigene.

Since 2000, as a transformational leader, Margaret envisioned the role of the professional coach on the health care team and cofounded two coaching organizations to realize that vision—Wellcoaches Corporation (2000) and the National Board for Health and Wellness Coaching (2010).

Margaret led Wellcoaches to become the first and leading coaching school for health professionals. Modeling coaching excellence, Wellcoaches has trained more than sixteen thousand coaches in fifty countries. In 2010, Margaret cofounded the National Board for Health and Wellness Coaching (NBHWC), now a nonprofit subsidiary of the National Board of Medical Examiners (NBME, which develops physician licensing exams). Margaret led the negotiation with NBME, which secured a multimillion investment to form NBHWC as an NBME affiliate. NBHWC delivers national standards and certification for health and well-being coaches and has now certified eleven thousand coaches.

Since 2019, Margaret has forged the industry's path to national reimbursement of health and well-being coaching services in medical practices. She is also starting a new business venture, expanding Wellcoaches to operationalize a vision—a turnkey, scalable coaching solution for medical practices.

SCIENCE TRANSLATION

Combining a biology degree and MBA in her biotech career in UK, Canada, France, and US, Margaret led global teams of scientists, helping them navigate the business world. She helped nonscientist board members, investors, and media understand how science was translated into medical treatments.

At Wellcoaches, she led the translation of science into coaching, culminating in the publication of a peer-reviewed textbook—the *Coaching Psychology Manual* (2008, 2015, and a forthcoming 2026 edition), which has now sold more than fifty thousand copies. Although the manual's focus is coaching for health and well-being, the scientific translation is foundational to leadership coaching and this book's translation of leadership science. The human building blocks of well-being, leadership, and coaching are one and the same.

Margaret has coauthored ten peer-reviewed book chapters and twenty-eight peer-reviewed papers on coaching. She coauthored two Harvard Health books—*Organize Your Mind, Organize Your Life* (Harper Collins, 2012) and *Organize Your Emotions, Optimize Your Life* (William Morrow, 2016). Margaret is an editor and chapter author of the American Medical Association's book *Coaching in Medical Education* (Elsevier, 2022)

In 2009, Margaret cofounded the Institute of Coaching (IOC) at McLean Hospital to broaden the integration of science into coaching practice across the coaching industry. She co-led from 2008 to 2024 the Coaching in Leadership and Healthcare conference offered by IOC, McLean Hospital, and Harvard Medical School. She has written more than a hundred articles (called research doses) for IOC, translating scientific papers into coaching practice.

As IOC chair from 2021 to 2024, Margaret co-led an IOC study of leadership and coaching during the pandemic and was the lead editor and writer of the report: *Leading with Humanity: The Future of Coaching and Leadership*. Next, with Jeff she inspired and mentored forty-five leadership coach members of IOC to write a handbook on science-based leadership models and educate coaches on leadership science. In 2023, she raised a $500K grant from IOC sponsor AceUp to build a science-based model of human-centered leadership and coaching. She also led a $500K investment in 2022 by the International Coaching Federation to fund IOC coaching research grants.

COACHING

Margaret, aka Coach Meg, is a seasoned professional coach, coach trainer, and educator; she has coached hundreds of clients and leadership teams and has trained thousands of coaches and leaders over the past twenty-five years. Her coaching is devoted mainly to supporting physicians and health care and biotechnology industry leaders and teams. Her ability to translate science into coaching and leadership is in good part built on her hands-on coaching experience as a transformational coach. Her vision for this book is to help bring scientists, leaders, and coaches together to foster leadership excellence and support everyday leaders far and wide.

Margaret lives in Wellesley, Massachusetts, with her husband, Paul, in a house built in 1836. When not working out, cooking, and listening to jazz and classical music, they enjoy their lively and smart tribe of three kids (Margaret's step-kids) and five grandkids—all emerging leaders.

Berrett–Koehler
Publishers

Berrett-Koehler is an independent publisher dedicated to an ambitious mission: *Connecting people and ideas to create a world that works for all.*

Our publications span many formats, including print, digital, audio, and video. We also offer online resources, training, and gatherings. And we will continue expanding our products and services to advance our mission.

We believe that the solutions to the world's problems will come from all of us, working at all levels: in our society, in our organizations, and in our own lives. Our publications and resources offer pathways to creating a more just, equitable, and sustainable society. They help people make their organizations more humane, democratic, diverse, and effective (and we don't think there's any contradiction there). And they guide people in creating positive change in their own lives and aligning their personal practices with their aspirations for a better world.

And we strive to practice what we preach through what we call "The BK Way." At the core of this approach is *stewardship,* a deep sense of responsibility to administer the company for the benefit of all of our stakeholder groups, including authors, customers, employees, investors, service providers, sales partners, and the communities and environment around us. Everything we do is built around stewardship and our other core values of *quality, partnership, inclusion,* and *sustainability.*

We are grateful to our readers, authors, and other friends who are supporting our mission. We ask you to share with us examples of how BK publications and resources are making a difference in your lives, organizations, and communities at bkconnection.com/impact.

Dear reader,

Thank you for picking up this book and welcome to the worldwide BK community! You're joining a special group of people who have come together to create positive change in their lives, organizations, and communities.

What's BK all about?

Our mission is to connect people and ideas to create a world that works for all.

Why? Our communities, organizations, and lives get bogged down by old paradigms of self-interest, exclusion, hierarchy, and privilege. But we believe that can change. That's why we seek the leading experts on these challenges—and share their actionable ideas with you.

A welcome gift

To help you get started, we'd like to offer you a **free copy** of one of our bestselling ebooks:

bkconnection.com/welcome

When you claim your **free ebook**, you'll also be subscribed to our blog.

Our freshest insights

Access the best new tools and ideas for leaders at all levels on our blog at ideas.bkconnection.com.

Sincerely,

Your friends at Berrett-Koehler